Brunel's Ships

BRUNEL'S SHIPS

Denis Griffiths, Andrew Lambert, and Fred Walker

CHATHAM PUBLISHING

LONDON

In association with the National Maritime Museum

FRONTISPIECE: *The survival of the* Great Britain *in a state which allows her restoration is a tribute to the quality of Brunel's work; the fact that so many people felt the restoration a worthwhile project is a reflection of the historical importance of his contribution. The ship is seen here returned to the dry-dock at Bristol in which she was built.* (By courtesy of Denis Griffiths)

Text copyright © Denis Griffiths, Andrew Lambert
and Fred Walker 1999
All photographs copyright © The National Maritime Museum

First published in Great Britain in 1999 by
Chatham Publishing, 61 Frith Street, London W1V 5TA

Chatham Publishing is an imprint of
Gerard Duckworth & Co Ltd

British Library Cataloguing in Publication Data
A catalogue record for this book is available from the British Library

ISBN 1 86176 102 3

Designed and typeset by Martin Richards
Printed and bound in Great Britain by
Hillman Printers (Frome) Ltd.

Contents

Foreword

This book began life on 15 November 1997 during a one-day Open Museum course about Brunel and his ships at the National Maritime Museum, Greenwich. The first pleasant surprise was the discovery that the course was sold out, persuading more than a hundred people to attend on one of the coldest, wettest days of the year. The second was the obvious benefit that accrued from approaching the subject from different perspectives, the varied insights available to a marine engineer, a naval architect and a historian proving to be mutually beneficial. Over lunch the speakers agreed that a book should be produced, and with the support of the Open Museum (an education programme co-funded by the National Maritime Museum and Goldsmiths University of London), the project could be taken to a publisher. Robert Gardiner at Chatham was the obvious person to approach. His contribution to this project, as with so many others, has gone far beyond the usual role of a publisher.

Susan Baylis
The Open Museum®

Introduction: The Man and his Ships

This book examines one important aspect of the life of a truly remarkable man. It is a testimony to the breadth of Isambard Kingdom Brunel's engineering genius that he is the one Victorian engineer to achieve the immortality of enduring popular fame, the man who symbolised and dominated the second 'Olympian' age of engineering. Where the men of the eighteenth century had struggled to escape the limits of natural materials and limited technology to produce the foundations of the industrial age, steam engines, machine tools and simple machines, their successors could call on a far wider base of technical support, and a pool of skilled labour to develop the limitless potential of the machine age. Through his education, ability, ambition and application Isambard Kingdom Brunel took the profession of engineer from grimy artisan to feted celebrity, earning himself a colossal reputation and undying fame. Brunel's range was simply astonishing, creating tunnels, bridges, railways, docks, vast open span buildings, prefabricated huts, and ships. He worked in timber, stone, brick, and especially iron, to transform the world in which he lived and lay out the guidelines for much of the one we live in today. Although his projects were largely successful, his ambition occasionally outran his ability, the materials technology of the time, and more often the intellects of his more pedestrian contemporaries. His was a genius largely untrammelled by money; his cost estimates were invariably too low, and he insisted on first class work and materials; for him there was only one standard of work, the best.

Ships were a permanent feature in the life of Isambard Kingdom Brunel. He was born in Portsea on 9 April 1806, at the time his father, the *émigré* French engineer Marc Brunel, was working on his epochal block mills in Portsmouth Dockyard. Sir Marc went on to develop steam saw mills, boot factories, a veneer plant, steamships and the Thames tunnel. His post-war attempts to interest the Admiralty in steamships were commercially unsuccessful, hampered by the opposition of powerful conservative forces within the Navy Board, especially the Surveyor of the Navy, Sir Robert Seppings.[1] His father's experience, while Isambard was still a youth, may well have coloured his attitude toward the Admiralty in the 1840s. Certainly Marc Brunel had far better reason to complain of his treatment by the Admiralty than Isambard. There was a delightful symmetry in the situation of the two Brunels: both

Isambard Kingdom Brunel, after a portrait by J C Horsley, 1858. (National Maritime Museum neg 8848)

recognised as the leading engineer of their era, both working as consulting engineer to the Admiralty, pioneering new technology. This point would not have escaped Isambard's notice.

Marc Brunel had provided his son with a unique, bilingual scientific, technical and engineering education. After studying mathematics in Caen and Paris, Isambard spent time in the Paris works of Louis Breguet, the leading French maker of chronometers and scientific instruments, and completed his education in the workshops of Henry Maudslay, the leading British engineer. Marc Brunel also introduced his son to a group of scientists, patrons and politicians who would play a critical part in his life. Men like Earl Spencer, the Duke of Somerset, Lord Lansdowne, Admiral Sir Edward Codrington and Lord Holland feature prominently in Brunel's career. Another prominent member of that circle was Charles Babbage, the pioneer of the mechanical analogue computer.[2] Babbage combined advanced liberal politics with a unique understanding of mathematics, science and engineering. He devoted much effort to his attempt to improve the standard of technical education, for the benefit of British industry. Babbage would play an important part in Brunel's life, from his earliest attempts to find work to the beginnings of Operational Research on railway gauges. Brunel regularly sought his advice for, unlike the majority of his engineering contemporaries, Brunel had the intellectual capacity to work with Babbage. Brunel's peculiar genius lay in straddling the then largely separate worlds of science and engineering. At the famous discussion of Dionysius Lardner's lecture claiming that ships could not steam across the Atlantic, Babbage and Brunel jointly destroyed Lardner's case, deploying a devastating combination of theory and experience.[3]

As might be expected of the son of a great engineer, Brunel's dominant ambition was to stand at the head of his father's profession, recognised by his peers and a wider public as *the* engineer. He neither sought, nor accepted, the usual rewards of public fame, honours and titles, and left precious little by way of personal fortune. Money was spent to demonstrate his status, on his house in Duke Street, a prestigious address in the heart of Westminster, which was presided over by a wife more noted for her beauty and accomplishments than any depth of emotional attachment. For Brunel

the advance of engineering, in due subordination to his God, was the ultimate reward.

In seeking a more human Brunel, to replace the selfless Victorian hero of engineering, we need to consider the man behind the achievement. Brunel was driven by an obsessive-compulsive personality, something that found outlets in his unceasing schedule of work and the habitual chain-smoking of cigars. He would empty his trade-mark humidor of fifty in a single day of frenetic movement that began early, and rarely ended in a night's sleep. Insomnia was one of the curses of his life, but characteristically he simply used the extra time to carry on working. He was reckless of his own life, and not always careful with those of his friends; he needed to try everything, to be at the head of progress, be it in the Thames Tunnel, first across the Clifton Gorge, hurrying into the engine room of the *Great Western* or driving himself home from Swindon one night, on the wrong side of the track, coming within minutes of a collision with the research train being used by his friend Babbage.[4] Furthermore, Brunel cannot have been an easy man to work for, demanding the same total commitment and perfection from his subordinates that he required of himself. His clashes with other engineers were almost as remarkable as his friendships: both Francis Humphrys and John Scott Russell saw the other side of the man, and only Russell survived the experience. Yet he was also a good friend to many, notably Francis Pettit Smith, the patentee of the screw propeller system, who he continued to support a decade after their collaboration.

By 1840 Brunel had succeeded in his greatest ambition, being then widely recognised as the leading engineer of the day. His work on the Great Western Railway was critical, but the related Great Western Steam Ship Company of 1835, which built and operated the first true Atlantic steamship, the eponymous *Great Western* was, if anything, more revealing. Brunel took no fee for this work, and invested his own money in the company. For Brunel the development of the steamship was an engineering legacy from his father, and an opportunity to test his vast range of engineering skill, and limitless vision, against the most demanding engineering environment of the age. In the space of twenty years he would perfect the wooden paddle-wheel steamship that his father had pioneered, introduce new materials into every aspect of ship structure and design, and apply a new propeller system to create the modern ship. By the time he died, tragically young, he had taken the ship to a scale and power that dwarfed the imagination of his contemporaries, to such an extent that his ship would never find a commercial use.

While Brunel's three 'Great' ships are relatively well-known, and show the full range of his intellect at work, this book introduces his fourth ship, one which demonstrated another side to this genius. HMS *Rattler*, the world's first screw propeller warship was fitted with an engineering plant conceived by Brunel, executed to his instructions, and tested under his supervision. For all the inspired genius of the myth his work on *Rattler* revealed the attention to detail, insistence on accurate trials and careful recording of data that remain the basis of development engineering. Brunel did not invent the screw propeller, but he, more than anyone else, ensured its success. At the same time his first two ships benefited greatly from close contact with the Admiralty.

Brunel worked on ships to the very end. He was on board the *Great Eastern,* supervising preparations for her sea trials, when he had a stroke on 5 September 1859. He lingered just long enough to hear of the disastrous explosion on board before he died, on the 15th. He was only 53. Daniel Gooch, who built the locomotives for the Great Western Railway, and later ran the *Great Eastern* as a cable-layer observed in his diary Brunel was:

> the greatest of England's engineers . . ., the man with the greatest originality of thought and power of execution, bold in his plans but right. The commercial world thought him extravagant; but although he was so, great things are not done by those who sit down and count the cost of every thought and act.[5]

In the years that have followed engineering has developed in such ways that the all-encompassing work of Brunel remains unequalled, and Gooch's tribute will stand for all time.

PART I: Brunel and Shipbuilding

The original sketch of the bow of Great Britain *at Dundrum done on the spot by Smyth, the artist for the* Illustrated London News. (National Maritime Museum neg PU6718)

A contemporary print of the Great Western *being floated out of her building dock, 19 July 1837. At this point she did not have her machinery fitted, so there is no funnel visible. (By courtesy of Denis Griffiths)*

1 Formation of the Great Western Steam Ship Company

Isambard Kingdom Brunel is given credit for originating the idea of a steamship line between Bristol and New York, the proposition being raised at a meeting of the Great Western Railway Company directors in October 1835. Concern was expressed that the proposed line between London and Bristol exceeded in length any railway then planned, but Brunel countered with the remark, 'Why not make it longer, and have a steamboat go from Bristol to New York?'. Most of those present treated the remark as a joke but following the meeting Brunel discussed the idea with Thomas Guppy, an engineer, and a number of other people including the businessmen Robert Scott, Thomas Pycroft and Robert Bright.[1] This, at least, is the story according to Brunel's son Isambard and although there is no reason to question the claim he makes on behalf of his father there is no evidence to authenticate it either. Whilst writing the biography and at the checking stage prior to publication Isambard sought help on marine matters from an associate of his father, Christopher Claxton,[2] the former Managing Director of the Great Western Steam Ship Company (GWSS Co) and one of the group who drew up the initial company prospectus. Brunel and Claxton had been close friends since 1832 when Brunel had been asked by the Bristol Dock Company to survey the Floating Harbour with a view to improving its operational efficiency, Claxton, a half-pay naval officer, then being Quay Warden at Bristol. This was a Municipal appointment and Claxton was not one of the Bristol Dock Company's employees.[3] Claxton was certainly in a position to know what went on prior to the founding of the GWSS Co as he quickly became involved but he was not at that initial meeting and any comments made to support the assertion would be hearsay.

Whether the claims of Isambard Brunel on behalf of his father are true does not really matter but what is certainly true and more important is that Isambard Kingdom Brunel played a significant part in getting the venture started and keeping it going. The establishment of the GWSS Co was something of a secretive affair as only six hand-written copies of the prospectus were made and circulated amongst the business communities of Bristol and Bath. Apart from a substantial holding taken by Brunel,[4] the majority of shares were held by residents of those cities, making the company somewhat parochial and, more importantly, under-capitalised. By the time the share list closed and the first meeting of the company was held on 3 March 1836 only about 1500 of the 2500 £100 shares had been taken; a deposit of £5 was required on each share and calls of £5 or £10 were expected to be made over a period until the shares became fully paid.[5]

Following Brunel's alleged comments at the GWR board meeting Thomas Guppy, a young engineer of similar age to Brunel, became enthusiastic and the pair soon found that other people held similar views on the possibility of a trans-Atlantic steamship service. A provisional committee was established and a prospectus issued; although Brunel appears to have avoided becoming involved in the management of the Great Western Steam Ship Company, he certainly played a part in acting as an adviser and became its consulting engineer. The initial prospectus called for two 1200-ton ships of 400 horsepower. Whilst the prospectus circulated Thomas Guppy, Christopher Claxton and William Patterson, a respected Bristol shipbuilder, made a tour of British steam ports in order to assess the current steamship situation. Naval contacts of Brunel and Claxton were also used in order to gain access to information from the Admiralty.

During the early years of the 1830s steamships were fairly common in the coastal waters around Britain and steamship services operated to European ports as far south as Gibraltar. A limiting factor in any steamship's operation was its coal consumption and coal bunkers occupied valuable cargo space; a small bunker capacity meant that more cargo could be carried but it limited the time which could be spent under steam and hence distance between ports if steam power was to be continuously employed. Naturally, sails could be used with or without steam assistance but the whole idea of employing steam was to enable the ship to operate irrespective of wind. On short-sea routes a ship could carry sufficient coal and cargo to make the venture worthwhile but on longer routes steam power was considered as auxiliary and only employed to supplement sail propulsion, particularly in light or contrary winds.

The Admiralty also appreciated the advantages of steam propulsion and in 1827 the steamers *Lightning*, *Meteor* and *Echo* appeared in the Navy List, whilst three years later the sailing packets which operated between Falmouth and the Mediterranean were replaced by steam vessels. In 1832 five 800-ton paddle-driven, steam-powered warships, *Medea*, *Rhadamanthus*, *Phoenix*, *Salamander* and *Dee,* were built by the Admiralty.[6] The 200-horsepower side lever engines fitted in HMS *Dee* were built by Maudslay, Sons and Field of Lambeth, this type of engine being an adaptation of the Watt beam engine and the most common employed for ship propulsion at that time. The rated or nominal power was not an actual measured power but was a function of cylinder dimension and boiler pressure, and this system of measuring engine power remained in common use for many years, even after adoption of the cylinder indicator, which could be employed to determine actual cylinder power, known as indicated power. Maudslays had a good reputation for quality machinery and was one of the few companies then able to construct high-powered steam plant. The Brunel family also had close connections with the company, Marc Brunel, Isambard Kingdom Brunel's father, having made the acquaintance of Henry Maudslay, founder of the company, shortly after he arrived in England at the end of the eighteenth century. The elder Brunel turned to Maudslay for construction of models, and subsequently the actual working plant, of his new block-making equipment and a long-term relationship between the Brunel family and the Maudslay company began.[7]

Without doubt Isambard learned much from this association with Maudslays, and it is likely that he gained an appreciation of the marine engine and its problems, but there was more to steam navigation

STEAM TO NEW YORK.

THE

Great Western,

Of 1340 *Tons Register, and* 450 *Horse Power,*

Strongly built, Coppered and Copper-fastened, with Engines of the very best construction, by Maudslay, Sons, and Field,

AND EXPRESSLY ADAPTED FOR THE BRISTOL AND NEW YORK STATION,

Lieut. JAMES HOSKEN, R.N., Commander,

Will Sail DIRECT *from Bristol*

On the 7th APRIL, 1838,

AT TWO O'CLOCK IN THE AFTERNOON.

The rate of Cabin Passage is 35 Guineas, to be paid on securing State Rooms, for which please to apply at

The GREAT WESTERN RAILWAY OFFICE,
Prince's-Street, Bank, London.
Messrs. GIBBS, BRIGHT, & CO., Liverpool.
Messrs. HAMILTON, BROTHERS & CO., Glasgow.
Mr. ROBERT HALL, Cork.
Mr. C. CLAXTON, *Managing Director,* Great Western Steam Ship Office, 19, Trinity-Street, Bristol.

To Officers on duty in her Majesty's Service, and their Families, some allowance will be made for their travelling expenses to Bristol ; and those from the Depot at Cork will have their passage-money, by the regular Steamers to Bristol, allowed. For Families, a reduction will be made in proportion to their numbers and the berths they require. Children under 13 years and Servants half price. No Letters will be taken except on payment of 1s. the single sheet each. Newspapers and Slips, 3d. each. Parcels in proportion to size and weight, and a small quantity of Light Goods at £5 per ton. Specie and Valuables, one-half per cent.

This Ship has Coal Stowage for 25 Days' constant Steaming, and therefore will not require to touch at Cork for Coal.

Printed at the Bristol Mirror Office by John Taylor.

than simply fitting a steam engine in a ship. By 1830 the reliability of the marine engine and boiler had improved to the extent that short-sea and coastal services could be operated effectively and economically, particularly in the high-earning mail and passenger trades. However, the real prize was oceanic transport, particularly on the Atlantic.

At that time it was generally believed that a steamship could not carry enough fuel for a direct voyage from Britain to New York and that the voyage would have to be accomplished in stages. One route proposed was via the Azores whilst another involved the Atlantic crossing between Valentia on the west coast of Ireland and Halifax, Nova Scotia. Champion of the Valentia scheme was Dr Dionysius

A poster advertising the maiden trans-Atlantic voyage of the Great Western. *The terms and conditions are interesting, and in particular the allowance that had to be made for Bristol's relative novelty as a packet station. (By courtesy of Denis Griffiths)*

Lardner, a cleric with some scientific knowledge and a self-styled authority on all forms of steam-powered transportation. Lardner, and others, believed that the power needed to drive a ship was directly proportional to the size of the ship and he founded his trans-Atlantic steamship plans using this opinion. Lardner based his views on results obtained from a pair of naval steamers, HMS *Dee* and HMS *Medea*, the most economical steamers then in service, and concluded that the best ship for a voyage to New York would be of 800 tons with a 200-horsepower engine. Why he concluded that such a ship was ideal for the journey between Britain and New York is not known but at that time *Dee* and *Medea* were the largest and most powerful steamers afloat. Ships of such size would be able to carry 400 tons of coal whilst machinery of the power envisaged would consume 20 tons per day on the 15-day voyage,

allowing a fuel reserve of 100 tons. Given the daily distance covered by a steamer of this size and power to be 170 miles, Lardner concluded that the distance which could be covered in 15 days was 2550 miles, insufficient to get from Liverpool to New York. He was of the opinion that to increase the size of the ship in order to carry more coal would require a proportionate increase in engine power to drive the ship through the water at the desired speed. With statistical data to back his claims, Lardner's opinions were treated seriously. Lardner put forward his views on a number of occasions, one of the first being at a meeting of the British Association for the Advancement of Science in Liverpool in December 1835. When plans for a direct steamship service between Liverpool and New York were announced at the end of 1835 Lardner commented that the proposal was '…perfectly chimerical, and they might

The maiden voyage of the Great Western, *a print by Cotman and Ackerman published on 21 July 1838. The passengers are gathered on the short poop to wave farewell to Bristol in the background.* (National Maritime Museum neg 3735)

as well talk of making a voyage from New York or Liverpool to the moon.'[8] At about this time the GWSS Co was attempting to attract shareholders and it is possible that Lardner's intervention had the effect of deterring some of the less committed businessmen of Bristol and Bath.

Brunel challenged Lardner's reasoning as fundamentally unsound, and he stated his opinions on oceanic travel. Brunel argued that the carrying capacity of a ship, including bunkers, increased with the cube of a dimension whilst the power requirement only increased with the square of a dimension. (This is accurate in terms of capacity but was not strictly true with respect to power requirement; however, it was certainly closer to the real operating conditions than Lardner's case.) Brunel asserted that doubling the size of a ship would not necessitate doubling the power and coal consumption: larger

ships would be profitable on the Atlantic and it would be possible to construct a steamer to make a voyage from Bristol to New York. The matter came to a head during Lardner's lecture to the British Association in Bristol during August 1836; unfortunately Brunel could not attend, but Joshua Field (the Field in Maudslay, Sons and Field, and a close friend of Brunel) was present and convincingly argued against the Lardner doctrine. Realising that he had no defence against good engineering reasoning, Lardner amended his views and stated that he '… considered such a voyage practicable, but wished to point out that which would remove the possibility of doubt, because if the first attempt failed it would cast damp upon the enterprise and prevent a repetition of the attempt.'[9]

Although incorrect in his reasoning with respect to steam power Lardner did have other reservations

Great Western in heavy weather, undated print by H E Hobson. The performance of paddle-wheels in oceanic conditions was a source of concern, but the officers soon learnt how to use steadying canvas to effect. (National Maritime Museum neg 2015)

about paddle-wheel propulsion which were more accurate. He correctly contended that paddle floats which were immersed at the ideal depth at the start of the voyage would not have full immersion at the end of the voyage due to the reduction in draught caused by the coal consumption. If wheels were immersed deeply at the start of the voyage in order to give a reasonable immersion at the end, then their efficiency at the start would be adversely influenced. A further disadvantage with paddle wheels, he argued, was that during bad weather, frequently to be found on the Atlantic, their floats would be immersed by varying amounts as the vessel rolled or waves passed.[10] If Brunel was not already aware of this he quickly accepted the argument and later became a convert to screw propulsion, because the screw did not suffer in this way.

Whilst Guppy, Claxton and Patterson made their tour of British steamship ports Brunel was engaged upon other work, most notably for the Great Western Railway – he was, after all, a professional engineer who had to earn a living and he was giving his services free to the GWSS Co. At that time there were no arbitrary distinctions between the likes of mechanical, marine or railway engineering, and all good engineers could apply themselves to whatever was required or get specialists to deal with the areas they were unhappy with or preferred others to tackle. Brunel was not just a solo engineer who went around Britain, and Europe, solving various problems and building the odd railway here and there: he was essentially an engineering consultancy with a staff of draughtsmen, assistants and pupils, who did much of the basic work for him. He directed operations and checked other people's work before it was passed to contractors. Without that staff he could not have become involved with the variety and number of contracts with which he was concerned at any one time. Undoubtedly he found great satisfaction in the work and certainly enjoyed the fame and fortune it brought; one only has to read a biography of the man to appreciate that he had a very full life. Whilst it is considered that the Great Western Railway was his major achievement, and one of which he was certainly proud, he was paid for that work whereas his services to the GWSS Co were given without expectation of financial gain, apart from anticipated earnings from his shareholding. That must say a great deal about his concern for the venture and his views on its ultimate success.

Upon conclusion of the tour by Guppy, Claxton and Patterson a report, dated 1 January 1836, was presented and this contained recommendations concerning the size, type of construction and power of steamships which would be suitable for Atlantic trade. After reading the report and discussing the tour with the committee Brunel decided that the engine power could safely be reduced to from 400 to 300 horsepower. At that time steamships belonging to the Royal Navy had a tonnage-to-power ratio of four to one, and a proposed 1200-ton ship could, therefore, be powered by a 300-horsepower engine.[11] This indicates that the powering of ships was still very much on a 'rule of thumb' basis rather than from any deep scientific reasoning.

The Genesis of the *Great Western*

As a result of the January 1836 report a new prospectus was issued and this proposed construction of two 1200-ton steamships of 300 horsepower, the estimated cost of each being £35,000.[1] The committee acknowledged problems in estimating the coal consumption and bunker capacity requirements for an Atlantic voyage due to the variable nature of coal. Because of his railway work Brunel was well aware of the problem with coal. Welsh steam coal was by far the best and for a service across the Atlantic from Bristol this could be classed as local and readily obtained; however, bunkers would need to be lifted in New York as it would be totally impractical to bunker the ship for a round trip. An initial idea to shut down the machinery when winds were favourable was abandoned by the committee in its report. Ships of the GWSS Co would steam all the way across the Atlantic. The first formal meeting of the Company took place in March 1836 when directors were elected and a decision taken to make the concern a 'large partnership' rather than a public company.[2] The reasoning behind this appears to have been that it would avoid the need to hold public meetings and enable matters to be kept between the rather small band of shareholders. Whilst this may have had certain advantages the rather parochial nature of the company limited its ability to attract finance when urgently needed in later years.

Although not a member of the committee Brunel

Hull lines of the Great Western. (By courtesy of Denis Griffiths)

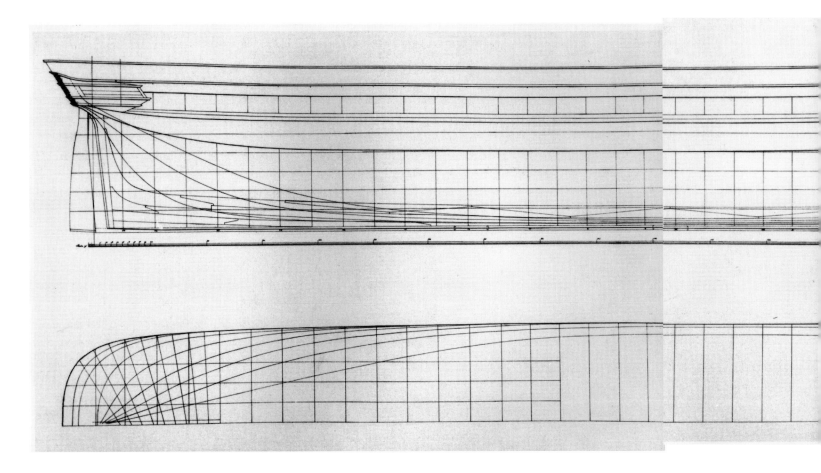

was constantly busy on behalf of the company and his contacts with engineering concerns (particularly Maudslay, Sons and Field) enabled him to keep abreast of current engineering matters particularly as they related to ship propulsion. Having decided to construct two 1200-ton ships with 300-horsepower engines at its first meeting the directors appear to have quickly changed their collective mind and Brunel would appear to have been involved in assisting that change of mind. A single ship would be built and this would also be constructed by the company and not by means of a contract to a shipbuilder, as a contract would have limited the ability to incorporate modifications. There was much to be said for taking this step as the intended vessel was the largest steamship which had been built to that time and construction would have to be carefully undertaken. Brunel suggested that a building committee be established to oversee construction of the hull; this committee comprised Brunel, Guppy, Claxton and William Patterson, a local shipbuilder who had been selected to superintend construction of the hull. The hull itself was to be built in the yard of Patterson and Mercer located on the Floating Harbour in Bristol, close to the Princes Street bridge. The building

committee met at Claxton's or Guppy's house whenever Brunel was in Bristol on railway business, which was usually about once every week.[3]

Even though he was not a shipbuilder nor had any real maritime experience, maybe even because of these facts, Brunel took a close interest in the actual construction of the hull and, with Patterson's assistance, was responsible for the implementation of strengthening measures thought desirable to meet the rigors of Atlantic crossings. Patterson had drafted the lines of the hull and had supervised the building but he would have worked closely with Brunel on matters related to the strength of the hull construction. Brunel quickly decided that the ship should be larger than originally intended but, influenced by Patterson's concern regarding stability, the directors decided, at first, to leave any increase in size to the second vessel. An increase to 1400 tons was sanctioned when Brunel suggested to the directors that it would be advantageous to install more powerful engines of 400 horsepower.[4]

Although Brunel was a good structural engineer and readily appreciated the need for a strong hull, he had to be made aware that a ship was not simply a floating building. During construction, and supported by Guppy, he expressed a wish to have the stern cabin windows made like drawing-room windows of a house in order to make the ship seem more hospitable to the passengers. Claxton and Patterson took the liberty of reminding their shore-based engineers that the sea could get very unpleasant at times and they agreed that suitable nautical proportions should be applied to these stern windows.[5]

Brunel was given complete responsibility for selection of the machinery to propel the ship and he invited tenders for machinery of about 400 horsepower from a number of manufacturers. Three tenders were received: from Messrs Winwood, a local Bristol concern; from Messrs Fawcett & Company; and from Messrs Maudslay, Sons and Field of Lambeth. The tender called for supply of boilers and engine(s); at that time a cylinder was referred to as an engine and so a two-cylinder side lever engine would be classed as two engines even though both cylinders drove the same paddle shaft. After careful consideration of the tenders Brunel recommended that Maudslays be awarded the contract to supply the engines and boilers. A major factor in his decision to recommend Maudslay, Sons & Field was that concern's experience in building large marine engines

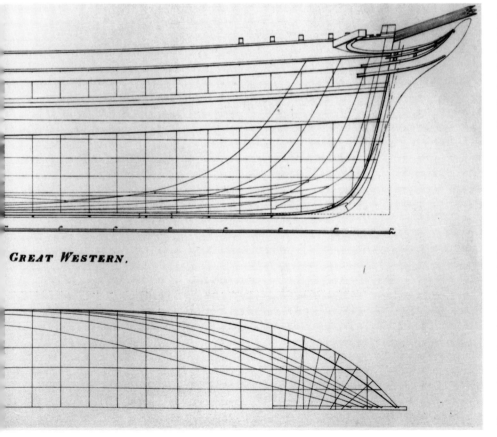

GREAT WESTERN.

for the Admiralty, but there was also the fact that Brunel had known the people at Maudslays and the company's workmanship and he knew that he could trust them to deliver. In recommending Maudslays Brunel wrote to the directors:

> In considering the three tenders for the supply of marine engines for your first vessel, which you have submitted to me for my opinion, I have assumed that the interests of the company are paramount, and that all feelings of partiality towards any particular manufacturer or any local interest must yield to the absolute necessity, in this the first and the boldest attempt of the kind yet made, of not merely satisfying yourselves that you will obtain a good engine, but also of taking all those means of securing the best which in the eyes of the public may be unquestionable. In this view of the case, if you agree with me, I think you will consider that, provided the prices are fair individually, the relative amount of the tender is of secondary consideration.

Showing his concern that the first voyage must be a success, he went on to add:

> You will remember, also, that it will be the longest voyage yet run; that in the event of unfavourable weather a total failure might be the result of the engine not working to its full power, or consuming too great a quantity of coals – a very common occurrence with engines apparently well made, after six or seven day's constant work; and, lastly, that the future success of the boat as a passenger ship – nay, even of the company's boats generally, and, to a great extent, and for some time, the reputation of Bristol as a steamboat station, may depend upon the success of this first voyage. It is indispensable, therefore, to secure as far as possible a machine that shall be perfection in all its detail from the moment of its completion.

The letter concluded with his recommendation:

> With these facts before you, it remains only for you to consider how far you agree with me in the conclusions that I have come to, and which I have no hesitation in expressing – that I think

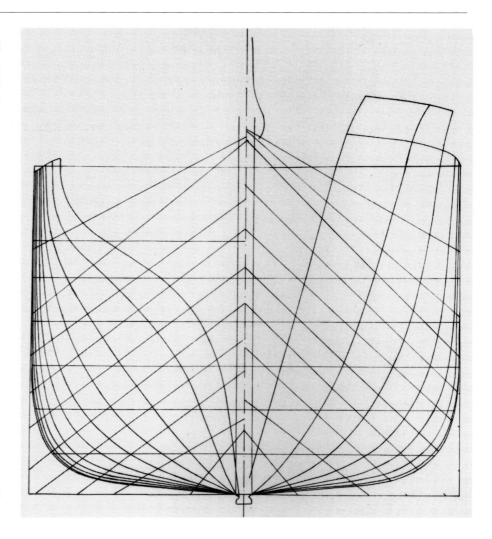

you will be safest, in the peculiar case of the first ship, in the hands of the parties who have had most experience, and that Messrs Maudslay are those persons. Their price is, I think, moderate.

The board did agree and Maudslay, Sons and Field were awarded the contract for the machinery.[6]

Whilst construction of the hull continued – the keel had been laid in June 1836 – Brunel made regular visits to Maudslay's factory at Lambeth in order to monitor progress on the machinery. This was necessary from a professional point of view in order to ensure quality but also for financial reasons as payment for the machinery had been arranged in instalments, each instalment being due at a particular stage of construction. Brunel had to authorise payment of particular instalments. It had been the intention that the *Great Western* would make her maiden voyage to New York in the autumn of 1837 and in a letter dated 4 April 1837 Brunel advised the directors that the machinery would be ready, work being in such a state as to justify the second stage payment.[7]

Great Western *body plan.* (By courtesy of Denis Griffiths)

TOP RIGHT *This locally printed engraving, which was accompanied by fulsome details of the* Great Western, *shows how much the ship was regarded as a Bristol venture and a source of local pride.* (By courtesy of Denis Griffiths)

RIGHT Great Western *as completed with short poop. The print by Robertson is dated 1838.* (National Maritime Museum neg 4822)

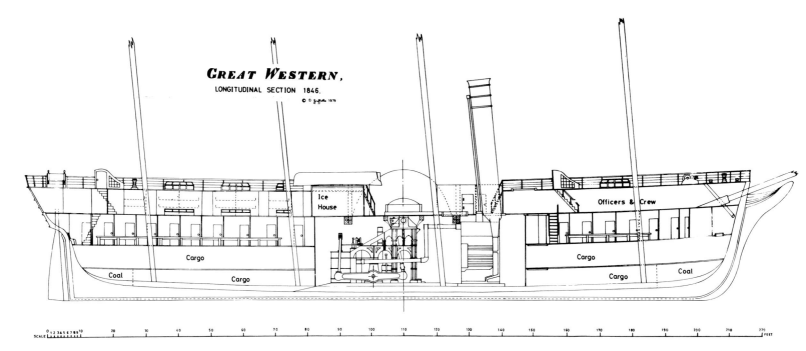

GREAT WESTERN,
LONGITUDINAL SECTION 1846.

It had been decided to have the machinery installed in London rather than Bristol for a number of reasons, including the fact that modifications to the engines, the largest built to that date, would be easier close to Maudslay's engine works at Lambeth rather than in Bristol. There was also likely to be a significant cost saving in having engines and boilers installed in London; the actual cost difference between installation at Bristol and in London for *Great Western* are not known but in 1839 Brunel estimated a difference in cost for slightly larger engines to be £3150 in favour of London.[8]

Selection of the Chief Engineer and all engine room staff had been left to the machinery builders to arrange and George Pearne had been appointed Chief Engineer on the strong recommendation of Maudslays.[9] This was a reasonable move, probably at the suggestion of Brunel, as Maudslays had a complete understanding of the requirements for operating the machinery and there were no experienced deep-sea marine engineers then available.

It is certain that Brunel visited the ship in the East India Dock whilst her machinery was being installed although there are no records of such visits. The need for inspections in order to sanction payments due to Maudslays would have necessitated such attendance but the concern he had for the ship and the venture as a whole would have guaranteed his presence on board whenever time allowed. With installation of the machinery complete, *Great Western* moved to a river berth at Brunswick Wharf early in March 1838 in order to prepare for engine trials. Two trial trips

were arranged during that month, these taking the ship down to Gravesend and back. Prior to the first trial on 24 March the boilers had been under steam for two days and slow turning of the engines whilst at the berth confirmed that all was well. Brunel was present for that first trip, and so were many other people, including a number of interested engineers.[10] It is not known if Brunel was present during the second trial trip on 28 March, but representatives from Maudslays were, including Joshua Field, and they expressed complete satisfaction with the machinery. Field and other representatives from the engine builders, including Joseph Maudslay, carried out experiments, including the taking of indicator diagrams in order to assess the actual engine power being developed.[11] Adjustments were made to the paddle wheels during the second trial trip and an average speed of 11 knots was achieved for a period whilst near Gravesend.

With all aspects of the ship performing to expectation *Great Western* could be moved to Bristol in order to prepare for her first voyage. The trip to Bristol commenced on 31 March with a number of distinguished visitors on board, including Brunel's father, Sir Marc Isambard Brunel. On passage down river Brunel, Field and Joseph Maudslay conducted further engine tests, again including the taking of indicator diagrams from the cylinders.

The visitors left when the ship was off Gravesend but about half an hour later a strong burning smell was noticed with smoke and flames being observed near the base of the funnel. Fearing for his ship, the

Longitudinal section of the Great Western *as modified 1846.* (Drawn by Denis Griffiths)

master, James Hosken, put *Great Western* aground on the mud of Leigh. The chief engineer, George Pearne, entered the smoke-filled engine room and opened the feed water supply to the boilers in order to fill them and so prevent rapid rise in pressure due to the additional heating caused by the fire; had he not taken this action an explosion could have resulted. An extract from the Pearne's engine room log details the events.

SATURDAY, 31st MARCH
3h. 45m., A.M., lighted fires.
6h. 10m., A.M., started; calm and inclined to be foggy.
7h. 30m., A.M., stopped to put out some persons at Gravesend; all going on well.
8h. 30m., A.M. a fire broke out in the region of the chimney, from the oil in the felt on the steam chests having ignited, which threatened destruction to the ship; the fore stoke-hole and

engine-room soon became enveloped in dense smoke, and the upper part in flame. Thinking it possible the ship might be saved, and that it was important to save the boilers, I crawled down, after a strong inhalation of fresh air, and succeeded in putting on a feed plunger and opening all the boiler feed cocks, suffering the engines to work to pump them up, as the steam was generating fast from the flames round the upper part of boilers. A small fire-engine was got to work on deck; C. Claxton, Esq., and the Chief Officer, descending with the hose, at great risk. We shortly after got the engines and hand pumps to work, and all hands baling, pumping, &c., succeeded in extinguishing the fire. The most melancholy part of the catastrophe was that I. K. Brunel, Esq., in attempting to go down the fore stoke-hole ladder, stepped on a burnt rung, several of which, in this state, giving way. Precipitated

Great Western sailing from the Avon; another contemporary print. (By courtesy of Denis Griffiths)

him down to the bottom, about 20 feet, falling on Mr. Claxton. He was taken up apparently seriously injured, and ultimately sent on shore. The vessel was run aground, in soft mud, not far from the Chapman Beacon. During the confusion, three or four stokers got over the side, into a boat, and left the ship. After a few hours, no very material damage having been done, got steam up, and started down the river.[12]

Claxton's action saved Brunel's life: he not only broke the fall but Brunel landed face downwards in a pool of water and if his friend had not pulled him clear one of Britain's foremost engineers may well have drowned. Brunel was not seriously injured but had to be confined to bed; however, within three days he had recovered enough to dictate a long letter to Claxton about the state of the ships and its machinery.[13] In rushing to the engine room without regard for the danger Brunel expressed his feelings for the *Great Western*, his ship, his concept. He was an engineer, Consulting Engineer to the Great Western Steam Ship Company and a shareholder in the company, but he gave his services free of charge and had no responsibility other than as a professional engineer. It was not his job to extinguish the fire but he risked his life to do so. In his other engineering ventures he certainly gave full value for the fees he was paid but his actions at the time of the fire and from the formation of the company indicate a passion for the venture which was not financially induced.

During the passage to Bristol Joshua Field, Joseph Maudslay and George Pearne continued with their engine experiments but there were difficulties in keeping steam pressure due to the reduced number of stokers remaining on board. This problem remained and during the first crossing to New York considerable troubles were experienced in maintaining steam due to the difficulties in getting coal to the boilers from the far ends of the ship. Coal had to be transported in barrows or baskets and as coal stocks close to the bunkers were used it was necessary for the coal trimmers to collect coal from bunkers further and further away from the boilers – not an easy task with the ship pitching and rolling. On the fifth day out Pearne decided that the trimmers and stokers should work twelve hours instead of eight. Conditions did not improve when the trimmers and stokers went off watch as their sleeping berths had been placed close to the boilers and they became too hot for effective sleep, resulting in considerable fatigue. At times the coal supply rate became so low that two out of the four boilers had to be shut down. On 17 April, eleven days after leaving Bristol and four days before arrival at New York, Pearne had to turn all engine room hands out, with the promise of an extra half dollar pay, in order to shift coal from the extreme end bunkers. On a number of days seamen had to be assist the trimmers and stokers with the moving of coal and disposal of ashes.[14]

These events illustrate that, despite great care having been taken with purchase of the machinery, little understanding existed with regards to operating a steamer on a long oceanic voyage. The company and its servants had no experience upon which to base the design of its ship or its operation as no steamer service between Britain and New York had at that time been operated. In publishing the logs of the first voyage (C Claxton, *Logs of the First Voyage of the Great Western*, Bristol 1838) the GWSS Co performed a valuable service to the shipping industry in general as it released some valuable information which, possibly, helped later companies avoid similar problems of manning levels and bunkering arrangements. The published logs did not, however, tell the full story as Claxton wished to avoid some bad publicity relating to a mutinous event on the part of one of the stokers and the published log book was an edited version of the actual engine room log. The stoker in question, by the name of Crooks, described by Pearne as a lazy shuffling fellow, decided that the extra work was too much and took to the bottle. At the time alcohol was not available on board for crew members but there was ample opportunity to smuggle some on board in London or whilst anchored in the River Avon before the voyage. Being drunk Crooks did not turn up for his watch on 20 April and upon being brought before the Chief Engineer and Master became abusive to both of them. He was restrained on the poop but broke free and attempted to throw the Master, James Hosken, overboard. Crooks was restrained more securely and the remaining engine room hands 'knocked-off' until he was released. The mutiny petered out when Crooks, a little while later, complained of being ill and, after being given some medicine, retired to bed.[15] The only reference to the period of the incident in the published log was '10.00am, scarcely any steam produced'

3 Brunel, the Navy and the Screw Propeller

The success of the *Great Western*, coming on top of the enormous critical success of the railway project that spawned her, provided Brunel with the status he craved. He was now *the* Engineer. The ship expanded his repertoire, and provided him with an opportunity to stand on the national stage, at the head of his profession, as an advisor to the Government on a matter of profound importance. While this was, no doubt, extremely flattering, it also enabled the Great Western Steam Ship Company (GWSS Co) to recoup something from the wreck of their hopes for a mail contract. Through his pioneering work in adapting the *Great Britain* for the screw propeller Brunel became the leading *independent* source of advice on the new system. He was the only engineer of note in the field who was not trying to *sell* propellers or patents, and one of very few who believed in the screw. That did not mean that his advice was entirely disinterested, merely that he provided it for a different form of reward.

Brunel's work with the Admiralty has been widely misunderstood, becoming an integral part of the mythology of naval opposition to technological progress. Re-examining Brunel's role in the introduction of the screw propeller into the Royal Navy provides a critical insight into the process of technical change, the role of government in managing progress. There is an enduring myth that the world's navies were reactionary, or at best unduly conservative in their handling of technical change in the nineteenth century. This, it has been argued, was symptomatic of large hierarchically structured bureaucracies which were opposed to change in any area, from uniform regulations to weapons procurement. This view is reflected in the work of historians of the liberal progressive school for whom conservatism in technology, as in politics, is the mark of an unthinking and bigoted reactionary. They contend that, had the world's navies been more adventurous, technical progress would have been more rapid, and more economical.

CREATING A MYTHOLOGY

Existing accounts treat the introduction of the screw propeller as a technical issue, isolated from politics, finance, strategy, tactics, and even the inner workings of naval administration. For too long the underlying assumptions about the propeller, and the engineers who worked with it, have been based on self-serving contemporary pamphlet literature, the latter-day complaints of disappointed speculators and the anti-establishment outpourings of advanced *laissez faire* liberals of the mid-century, who really believed the millennium was at hand. By failing to question the underlying assumptions of this literature, subsequent generations have done a grave disservice to the memories of several hard-working, professional men.

The essential argument is that a 'conservative' bureaucracy either misunderstood or deliberately opposed each new manifestation of progress. This line of attack can be traced back through contemporary pamphlets, which were little more than glorified sales brochures, into the more durable biographies and general histories. Perhaps the first, and most influential renditions of this 'critical' version was provided by Isambard Kingdom Brunel junior's biography of his father, of 1870. Isambard junior largely created the genre, linking his father with other engineers and inventors of the era. He suggested that these men worked for the good of mankind and the benefit of their country. Consequently the opposition of the Admiralty could only be explained by stupidity or malice. Isambard junior based his case on his father's favourite anecdote, concerning the 'adverse influence which had been exerted in some departments of the Admiralty to prevent the successful issue of these experiments'.[1] This story was perpetuated in the standard modern life.[2] The source for the anecdote was Brunel's friend 'Captain' Christopher Claxton, RN (1790-1868). Claxton provided Brunel with 'liberal' naval connections that were vital to his work on the *Great Western*, and later the propeller. An important contributor to the GWSS Co, and other shipbuilding and railways projects around Bristol, Claxton was actually only a half-pay Lieutenant in the Royal Navy. Despite an active and successful naval career Claxton received little reward; he was only promoted Commander in June 1842, in recognition of his assistance with the propeller, and became retired Captain in 1860.[3] Evidently Claxton bore a grudge against the post-war tory Admiralty boards, elaborating the most extreme version of an anecdote that his friend had told so often that it became a parody of truth. Not everyone connected with Brunel believed Claxton's version. His younger son Henry did not believe Claxton's stories, and was disappointed to find his brother retelling them in the biography.[4] They were good stories, but they do not stand up to close scrutiny.

When Brunel's near contemporary, the brilliant Swedish engineer John Ericsson received his valedictory biography, his brief relationship with the Admiralty Board was portrayed in equally bleak terms.[5] By that time the liberal progressivist version, in which the Admiralty was the source of all obstruction, had been adopted by the standard history of the Royal Navy.[6] It would be followed in the standard study of the development of marine engineering.[7] These accounts assume that anyone but a fool, and a peculiarly conservative fool at that, would have seen the merits of the propeller from the beginning, and pressed for its immediate adoption. They ignore the key questions that surrounded the process. These were financial, technical, political, tactical and strategic. When they have been addressed it is possible to see the propeller in a wider context, providing an altogether more complex chain of events. And Brunel's role in the process was far from straightforward.

The Admiralty was not dragged reluctantly into the adoption of the propeller. It was well aware of what was happening from the beginning, maintained a careful watching brief, intervened in particular experiments to great effect, forced the private sector to conduct much of the fundamental research and early trials without adequate recompense, and then took control of in the process at a decisive moment, just as the technology matured, to secure all the patent rights and build the world's first all-steam fleet. By bringing Brunel into the process they secured the best engineering advice for a pittance. Far from the reactionary image created by the engineers and their hagiographers, the most common complaint of contemporaries was that they had been 'defrauded', and that the Admiralty would only deal with people it could 'bully or defraud'.[8] Such problems as there were reflected the impact of political change and internal friction on a semi-reformed naval administration.

STEAM, STRATEGY AND TACTICS

By the mid-1830s intelligent naval officers understood steam technology, and recognised the implications of each new development without any prompting from the host of inventors, speculators and cranks who pestered the Admiralty. The naval response to new technology was not one of unthinking animosity or blind worship of the past. Naval officers were well informed because the development of naval strategy and tactics between 1805 and 1840 made steam increasingly important. After the crushing victory of Trafalgar the whole thrust of naval operations had shifted from fleet combat to littoral warfare, the projection of power from the sea. Large vessels could only operate close inshore with steam power; consequently steam propulsion was critical to the maintenance of naval mastery.

The earliest naval steamers were paddle-wheel tugs and packet boats. As they became larger they mounted some guns, making them useful auxiliary warships, and capable of tactical towing. By the 1850s large paddle-wheel frigates, such as HMS *Terrible*, were capable of strategic towing, mounted 24 guns, and cost as much as a small battleship. However, they were too vulnerable for the line of battle, their large wheels blocked much of the broadside, and the machinery, wheels, shafts, cranks and even boilers, were exposed to gunfire. They were also poor performers under sail, which limited their strategic utility. Their real value lay in the projection of naval power ashore, where their mobility and large paddle-box boats made them ideal for amphibious assault and inshore bombardment. Because there were no regular fleet actions between 1805 and 1866 the paddle-wheel steamer achieved a misleadingly high profile as a naval weapons system.

The fundamental problems of the paddle-wheel warship had been recognised by the mid 1830s, and intelligent officers were already looking for solutions.[9] Ultimately the screw propeller would answer all of their requirements, enabling the standard

The Royal Navy first embraced steam tactically for the towing of line of battle ships. This was not just to facilitate getting these unwieldy ships in and out of harbour, but paddle vessels were also used to manoeuvre them in action. Here the paddle sloop Virago *is shown towing the* Queen, *110 guns, to sea from Grand Harbour, Malta.* (National Maritime Museum neg 3553)

wooden sailing warship to be fitted for steam power without the loss of its broadside battery or efficient sailing rig. The screw transformed steam from an auxiliary power installed in auxiliary warships to an auxiliary power installed in front-line warships. Before examining Brunel's role in the introduction of the new system it is necessary to consider the administrative structure that had to manage the change.

THE ADMIRALTY AND THE STEAM WARSHIP

While there has been much criticism of the 'Admiralty' response to the screw propeller, the real problem was one of administrative structure. In 1832 British naval administration had been subjected to the first comprehensive overhaul in three hundred years. The age-old distinction between the Board of Admiralty, charged with the political and military direction of the service, and the Navy and Victualling Boards, which maintained the fleet, ran the dockyards, and fed the men, was ended. Day-to-day administration was turned over to the Board of Admiralty, the other Boards being abolished. At one level this saved a small amount of money, in accordance with the political programme of the new whig government. More fundamentally the whigs had long wanted to abolish the Navy Board, which they believed was dominated by conservative nominees. The 1832 reform was triumph of ideology and political revenge over common sense.[10]

Hitherto the Navy Board had developed annual construction programmes, organised the dockyards and advised the Admiralty on shipbuilding and steam engineering. Led by experienced naval officers and ship designers the Navy Board even had its own engineer. Between 1832 and 1852, when the need for sound advice on technology and long-term policy was greater than ever, the Navy Board would be sadly missed. Under the new system the Admiralty would rely on the Surveyor of the Navy for this advice. Hitherto the Surveyor, a dockyard-trained naval architect, had been a member of the Navy Board, but the new Surveyor, Captain William Symonds, was a naval officer with some intuitive design ideas. The central tenet of Symonds' work was the primacy of speed in naval warfare, both under sail and steam. He was convinced the problem of the next war, as it had been in the last, would be to catch the enemy. Although tasked with developing construction policy Symonds was more interested in promoting his own designs, and lacked the funds to maintain the fleet. Appointed by the whig ministers his term in office would be dominated by party politics.[11] In addition the Surveyor's Office, like the Admiralty as a whole, was short of staff and money. The Admiralty simply did not have the manpower to conduct fundamental research, and, as this chapter will demonstrate, found it hard to exploit or even retain the results of the research it had already

conducted.[12] It was against this background, starved of funds, short-handed and lacking any coherent long-term policy, that the Royal Navy had to respond to the screw propeller. Despite these problems the Navy handled the introduction of the screw with remarkable success, demonstrating the inherent professionalism of British naval administration.

To add to the confusion a new Steam Department, under the Controller of Steam, was created on 19 April 1837. This was an official recognition that steam was now critical to naval operations. The first Controller, the Arctic explorer Captain Sir William Edward Parry, was selected because his brother-in-law, Lord Stanley of Alderley, was patronage secretary to the whig ministry.[13] Until his untimely death in 1842 the expertise of the new Department was provided by Peter Ewart, a conservative engineer trained at Boulton & Watt. As the relationship between the two departments was never formally settled Symonds, by far the stronger character, effectively ignored Parry and left the

ABOVE *Sir William Symonds, the Surveyor of the Navy from 1830 to 1847. Although invariably cast as the villain in the propeller story, his input was positve and valuable.* (National Maritime Museum PA18837)

LEFT *Captain Sir William Edward Parry was best known as an Arctic explorer, but an arguably greater contribution to the advancement of the Royal Navy was his stint as the first Controller of the Steam Department after 1837. Oil painting by Charles Skottowe.* (National Maritime Museum BHC2938)

personalities, and the failure to prepare long-term programmes had all influenced the handling of the new technology. Fortunately the private sector had been prepared to carry out the fundamental research.

THE SHIP PROPELLER COMPANY AND THE PROMOTION OF SCREW PROPULSION, 1836-52

In examining the Admiralty's response to the screw propeller it should be stressed that finance and politics were far more important than technological innovation. One of the perennial, irritating features of so much comment on the supposed 'failure' of the Royal Navy and the mercantile community to adopt steam and the various improvements in power and propulsion at the proper time is the conceit that Ericsson, Francis Pettit Smith and others were attempting to 'interest' their fellow men in the new technology for the good of mankind.[17] In truth the engineering community wanted to sell their ideas. Ericsson's disgust at the commercial failure of his

ABOVE *Peter Ewart, the engineer on whose expertise the Navy's Steam Department depended until his death in 1842* (National Maritime Museum PAG6534)

RIGHT *Francis Pettit Smith shown with a model of the* Archimedes. *The print credits the introduction of screw propulsion to Smith's 'talent & untiring energies', and is part of the mythologising process that turned Victorian businessmen into heroic benefactors of mankind in the eyes of the public.* (National Maritime Museum PAH5593)

Steam Department to fit engines into his ships, rather than developing integrated steam warship designs.[14] This was particularly problematic as Symonds' hull form, which combined a broad beam with sharply rising floors, was peculiarly ill-suited to the installation of machinery. Symond's deputy, the senior constructor John Edye, was a cautious man. He was responsible for the structure of warships, and was well aware that paddle-wheel propulsion, which applied the drive above the upper deck, made less fundamental demands on the structure of the ship than a submerged propeller. His structural concerns had been heightened and focused by recent problems with the stern frames of large sailing warships.[15]

The relationship between steam engines and warships was only rationalised in March 1850, when the Steam Department was subsumed into the Surveyor's Office. This was a recognition that an all-steam navy, propelled by the screw, was only months away.[16] In the interval the fractures and divisions within the Admiralty, lack of manpower and money, the clash of

design in Britain should be viewed in purely pecuniary terms: it is simply incredible to argue that commercial success was not his prime motive. His sense of outrage reflected the failure to secure financial support from the Admiralty, and the brief confinement in the debtors' prison that followed. The prison term demonstrated that Ericsson did not have access to the capital required to develop the screw. His system, whatever its merits, needed Admiralty support to complete its development. The requirement for the Navy to fund this work doomed it to fail. The Navy simply did not have the money, the Naval Estimates of the 1830s being trimmed to the bone. Similarly Smith and his backers were not interested in science and experiment, but in royalties and financial success. While the Admiralty demonstrated remarkable skill, or an incredible degree of luck, both in avoiding such entanglements, and securing proven technology for the country at a reasonable price, the mercantile community made relatively little use of the patented system. In fact the screw was of little utility to the mercantile community before the development of compound engines and iron hulls.

The wooden hull of an ocean-going steamship lacked the rigidity to withstand the vibration of large, unbalanced engines driving a massive propeller through a long, heavy and imperfectly secured shaft. Only the world's navies could afford the cost of large wooden screw-propelled ships, since both the capital outlay and the alarming frequency of major repairs made them uneconomic.[18] It should be recalled that any number of speculators and cranks were also trying to lighten both private owners and the Government of funds, making caution essential. One of the main reasons for creating the post of Controller of Steam had been to filter out the 'cranks' before they troubled the Board.[19] The Admiralty, like the Navy Board before it, preferred to work with large, reliable contractors. For the screw propeller this role would be filled by the Ship Propeller Company. The brief life of the Ship Propeller Company (SPC) demonstrated the complex relationship between industry, commerce and government in the transitional era. While it proved vital to the success of the screw in the period 1840-45, it failed utterly in its main object, to make money, quickly split apart and collapsed.

Contrary to popular myth the screw propeller was not 'invented' by Francis Pettit Smith and John Ericsson. Marine screw propellers had been in use

for thirty years before these two men took out their patents. Furthermore when Smith refined his original general patent of 31 May 1836, he restricted his claim to the position of screw in the deadwood,[20] under the patent of 30 April 1839. Similarly Ericsson's patent of 13 January 1837 was for 'An *improved* propeller applicable to steam navigation'. There had been at least five worthwhile 'inventions' of the screw propeller, for use with steam engines, before 1836.[21] The deserved primacy in the field of Smith and Ericsson reflects their ability to secure the funds to develop and exploit the new technology, not a leap in design or technology. The Ship Propeller

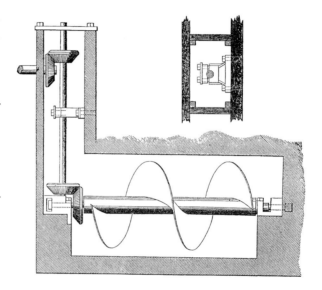

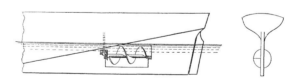

The form and position of Smith's original screw propeller. From A Treatise on the Screw Propeller, *by John Bourne.*

Company was incorporated by an Act of Parliament on 29 July 1839 to exploit Smith's Patented *location* for the screw propeller.[22] While the company demonstrated the technical success of the system, their commercial objects were restricted to selling licences to install propellers in the patented location, between the stern post and the rudder, rather than any tangible product. This was to be their downfall. At the time intellectual property rights, as protected by the Patent System, were ill-defined, and almost unenforceable at law.[23] Despite that, the introduction of the screw propeller into the Royal and United States Navies would be dominated by patents. The SPC wanted to sell their concept to the Admiralty, as

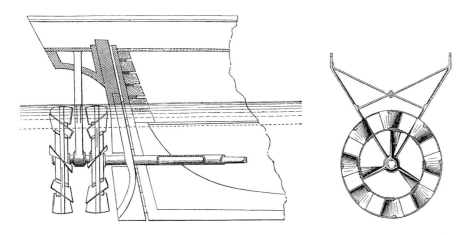

The form and position of Ericsson's original screw propeller. From A Treatise on the Screw Propeller, *by John Bourne.*

the largest shipbuilding concern and the richest purchaser. However, the Admiralty was more astute than they anticipated.

The leading members of the SPC recognised that access to the key decision-makers would be critical. Unlike the penniless, friendless Ericsson, they were an impressive group: John and George Rennie, recognised Admiralty engineering contractors,[24] the banker John Wright, the shipbuilder Henry Wimshurst and a colonial Governor and close friend of the whig ministers, Lord Sligo. Naval recommendations were also secured.[25] With a share capital of £100,000 and a London office the SPC was taken seriously by the Admiralty. The Admiralty exploited the SPC's anxiety to sell the system, effectively forcing it build the 200-ton *Archimedes* to prove the concept at sea, employed her while she remained useful, and then refused to take out any more licences than were absolutely necessary, or to buy the ship.[26] The private sector had conducted the fundamental research and development. The *Archimedes* was demonstrated to the Admiralty *before* the mercantile community. The officers and engineers on board for the first trial near London Bridge on 16 October 1839 included Parry, Symonds and Ewart. They recognised the experimental nature of the vessel, and the auxiliary nature of her machinery. They could also see that the ship was fatally flawed by the extremely long screw aperture, the convoluted bevel drive to the propeller and the cog-wheel gearing, while the inability of the company to settle on the purpose of the experiment, as an auxiliary steamship or a full-powered competitor for the paddle wheel limited her performance. Having proved that the screw was a useful propeller she was of no further use as a trials platform, being restricted to the role of commercial demonstrator. Almost immediately the Board instructed Captain Chappell and the Steam

Department engineer Thomas Lloyd to report on the ship and the system.[27] The Admiralty then hired the ship for further trials.[28] Although the *Archimedes* had proved the propeller concept, the Admiralty was unwilling to rely on the Ship Propeller Company, which had a fundamental commercial interest in the project. Fortunately they were able to call on an entirely different source of advice, from a man who did not have a financial stake in the success of the propeller.

BRUNEL AND THE SCREW PROPELLER

After her initial trials the *Archimedes* had been sent on a 'Round Britain Tour' to publicise the screw, and while at Bristol in May 1840 had been hired by the Great Western Steamship Company for a series of trials. Although Brunel recognised *Archimedes* was an inefficient compromise, he had the vision to modify his new iron transatlantic steamer into a screw vessel, bringing together for the first time the two key developments that created the modern ship. Alone of all those who saw the experimental ship he recognised the fundamental advantages of the screw for full-powered ships of the largest size, and was prepared to make a complete commitment to its success as the drive for a massive ocean-going vessel.[29]

In late 1839 and early 1840 Brunel had been anxious to improve the performance of the paddle wheels on the *Great Western*, examining more advanced board designs. Consequently the appearance of *Archimedes* at Bristol was particularly timely. After a cruise at sea the Great Western Company's Building Committee had sent Thomas Guppy with the little ship when she steamed to Liverpool, during the voyage she encountered heavy weather, and proved eminently seaworthy. The Building Committee then halted work on their new iron paddle-wheel vessel and her massive engines, while Brunel, who supported the decision, reported on the new system. This required him to hire the ship, and experiment with eight different screws. These experiments were conducted with the latest engine indicators to establish performance.[30] They were the first 'scientific' attempt to generate useful data from a screw ship.

After *Archimedes* returned to London Brunel advised the SPC to continue his work, notably on the frictional resistance of the screw, by towing her, and suggested that Captain Chappell RN of the

Packet Service would be able to provide a steamer for the task. He considered such experiments would help to promote the system, and left it to the SPC to publish the results. His only interest was to advise the Directors of the Great Western Steamship Company. Clearly he was aware of the Admiralty's involvement.[31] During the trials Brunel kept the SPC fully informed of his work, and provided important suggestions on how to transmit power from the crankshaft to the propeller, obviating the need for the bulky, inefficient and noisy spur wheel drive used on *Archimedes*. In return the Great Western Company was offered one or two free licences to use the patented location.[32]

Brunel left the day-to-day running of the propeller trials to others, particularly Claxton, his son Berkeley Claxton, and Thomas Guppy. In mid October he reported to Claxton:

A promotional print designed to show the superiority in heavy weather of the screw-driven Archimedes *(above) over a paddle vessel; and (below) a schematic layout of the ship that accompanied the print. (National Maritime Museum neg A8312)*

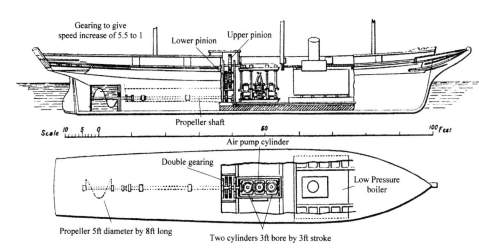

Gearing to give speed increase of 5.5 to 1

Lower pinion Upper pinion

Propeller shaft

Scale 10 5 0 50 100 Feet

Air pump cylinder

Double gearing

Low Pressure boiler

Propeller 5ft diameter by 8ft long

Two cylinders 3ft bore by 3ft stroke

A short time back Barnes,[33] who was with us on the *Archimedes* told Phipps[34] that he had considered the results of our experiments had made the screw <u>better</u> than the common paddle wheel as 4 to 3, but a little under Morgan's [paddle wheels] . . . but that taking into consideration all the advantages of the screw it was better than any paddle and that he had no doubt it would soon supersede the paddle. I never heard this till today. Phipps is positive of the whole. This is satisfactory, but except to Guppy or Bright[35] do not mention it.[36]

Within days Brunel had compiled a powerful report to the Directors of the Great Western Steamship Company, as their engineering adviser, recommending that the new iron Atlantic steamer then under construction, should be adapted for the propeller. The justly famous document demonstrated Brunel's considerable theoretical knowledge of hydrodynamics, the detailed experiments conducted under his guidance, the success of the principle, as demonstrated by *Archimedes*, and the allowance that to be made for the inferior design and manufacture of that vessel's engineering installation, from her engines and boilers to the dog leg shafting, and geared drive.[37] In December the Building Committee accepted Brunel's recommendation.

However, even before this decision had been ratified the Steam Department of the Admiralty was anxious for reports on 'the large iron ship, including the <u>Screw</u>'.[38] At this stage the process of adopting the screw for the Navy, and for the Great Western Company, was going ahead smoothly. Brunel dined with Captain Chappell and Francis Pettit Smith.[39] At Parry's request Brunel submitted an unofficial copy of his propeller report to the Admiralty, suggesting that Lord Minto, the First Lord of the Admiralty, might like to read it.[40] The following day Ewart, Chappell, the Controller of Channel Packets, and the engine builder Seaward were directed to attend a Committee on the Screw at the Office of the Controller of Steam.[41]

At this time the relationship between the Great Western Steamship Company and the Admiralty was complicated by the negotiations for the Atlantic Mail contract. The Company had responded to an Admiralty advertisement by tendering for the service in December 1839, only to be curtly rejected the following month.[42] The final contract, awarded to the Canadian Samuel Cunard, was almost identical to the Great Western offer. Cunard wisely secured access to the Prime Minister, Lord Melbourne through his mistress, Mrs Norton.[43] Unlike Brunel and his friends, who were on the radical wing of the liberal movement, Melbourne was an ex-Tory. The rejection left a legacy of mistrust between the Great Western and the Admiralty, which influenced Brunel's subsequent work. Despite this Brunel was closely connected to the ministers by politics and family. His brother-in-law, the radical MP Benjamin Hawes, was a member of the government, while a number of leading political figures were personal friends.

Even before he had solicited Brunel's report, which had been drawn to his attention by the SPC, Parry, as Controller of Steam, had recommended building a screw vessel. Chappell, who was closely involved with the SPC, advised constructing a replica of an existing steam packet.[44] Symonds agreed, although he was concerned that the screw would not be as fast as the paddle-wheel, a serious flaw in his view. Symonds' report was adopted by Lord Minto.[45] Parry advised building an experimental ship, based on the 200-nhp packet *Polyphemus*, with her stern configured for testing various screws.[46] A model of *Polyphemus*'s stern was sent to the SPC so they could advise how it should be modified. Their reply alarmed Symonds: he considered that an aperture 8ft long and 9ft 3 in deep would 'weaken the ship … particularly if she strikes the ground'.[47] This early clash of priories between the Surveyor and the Steam Department was, in all probability, instrumental in bringing Brunel into the equation.

In mid-March 1841 Brunel was called to the Admiralty by Parry and invited to direct the project, working with Symonds and Ewart, but having sole charge of the mechanical arrangements and the experimental testing of the ship. After the treatment previously accorded to the Great Western Company this was 'gratifying'.[48] The details were settled, although it would appear only verbally, at the Admiralty in a meeting in Minto's office on April 27th. Brunel's first concern was to obtain reliable trials data from *Polyphemus*, primarily her resistance in proportion to her midship area, as the basis of his calculations. These could be compared with the figures he had already obtained from *Archimedes*. This evidence was, of course, equally applicable to his own project, *The Great Britain*. Symonds quickly made the

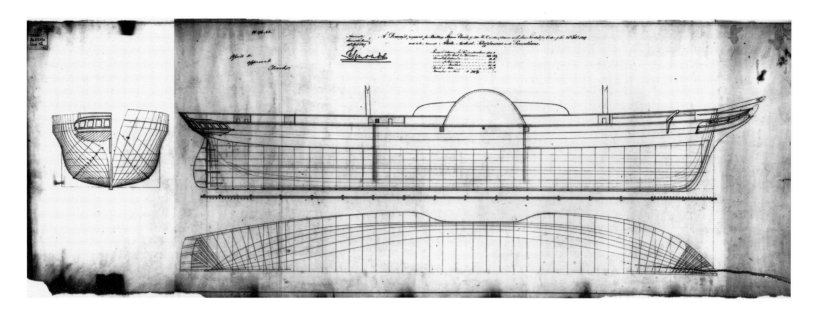

ship available, and attended the trials. Brunel appreciated the trouble he had taken and complemented the Surveyor on the excellent form of the ship.[49] He secured estimates for three different sets of 200 nhp engines and tried to persuade Minto to hasten the project. His report to Parry advised a propeller aperture 10ft 6in long and 11ft 6in deep. He recognised that if such a vast opening were necessary in all screw ships it would be fatal to the adoption of the system, but stressed that 'the construction of the vessel should, in the first instance, be made entirely subservient to the single object of making a full and complete <u>experiment upon this system of propelling</u>'. Once this was complete the screw aperture could be modified to suit the needs of the ship. He stressed that one of the major advantages of the new system would, 'undoubtedly be the facility it affords of carrying sail, either with or without the steam'.[50] Deputy Surveyor John Edye, writing in Symonds' absence, rehearsed all the Surveyor's concerns about structural integrity with a vehemence that revealed their source. While Symonds was an intuitive designer Edye was the professional shipbuilder in the Surveyor's Office. Edye objected that the elongated stern and sharp lines lacked buoyancy, and prevented the use of pivot guns at the stern.[51]

There was a minor crisis of confidence at this point, when Brunel believed that the Engineering Staff were reporting on his work. Parry hastened to assure him that this was not the case, and that Ewart was particularly anxious that Brunel should direct the whole project.[52] Whether this was out of admiration for his genius, or an unwillingness to

enter into any more quarrels with Symonds remains an open question. In order to place the process on a regular footing the main participants, Symonds, Parry, Chappell, Ewart, Brunel and Smith assembled in Minto's room at the Admiralty in late September 1841. Parry recommended that Brunel should be admitted to the 'conference' on the propeller, in view of the work he had already carried out for the Admiralty and the Great Western Company, and the fact that he had no financial stake in the project.[53] Although he agreed, Symonds objected that Brunel's proposed aperture was even greater than Smith's, which he considered a serious objections to the propeller.[54] Understandably Smith was far from pleased by this turn of events.[55] A year later he was still arguing that Brunel had no right to interfere. The Admiralty firmly rejected Smith's claims, informing him that he could not be given the overall direction of a project, and that he must work with Brunel, who would be responsible for installing the machinery and propeller. He was to confine himself to the design, location and aperture of the screw.[56] Brunel's superior education and all-round engineering vision were critical. Smith was only concerned to prove his idea, while Brunel conceived the screw steamship as an integrated machine, in which the ship, her structure, form and machinery, combined to create a harmonious and efficient vessel. Brunel could see the value of the new system in his grand design.

The original draught of the Polyphemus, *the paddler whose lines were the starting point for the Navy's first screw ship.* (National Maritime Museum DR7343)

POLITICS AND TECHNOLOGY

Admiral Sir George Cockburn, the First Sea Lord 1841-6, has suffered a largely undeserved reputation as a technological reactionary. In fact, he played a major role in the evaluation procedure before the screw was adopted widely. (National Maritime Museum PAH6657)

In late September 1841 the introduction of the screw propeller into naval service was thrown into confusion when Lord Melbourne's Whig ministry was replaced by the Conservative regime of Sir Robert Peel. As Brunel's relationship with the Board had been essentially a gentleman's agreement, based on political friendships, the change came at a particularly unfortunate time. Just as the personal relationships that were essential to the smooth functioning of nineteenth century administration had been established he would have to create a whole new series of links, with men he did not know. While Parry and Symonds survived, their influence with the Admiralty was greatly reduced by their notorious Whig politics; both had been appointed by the outgoing ministers.

The resulting period of confusion would have been an ideal opportunity for Symonds, had he been an outright opponent of the project, to have stifled or redirected the effort. Following Claxton's version both Brunel junior and Rolt have suggested that he was the villain of the piece, creating a wholly erroneous model of how the propeller would be applied which reduced the new First Sea Lord, Admiral Sir George Cockburn, to apoplexy.[57] In fact the problems arose in a different quarter, and their solution required Brunel to take Symonds' advice, not engage the Surveyor in open warfare.

Throughout the second half of 1841 the Great Western's experimental work with the *Archimedes* was continued by Thomas Guppy, and Brunel fed the results into his work on the new ship.[58] He hoped these would 'enable me to obviate some of the objections which I understand have been felt regards the construction of the vessel'.[59] When he was called to a new conference at the Admiralty late in 1841 he was 'most anxious' to have the latest Bristol results.[60] These turned out to be necessary, because on 5 January 1842 Cockburn called Brunel, Parry, Symonds and Ewart to a conference, where he decided that an existing vessel should be converted, and ordered Symonds to report on the suitability of the *Acheron*.[61] Symonds decided that an aperture 5ft long should suffice, and although he recognised that the conversion would make all the comparative results unreliable, he did not think it was necessary to do more than inform Brunel of the change.[62] Brunel had been too surprised by this sudden shift of direction to make an effective response, but he was convinced that it would be a wrong step. In a letter of the 12th he reminded Sir George that the SPC had already demonstrated that the screw would do the same work as the paddle wheel. What remained to be settled was:

> whether all the advantages claimed by the promoters of the invention anticipate, of the vessel being capable of being constructed with perfect sailing qualities – and of a press of sail

being advantageously carried, either with or without the working of the engines and without stopping to connect or disconnect, and of the efficient working of the screw in the heaviest sea, and whether when working against a very strong head wind which reduces the speed of the vessel to two or three knots – the screw does or does not enable you to keep the vessel's head to the wind and to prevent her falling off, which I think will be found to be the case.

In order to determine these questions, and to reach reliable conclusions about the relative efficiency of the screw and paddle wheels it was essential to build a vessel with a form suitable for the screw, and for good sailing. If a compromise were adopted now it would all have to be done again.[63]

His concerns increased when he discovered that Symonds had reported *Acheron* was suitable for conversion. He obtained a copy of her draft, and that of *Archimedes* for comparison. He then wrote to Symonds, asking him how he could convince the Admiralty that the conversion of *Acheron* would be a waste of time and money.[64] His letter to the Board, repeated much of what he had written to Cockburn, adding that *Acheron* was too full in the after body for an efficient use of the screw, and had built-in sponsons which would impair her sailing. He

protested that only a new vessel would answer.[65] The Board directed that Symonds and Parry should be consulted.[66]

Three weeks later Brunel exploited the fact that he would be away for several weeks to encourage Parry to have the matter settled. 'Is there any possibility of inducing their Lordships to do the thing properly and quickly?'.[67] In fact things were going his way, Symonds reporting that as the steamers then building were all too large for the 200 nhp engines already ordered, it would be best to return to the plan of December 1840, building a replica of *Polyphemus*, at Sheerness in place the projected paddle steamer *Rattler*, which had been suspended before construction had commenced.[68] Consequently the dockyard had seasoned timber of the correct scantling on hand. The order was approved by the Board on 24 February 1842, and a sheer draft was submitted on 6 April.[69] To hasten the construction Symonds was instructed to communicate with Smith, and send the remaining drawings and scantlings to Sheerness as soon as they could be prepared.[70] This urgency was largely generated by Symonds. *Rattler* was a wholly new design, built with seasoned timber already collected for a 280-nhp paddle-wheel vessel. The decision to build at Sheerness reflected the importance of seasoned timber to the post-1815 Royal Navy: it was the only dockyard with the materials to hand in a state for immediate use.[71] Following

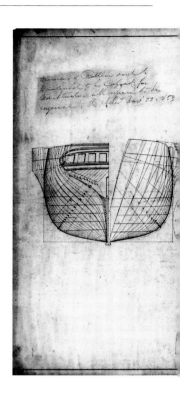

The naval dockyard at Sheerness where Rattler *was built. One of the covered slips can be seen just left of centre.* (National Maritime Museum neg 6141)

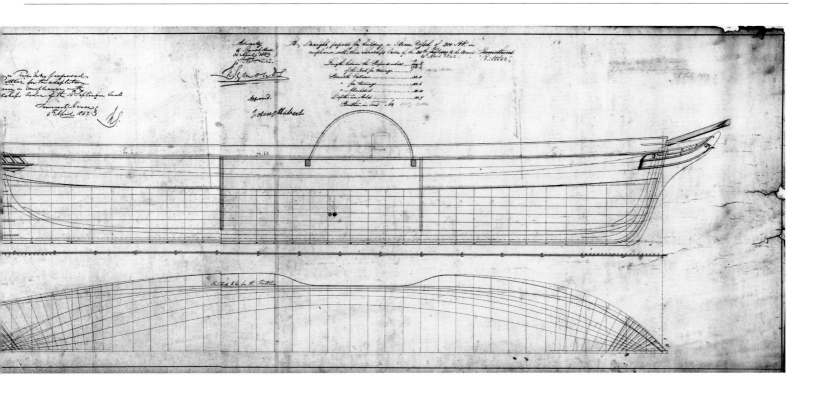

The original sheer draught of the Rattler *showing the conversion of the design from paddle to screw, 1842.*
(National Maritime Museum DR6170)

Claxton, Brunel's biographers have contended that Sheerness was chosen to hide the ship, but this is simply incredible.[72] She was laid down on 13 April 1842.

Brunel was not immediately informed, being in Italy on railway business. On his return he discovered that the work was already in hand, with Smith advising the Shipwright officers on the screw aperture, the screw, and the gearing. The latter point was one of the key areas where Brunel's superior engineering vision proved vital. Smith proposed a wooden cog wheel drive, like the noisy, bulky system used aboard *Archimedes*.[73] Brunel had long argued that oiled ropes operating on flat drums would be the most efficient experimental drive, until the correct gearing ratio had been settled. This system was ultimately adopted. Brunel had persuaded the Admiralty that Maudslays should design, manufacture and instal the entire machinery plant, and all related metal fittings for the screw. This would ensure the best fit, and the most effective operation. Maudslays remained involved as engineering consultants until the end of the trials phase, reflecting both their eminence as marine engineers, and Brunel's friendship with Joshua Field.

On his return to England Brunel realised he was being ignored, and complained to the Admiralty. The Board had simply forgotten to mention him in the order to proceed with *Rattler*, given on 6 April, leaving Symonds to surmise that he was no longer involved. After a meeting with Cockburn on 22 July Brunel was able to report to Claxton that the matter had been put straight, and would get straighter. Cockburn was 'evidently surprised to find that nobody had communicated with me and was rather angry when he was told by a clerk that the hole was making for Smith's long thread instead of the short one as he had supposed'.[74] This is the origin of the apoplectic Admiral of Claxton's account. The villain of the piece, as far as there was one, was simple bureaucratic weakness. The Board ratified Cockburn's declaration that Brunel was to be involved early the following month. He was now back where he had been during Minto's regime. He was to liaise with Maudslays and the Captain Superintendent at Sheerness on the installation of the machinery.[75] When Brunel and Smith discussed the vessel it became clear that their relationship had not been settled by the Board. Smith thought he was responsible for the aperture, the engines and other aspects which were in Brunel's domain. Brunel offered to give up his role, as he could not act to the benefit of the Board, or his own credit, in such confusion.[76] When the Board settled the lines of authority Brunel agreed that Smith should advise on the form of the propeller, and left it to him to decide if the screw should be fitted for unshipping without going into dock.[77] This was an unusual oversight on his part when the vessel would be shifting her propeller regularly.

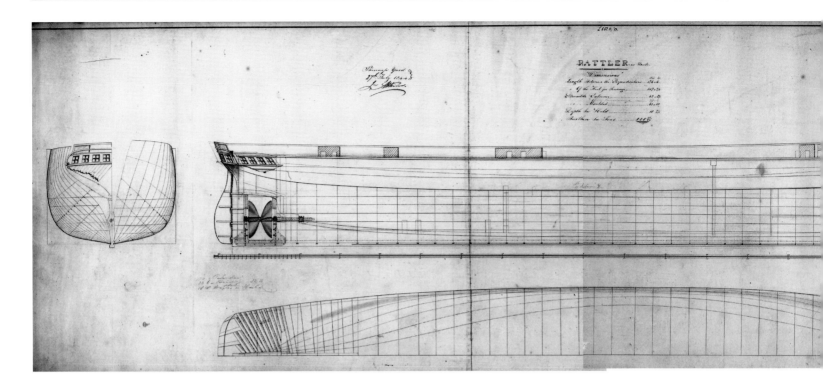

Far from wishing to delay the ship Symonds was annoyed to find, on a visit to Sheerness, that work was suspended 'on account of the indecision of the Engineers who are to provide a screw propeller for her'.[78] Brunel, stung by the complaint, hastened to excuse himself on grounds of ill-health, claiming that 'no avoidable delay has occurred on my part'. Cockburn endorsed the letter for Symonds 'information and guidance'.[79] From this point the correspondence reveals a fundamental conflict of ambition between Brunel, who was anxious to finish *Rattler* and try her afloat, and the Surveyor's Department, which was anxious to build the ship properly, which meant taking time to season the structure at various stages. Brunel's anxiety was not unconnected with the imminent completion of the *Great Britain*, for which *Rattler* would provide important experimental data for the design of propellers.[80]

THE *RATTLER* TRIALS, 1843–4

Rattler was built in a year, which was the average length of time taken to build a steamship of her size in the Royal Dockyards at this time. Although Sheerness had run up her paddle-wheel half sister, the *Prometheus*, in 3 months that was very much the exception.[81] *Rattler* was launched on 12 April 1843, making her the world's first screw propeller warship. The dockyard was specifically instructed not to copper her until after the engines had been installed, a common practice already familiar from work on the steamers *Cormorant* and *Styx*.[82] It would be counterproductive to devote much time to coppering the

The lines of the Rattler *as built, dated 27 July 1844.* (National Maritime Museum DR6169A)

The original profile draught for Rattler, *showing the diagonal bracing.* (National Maritime Museum DR6169)

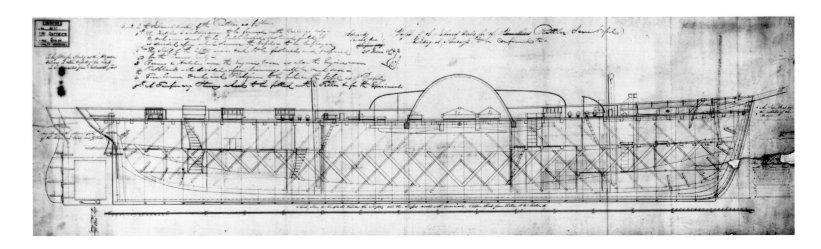

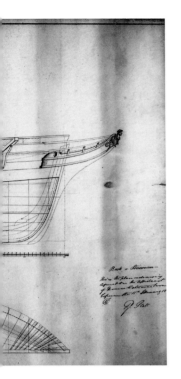

hull until the propeller was in place, and had been tried. The tendency of all large wooden screw vessels to shake their sterns loose was then unknown, but all steamships vibrated. After completion of the shipwright work and partial fitting out *Rattler* left Sheerness on 7 July 1843, being towed by *Archimedes* to East India Dock, as a publicity stunt for the Ship Propeller Company. The Admiralty was doubtless pleased to save the cost of the coal. She was then docked at the East India Docks to be fitted with her machinery and screw propeller. On the 11th shipwrights were sent from the nearby Woolwich Dockyard to lift her decks to enable Maudslay, Son & Field to instal her machinery.[83] Once he had floated out the *Great Britain* from her building dock, on 19 July, a gala to which he personally invited Smith,[84] Brunel began to press Joshua Field to complete the machinery. He hoped that he completion of work on the new Royal Yacht *Victoria and Albert* would speed the process, lamenting; 'the vessel was tediously slow in getting made, and you have caught the complaint'. He also advised him against conservatism, reminding Field that he had rejected Brunel's advice to instal direct acting engines in the *Great Western* 'do not run the risk of quarrelling with screws – they may also turn out good things'.[85] He also worked on Parry to

hurry the engineers. He was anxious to begin the trials which, at his insistence, were measured with early thrust meters, and the latest engine indicators. Brunel was determined to generate consistent data, which could be transferred to other vessels.[86]

Steam was first raised on board the *Rattler* on 24 October 1843 to work the engines and the screw in the dock basin. Brunel reported that everything went well, but advised that as the straps connecting the engines to the propeller shaft, with a multiplying effect of 1 to 4, needed to be worked for some days to bed in he advised running her in the river. On the 27th the paddle wheel Admiralty yacht *Black Eagle* was ordered to be tried with *Rattler* on the measured mile the following day.[87]

Between October 1843 and October 1844 *Rattler* ran a series of trials, under Brunel's direction, which were intended to ascertain the best length of screw for maximum speed. During this time the length of the screw was reduced from 5ft 9in to 1ft 3in, and the diameter increased as far as practical. Subsequently other propellers were tried, but the Smith type with flat blades was found to be as efficient as any other.[88] It is on the results of these trials that Brunel's work with the Admiralty must be judged. Did he advance the theoretical and practical understanding of screw

The launch of the Rattler, *the first of a number of appearances by the ship in the pages of the* Illustrated London News, *in this case for 22 April 1843.* (National Maritime Museum neg E0449)

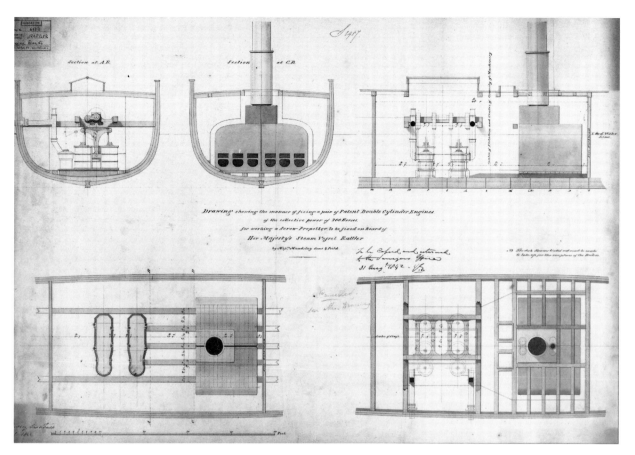

The boilers and engines of the Rattler *as seen in the original draught. It is annotated: 'To be copied and returned to the Surveyor's Office, 31 Aug 1842.' (National Maritime Museum* DR6173*)*

Black Eagle, *the powerful Admiralty paddle yacht, which was* Rattler's *first trials opponent, in October 1843. (National Maritime Museum* PAH8862*)*

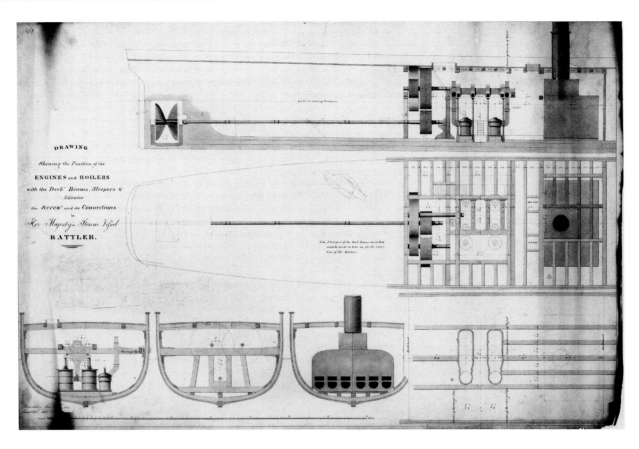

The boilers, engines and propeller arrangements of the Rattler. *This draught was actually furnished by Maudslay, Sons & Field, and is dated Lambeth 13 October 1842, just before the first trial took place.* (National Maritime Museum DR6173A)

The upper deck of Rattler *as finally fitted for service, dated Portsmouth 1 April 1846. The main armament of small steamers was a large pivot gun forward, the racers for which can be seen clearly.* (National Maritime Museum DR6172)

propulsion to a level where the screw could be adopted by the Royal Navy, without risk of failure, as a critical element in the design of modern warships? The answer to this question has to be an unqualified affirmative. Brunel effectively took over the development of the screw between 1840 and 1844, with two projects running concurrently, and established the best forms for screws, and the ships that were to be fitted with them, whether they were low-powered naval auxiliary steamers, or full-powered Atlantic liners. In order to understand this process, it will be necessary to examine Brunel's work on HMS *Rattler*, which is little known, and her

subsequent career, which is largely unknown, to assess the success of her machinery plant, wholly chosen by Brunel, and the concepts she was set to demonstrate, for unlike a modern trials platform, *Rattler* was always intended to be a front-line warship.

In accordance with Brunel's wishes, and to suit his convenience, *Rattler* ran her **First Trial** on Monday 30 October 1843, going down the river from Blackwall to Greenhithe and back to Blackwall. Her engines achieved a maximum of 22½ rpm for 8 knots. Brunel considered the results unsatisfactory, due to lack of immersion of the screw. Afterwards he ordered Maudslays to reduce the length of the screw,

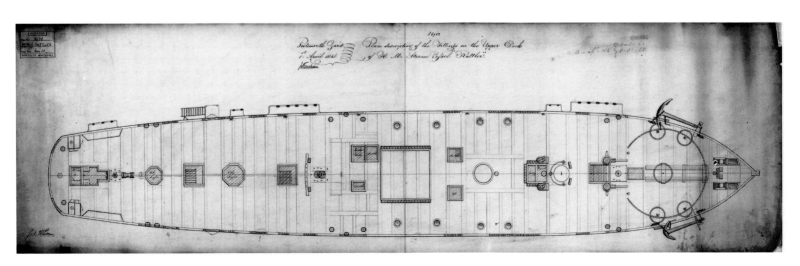

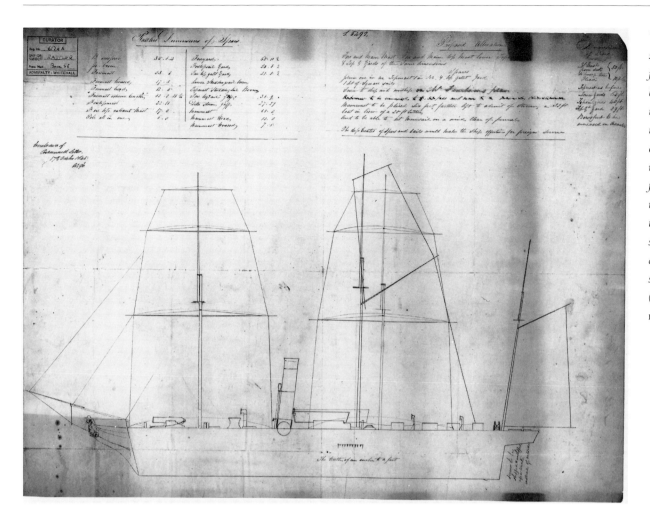

The Rattler spar plan, showing proposed alteration from a barquentine to a barque with similar sized masts and spars on fore and main, 1845. Annotated: 'The duplicates of spars and sails would make the ship effective for Foreign Service.' However reliable the machinery, at this time a full set of sails was still thought necessary to give a steamer the endurance that strategic mobility required. (National Maritime Museum DR6174A)

in accordance with Smith's directions.[89] The following day Brunel urged Joshua Field to provide and instal permanent engine indicators, at least one was needed before the next trial. Having instructed Field to alter the screw he then advised Smith that he should reduce the after end of the screw, leaving the fore part alone.[90] Smith requested that the next trial be run with Rattler one foot deeper in the water.[91]

As planned the **Second Trial** took place on Monday 6 November. This time the engines managed 23½ rpm, and Brunel calculated the slip at ⅙th. The best speed went up to 8.3 knots. During the trial ballast was shifted to alter the trim. However, she was still not deep enough, Brunel advising the Admiralty of the need to bring her down to average draft of the Polyphemus class 'keeping her about 1 foot by the stern, this being the trim that Mr Smith prefers'. He also reported that the oiled straps used to drive the propeller shaft worked well, and asked Parry if a shelter could be built on the upper deck, so that he would have somewhere to record his results.[92]

On the **Third Trial**, on 8 November the slip was slightly reduced, to ²⁄₁₁ths but the speed went down

to 8.2 knots. Brunel advised Parry to fix the next trial for the 15th, when he would be back in London after a trip to Ireland on railway business.[93] The journey to Wexford gave him time to reflect on the relatively low speeds achieved on the early trials. He advised Smith to measure the pitch of both blades of the propeller 'very accurately' as he suspected they might differ from the drawing, and from each other. Suspecting the worst he asked Field how long it would take to make another screw. He also wanted to know how large the small drum on the drive shaft could be, and what effect Rattler not being coppered had on her speed. He advised Field that 'I think I perceive the cause, but I am afraid of being led into theorising on insufficient data'[94]

Despite his best efforts Brunel missed the **Fourth Trial** on 16 November, for which he apologised to Parry. However, once the new Admiralty Chief Engineer Thomas Lloyd had supplied the data he required, he reported that the screw used for the Third Trial, as altered by Smith, had shown considerable improvement, despite the ship not being coppered. He told the Admiralty that it would be advisable to

Two of the propeller designs tried in the Rattler: *end and perspective views of the* Smith (left pair) *and* Steinman screws. From A Treatise on the Screw Propeller, *by John Bourne.*

find the best two-blade performance before trying a three blade screw of the same pitch and form. Smith concurred. In the mean time he wanted a four-arm screw prepared. He advised tapering the rudder and removing the slack from rudder pintles, tasks best undertaken in dock at Woolwich.[95]

The Board accepted his recommendations on the 23rd, directing Master Shipwright Oliver Lang to report on the proposal to taper rudder, and ordering the Surveyor to have her coppered at Woolwich or Deptford.[96] In a letter to Smith Brunel expected this to happen soon, and advised Smith to view *Rattler* while in dock. However, he was understandably less confident writing to Thomas Guppy the same day. With the *Great Britain* fitting out it would soon be necessary to design her propeller, and he did not think he would get the desired speed from *Rattler* for another two months. The data such trials would provide would be particularly useful when he came to design an effective screw for his high speed liner. So anxious was he to have *Rattler* coppered and tried with a multi-bladed screw that he enquired if the Great Western Steamship Company could cast a four armed propeller of 9ft 9in diameter for *Rattler*.[97] Three days later he advised Guppy to wait.[98]

Brunels' report on the first four trials was quickly sent to the Surveyor:

By contrast the proposed docking did not materialise. By 20 December Brunel was reduced to scare tactics, warning Parry, 'you know Louis Phillipe [the French King] is building an iron screw yacht'.[100] He probably acquired this information from John Barnes. At the end of the year he went to Italy for three weeks, and advised Parry that *Rattler* should be tried with her present two-bladed screw when she had been coppered. It was essential to proceed carefully and thoroughly as; 'a great deal may be done with the screw but that we are quite in the dark about it – and in these experiments now making I should hope that by proceeding very carefully and systematically we may enlighten ourselves'.[101]

Rattler was docked at Woolwich on 21 January 1844 to be coppered, and was undocked on 30 January. Brunel returned while she was in dock, to find Smith ill. He tried to cheer him up with some encouraging news:

> I find on my return a decidedly increased opinion, or conviction, on all hands that the days of paddle are numbered and that the age of screw in commenced. I sincerely hope you may reap the benefit of it.[102]

The **Fifth Trial** took place on Saturday 2 February, with the newly coppered ship using the two-arm screw, which had been sharpened. She achieved 9.2 knots, with a slip of 19.6 per cent. Brunel was pleased to find no perceptible slip of driving straps, and advised trying the three-bladed screw, which the Admiralty was pleased to confirm.[103] The latest experiment had convinced him that the screw being made for *Great Britain* should be bent at the tip, rather than all along the arm. He instructed the engineering manager accordingly, and then altered the pitch of the arms after the sixth trial.[104]

Brunel was also pressing Field to finish the four-

DRAFT

Trial		Fwd	Aft	Ballast	Coal	Knots	Remarks
1	30.10	9'2"	11'2"	60 t	80 t	not asc.	Screw double threaded 9ft diam. 5ft 6in long 11ft pitch
2	6.11	9'	11'½"	60	70	8.366	Length reduced 1ft 3in to 4ft 6in long
		8'6"	11'6"	60	70	8.343	
		9'6"	10'6"	60	70	not. asc.	
3	8.11	10'9"	11'9"	132	122	8.249	
4	16.11	10'9"	11'9"	132	122	8.751	Length of screw again reduced 1ft 3in leaving it 3ft long.[99]

arm screw for *Rattler*, complaining that the Admiralty had delayed coppering the ship as the screw was not ready. He was annoyed by the delay, as Maudslays' had already taken ten weeks.[105]

The **Sixth Trial** on 9 February used the three-bladed screw. The ship was still too high out of the water, but her speed was much lower, with 15.6 per cent slip. Brunel advised that the three-bladed screw would need reducing, which would take two or three days, and sought Admiralty authorisation to order such minor modifications.[106] By this time Brunel had recognised the limitations of Smith's preliminary work, and of Smith as a theoretical and experimental scientist. The future of the screw, as an efficient propeller, was very much in his hands. He advised Smith that the new four-bladed screw need only be 18in long, a figure that also applied to the new two-bladed screw. He also offered him the concept of the variable pitch on the blades of the screw, which he was already using in his design for the *Great Britain's* screw, so that Smith could patent it, 'and strengthen your original patent as it is more fully applicable to your screw than any of the forms claimed by others.' While Brunel did not consider the idea worth patenting, he hoped it would strengthen Smith's patent.[107] Evidently he had not read Smith's patent, which did not concern the screw, only the location. Smith, for his part, was too polite to point this out.[108]

On the eve of the next trial Brunel complained to Parry that he had not received a reply to his last letter to the Admiralty of the 10th, requesting authority to order minor alterations. Without this he feared progress would be delayed. He also reported that both Lloyd and Smith agreed that it was advisable to try the two-arm screw with 16in more diameter.[109]

In the **Seventh Trial** on 19 February 1844 the shortened three-bladed screw demonstrated a marked improvement, with the speed up to 8 knots. Brunel then advised Lloyd to try the three-bladed screw with similarly increased diameter, and in the meantime to reduce length of the three-bladed screw by 6in, as it now had the same surface area as the two-bladed version.[110] However, the **Eighth Trial** on 23 February used the further reduced three-arm screw, and achieved a speed of 8.56 knots. A **Ninth Trial** on the 28th, using the old 10ft diameter two-bladed screw, as lengthened to Brunel's design, proved inconclusive as one of the driving straps broke. Lloyd advised the Admiralty that it should be repeated on 5 March, and the Board concurred.[111]

Brunel's role in the development of the screw was attracting attention, not all of it welcome. In the *Morning Post* Captain George Pechell (liberal MP for Brighton) made what Brunel termed a 'ridiculous and unfounded attack' on the Admiralty, claiming that it was using Brunel and the *Rattler* trials for the purpose 'of robbing Mr Smith of the invention, and of marring the experiments'. Brunel's attention had been drawn to what was being said in the House of Commons by Cockburn, when he had called at the Admiralty on 2 March. Although he would normally have ignored such remarks, he asked Caldwell, the Secretary to the Ship Propeller Company if he could show Cockburn the letters that the SPC had sent him to refute this foolish nonsense.[112] The previous evening Cockburn, who was very much the directing intellect at the Admiralty, had told the House of Commons that he expected the screw to supersede the paddle.[113]

At the **Tenth Trial**, on 5 March, the modified screw drove *Rattler* to an impressive 9.235 knots. This, it should be stressed, was more than 50 per cent faster than the Admiralty had intended, and provided far more useful information for Brunel and his project than it did for the Admiralty, which promptly forgot everything that had been learnt. The success of this trial was particularly timely for the Directors of the Great Western Steamship Company who now decided that Brunel should design the propeller for the *Great Britain*. They had been deliberately waiting for further data from the *Rattler* trials. Brunel's six-bladed design has been demonstrated to be 'extraordinarily efficient', almost as good as the best modern designs.[114] This was hardly surprising, in view of the work he had been able to undertake at the Admiralty's expense.

The trend of Brunel's thinking on the screw can be traced in his correspondence. Following the tenth trial Brunel advised Smith that the two-blade screw should be 1ft 9in long. Smith was to draw a new screw, and this would be ordered by the Admiralty. He suggested making the blades sharper and better for passing through water than they had been hitherto.[115] The **Eleventh Trial** on 11 March led him to alter his mind; 'the results of yesterday's trials show 18 inches is long enough for the new 2 blade'. The value of increased diameter was so striking that he asked Smith to measure the screw aperture very carefully, so that they could try the deepest screw.[116]

His discussions with Lloyd centred on the strength of the experimental screws, which had been cast in iron for cheapness. Here practical engineering concerns which he, above all men, would have recognised, were ignored in his anxious search for an ideal form. While Brunel was urging increased radius, Thomas Lloyd was concerned that cutting the length of the cast iron screws would weaken them.[117] Lloyd's concern would prove well founded.

Although Brunel did not record it in his logs the **Twelfth Trial** occurred on 14 March, using the Smith three-bladed screw now of 9ft diameter and 1ft 2in long. The trial was abortive, as one of the arms broke off at the axis. Brunel took the opportunity to press on Smith the need to order a new screw, which they had discussed, to avoid delay.[118] Having missed the trial Brunel was anxious to know whether the screw had been particularly fast before it broke. This information would be required before a new one was cast. He asked Smith to call on him on the evening before the fourteenth trial.[119]

A **Thirteenth Trial** on 18 March used Bennet Woodcroft's four-bladed increasing pitch screw of 9ft diameter, and 1ft 7in long. The result of 8.2 knots did not add much to the process. Brunel was on board for the **Fourteenth Trial**, on 20 March, when the cut-down Smith two-blade screw broke. He immediately directed Maudslays to cast a new screw, and advised casting another two-blade screw using a different pitch. He hoped they could be cast together, to save time, and asked how soon they could be ready.[120] Brunel then advised the Admiralty that Smith had applied to him for an order to construct a two-blade screw 10ft in diameter, with the pitch at the centre considerably less than at the outside, like the screw Brunel had cast for the *Great Britain*. Lloyd would make a detailed report, but observed that the speed had now increased to 9½ knots and that he expected

to reach 10. However, with the present machinery the ship could not do much more with any other propeller – such as Woodcroft's now being built by Maudslays. If the Admiralty wanted to try the Ericsson screw he advised doing it now while it was still possible to alter the gearing through the straps.[121]

As *Rattler* had greatly surpassed the expectations of the Admiralty in terms of speed they lost interest in further experimental work, ignoring Brunel's request that they authorise a new screw, claiming that any further work would only be to the advantage of the Smith patent. Brunel urged Smith to have the screw made anyway, a course of action that would have benefited his own work far more than Smith or the Admiralty, but eventually the Admiralty relented, when Smith reminded the Board that he had not patented his screw.[122] At the same time the Admiralty decided to fit *Rattler's* armament, the same as that carried by her paddle-wheel half sisters, one 68-pounder 65 cwt 8in pivot gun and four 32-pounder carronades of 17cwt.[123]

For the **Fifteenth Trial** on 13 March Woodcroft's four-bladed screw 1ft 7in long and 9ft diameter was fitted, this created a large degree of slip and a mere 8.1 knots. Woodcroft and his friends were on board, along with Miller, John Penn, Lloyd and others. This was followed by a **Sixteenth Trial** on 18 March with Woodcroft's screw reduced to two blades. This recorded 27 per cent slip and a slightly improved 8.63 knots. Joshua Field, Captain Horatio Austin, and Smith were among those present.

Brunel did not attend the Woodcroft trials, already satisfied that they would confirm his decision that there was no need for any increase in pitch. Instead he continued to press Smith and Maudslay's to improve the Smith screw according to his own ideas, with a new two-blade screw of 10ft diameter.[124]

His interpretation was largely confirmed by the **Seventeenth Trial** on 23 April when the new Smith two-blade screw, following the form of the one that had broken on the fourteenth trial created only 16 per cent slip in reaching 9.8 knots. On board for this trial were Lloyd, Captain George Smith, John Barnes, Swedish and Danish officers and F P Smith. The Admiralty accepted Brunel's advice that they should purchase a thrust meter to his design, which would cost £50.[125]

While Brunel did not record the **Eighteenth Trial** on 29 April, or any of the remaining series, he

The Sunderland screw tested briefly on 3 January 1845. From A Treatise on the Screw Propeller, *by John Bourne.*

remained interested in the trials, and had hoped to attend on Monday 6 May, to discuss the thrust measurements with Lloyd.[126] By this stage the fundamental experimental phase was effectively over, Maudslay's had designed the gears that were to replace the experimental strap drive, and were directed to manufacture them at once.[127] Brunel approved Lloyd's design for the dynamometer, and his use of a 4 to 1 ratio, although Field had made the device with 4½ to 1.[128] Later he would confirm that Field was right.[129]

There was a **Nineteenth Trial** on 6 May. Brunel was still seeking higher speeds, asking Smith if it would be possible to enlarge the drum used for the gearing without hitting the keelson. If it was possible he hoped to try a larger screw.[130] In truth the Admiralty had no interest in any further speed trials, and *Rattler* was established as a second class steam sloop at the end of May 1844.[131] Brunel continued to press for further experimental work, at Admiralty expense, urging the Board to sanction the construction of a device Field had designed to measure water velocity, at a cost of £50.[132]

While the trials series continued, with a **Twentieth Trial** on 8 June, and a **Twenty-first** on the 13th, little was learnt. As the experimental work on screws was over it was time for the final stage,

which Brunel had outlined years before in response to the structural concerns of Symonds and Edye. The Admiralty directed that that part of the aperture no longer required by the short screw should be filled

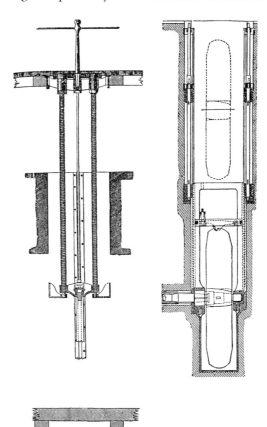

The form of two-bladed hoisting screws and their associated gear as finally adopted by the Royal Navy. Top right is the fitting for the line of battle ship Ajax, *and the remainder refer to the frigate* Amphion. *From* A Treatise on the Screw Propeller, *by John Bourne.*

up; 'to ascertain how much the length of the aperture can be reduced without affecting the efficient action of the propeller'.[133] On this trial, the **Twenty-second**, on 27 June *Rattler* made 10 knots with the Smith two-arm screw. She was then docked at Woolwich, between 29 June and 11 July to repair her copper. Following the **Twenty-third Trial** on 13 July Brunel observed that filling up deadwood to the extent tried produced no effect.[134] The ship was docked again between 27 July and 8 August to fit the new fixed gearing between the engine and the propeller shaft.

By late August Brunel was losing touch with the project, his last letter on the subject was a plaintive plea to Smith; 'will you let me know the exact state of things with the *Rattler?*'[135] The Admiralty had a new agenda, offering *Rattler* as a trials platform for

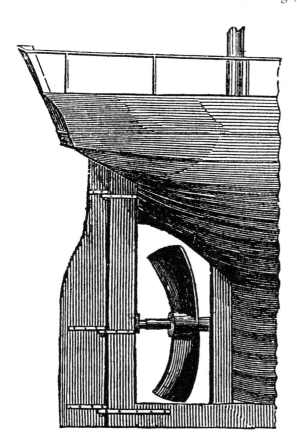

The Hodgson's screw used in the twenty-ninth trial. From A Treatise on the Screw Propeller, *by John Bourne.*

screw patentees, an offer that would ensure they were well informed about the state of development in an increasingly popular field. The patentees were free to try their propellers, at their own expense.[136] After a **Twenty-fourth Trial** on 4 October, the **Twenty-fifth Trial** on the 10th was of Sunderland's propeller, the **Twenty-sixth** two days later was of Steinman's design, followed by a **Twenty-seventh** on the 15th, with Sunderland's propeller, after it had been cut down. No improvement was observed. As if to confirm the success of Brunel's work the **Twenty-eighth Trial** on 17 October, with a Smith two-blade screw 10ft in diameter and 1ft 3in long drove the ship to 9.8 knots despite low steam pressure.

While docked at Woolwich *Rattler* was ordered to be commissioned for general service on 12 December 1844, but the trials programme continued. The ship was un-docked on 27 December, and on 3 January 1845 tried Sunderland's propeller while tied up alongside the dock. The **Twenty-ninth Trial** took place on the 10th using Hodgson's propeller. A speed of 6.5 knots was achieved. The following day the standard Smith propeller was refitted and a **Thirtieth Trial** occurred on the 13th, although there were too many ships in the river for any useful results to be achieved. It was observed that the shaft pinion was worn. The **Thirty-first Trial** on 22 January was with a Steinman propeller, modified to be closer in form to the Smith. After reaching 9.4 knots the Smith propeller was then refitted for the **Thirty-second Trial** on the 23rd which achieved 9.6 knots in a stiff breeze, despite low steam pressure.

The *Rattler* trials led to a gradual reduction in the length of the screw, and a steady lengthening of the blades. The Navy, which required the screw as the drive for an auxiliary propulsion system, would adopt a two-bladed hoisting screw. Brunel designed a five-bladed fixed propeller for the *Great Britain*, the world's first full-powered oceanic screw steamship. Although their direct collaboration on the *Rattler* ended in 1844 the close relationship between Brunel and Smith continued with the *Great Britain*, Smith was on board for her first sea trial on 8 January 1845, and was toasted at the banquet that evening. He was also in a position of honour when the Queen visited the ship in the Thames on St George's Day 1845.[137]

Brunel had provided a priceless input for the development of efficient screw propellers, but he had also benefited greatly from the opportunity to use naval vessels for full-scale propeller experiments. His combination of breadth of engineering vision, insistence on high-quality machinery, and meticulous recording of data demonstrated that he was the leading professional engineer of the age. Without his input the introduction of the screw propeller would have been significantly impeded. However, the *Rattler* trials had gone far beyond the original intention of the Admiralty, and the most significant results were quickly forgotten.

THE CREATION OF THE SCREW STEAM NAVY

Once the concept of the screw propeller had been proved the major problem for naval architects was the form of the stern run. Brunel had made it clear in February 1842 that a fine stern run was vital for the efficient use of the propeller.[138] However, this advice had been forgotten in the Board's enthusiasm for auxiliary, low-powered ships, and had to be re-learnt empirically, after much wasted effort with the first group of large screw steamships. In 1848 the Navy's Chief Engineer, Thomas Lloyd, declared that the fine stern run of *Rattler* had been accidental, occasioned by the long screw aperture. He had objected to the use of a square stern from a sense that it was wrong, and proved his case with trials. He believed the square form had been adopted on Smith's advice.[139] He seems to have forgotten that he had worked alongside Brunel throughout the *Rattler* trials. Once again the shift in the balance of political power in naval design circles had a major impact on the resolution of this problem. The 'tory' designers, those favoured by, and supporters of, the tory ministry, had adopted very bluff stern lines for their screw ships.

When the whigs returned to office their First Lord, Lord Auckland, needed little convincing that the screw was the future. In 1848 he declared:

> I am satisfied that the whole theory of ship building will be directed from the old notions of sailing ships to the manner in which the screw auxiliary may be best combined with good sailing qualities.[140]

To achieve the new balance of sailing and steaming qualities the Admiralty had to abandon the sharp floored form developed by Symonds. The Surveyor

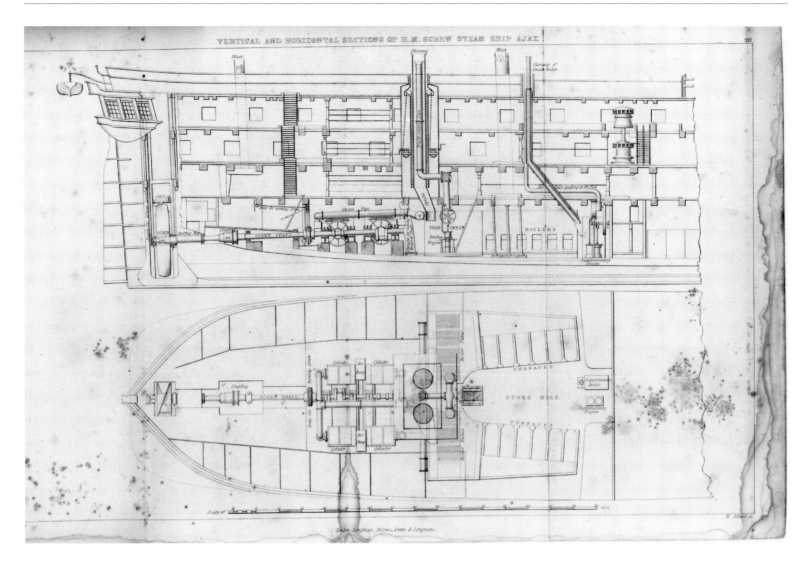

VERTICAL AND HORIZONTAL SECTIONS OF H.M. SCREW STEAM SHIP AJAX.

was manoeuvred out of office in mid-1847, not because he opposed the screw, which he did not, but because he was 'a very difficult man to deal with'.[141] The additional length of the screw ships, and their fine stern runs, sacrificed handiness and speed to windward for effective use of the screw, but as a bonus the new hulls also provided improved performance off the wind, leaving the engine to solve the age-old problem of windward sailing. This solution, of classic simplicity, made the screw steam auxiliary a far more effective warship than any that had gone before. In June 1848 the Board had directed that when designing ships converting timber consideration should be given to the possibility that the ship would be converted into a screw steamer.[142] When Smith's patent was granted a five-year extension the Admiralty decided to take control of the situation. Smith's leading financial supporter, John Wright 'claims the merit of having started the *Archimedes* and assisted Mr Smith by his money, and patronage, and complains of having been defrauded of his shares in

the *Archimedes* by a wilful depreciation of their value'.[143] The patent had been extended for five years on 11 February 1850 because the patentees had not obtained any significant economic advantage from their invention.[144] The Board then offered £20,000 for the patent rights of all patentees in 1851. Smith received one third of the money.[145] Having carefully monitored the development of the screw the Admiralty moved to secure the patent rights after the private sector carried out all the fundamental development work, albeit unwillingly. The private sector had been outmanoeuvred all along the line by the Admiralty.

This was reflected in a widespread belief within the engineering community that Smith had not received a proper reward for his efforts. Brunel agreed, when he was planning the *Great Eastern* he consulted 'my friend Mr F. P. Smith, to whom the public are indebted for the success of the screw'.[146] In 1854 the 'Smith Testimonial Fund' raised £3000, of which Brunel contributed £50, and secured him

The machinery installation of the Ajax. *From* A Treatise on the Screw Propeller, *by John Bourne. (*National Maritime Museum neg 0447)

Details of the Ericsson-designed US screw frigate Princeton. *From* A Treatise on the Screw Propeller, *by John Bourne.* (National Maritime Museum neg E0446)

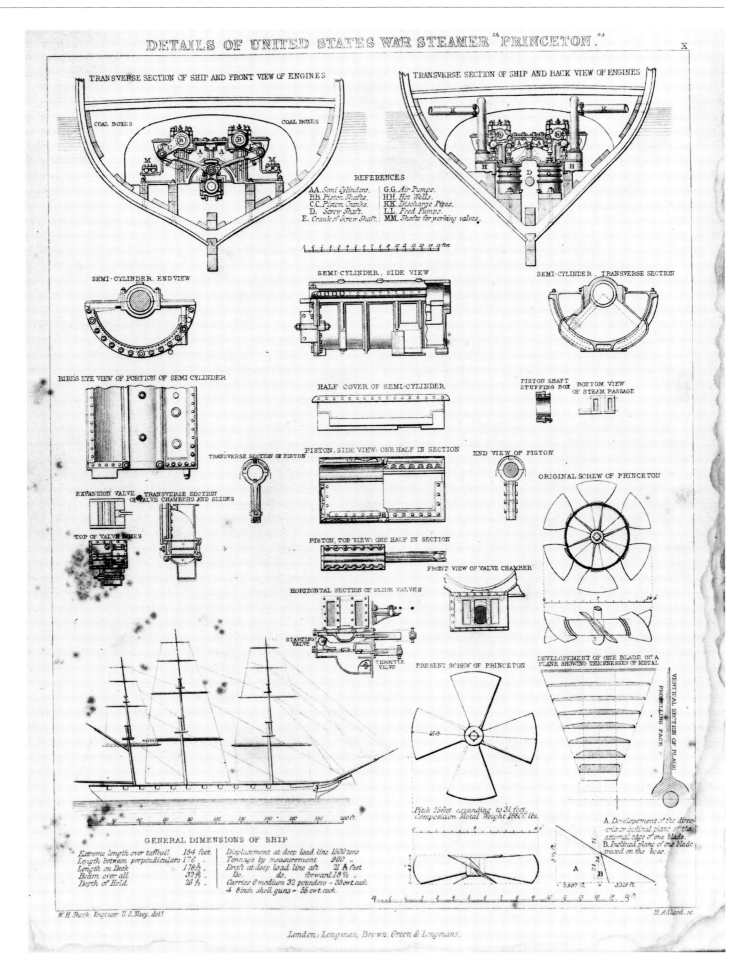

DETAILS OF UNITED STATES WAR STEAMER "PRINCETON."

TRANSVERSE SECTION OF SHIP AND FRONT VIEW OF ENGINES

TRANSVERSE SECTION OF SHIP AND BACK VIEW OF ENGINES

COAL BOXES COAL BOXES

REFERENCES

AA. Semi Cylinders.   G.G. Air Pumps.
BB. Piston Shafts.   H.H. Hot Wells.
C.C. Piston Cranks.   KK. Discharge Pipes.
D. Screw Shaft.   L.L. Feed Pumps.
E. Crank of Screw Shaft. MM. Shafts for working valves.

SEMI-CYLINDER, END VIEW

SEMI-CYLINDER, SIDE VIEW

SEMI-CYLINDER, TRANSVERSE SECTION

BIRD'S EYE VIEW OF PORTION OF SEMI CYLINDER

HALF COVER OF SEMI-CYLINDER

PISTON SHAFT STUFFING BOX

BOTTOM VIEW OF STEAM PASSAGE

TRANSVERSE SECTION OF PISTON

PISTON, SIDE VIEW: ONE HALF IN SECTION

END VIEW OF PISTON

ORIGINAL SCREW OF PRINCETON

EXPANSION VALVE

TRANSVERSE SECTION OF VALVE CHAMBERS AND SLIDES

TOP OF VALVE BOXES

PISTON, TOP VIEW: ONE HALF IN SECTION

FRONT VIEW OF VALVE CHAMBER

HORIZONTAL SECTION OF SLIDE VALVES

STARTING VALVE

THROTTLE VALVE

PRESENT SCREW OF PRINCETON

DEVELOPEMENT OF ONE BLADE ON A PLANE SHOWING THICKNESSES OF METAL

VERTICAL SECTION OF BLADE

PROPELLING FACE

Pitch 25 feet expanding to 31 feet
Composition Metal Weight 18800 lbs.

A. Developement of the direc-trix or inclined plane of the external edge of one blade.
B. Inclined plane of one blade traced on the base.

GENERAL DIMENSIONS OF SHIP

Extreme length over taffrail 184 feet   Displacement at deep load line 1500 tons
Length between perpendiculars 176 ,,   Tonnage by measurement   900 ,,
Length on Deck   178 ft.   Draft at deep load line aft   21 4 feet
Beam over all   32 ft.   Do.   do.   forward 18½ ,,
Depth of Hold   26 ft.   Carries 6 medium 32 pounders - 33 cwt. each.
                                          4 8 inch shell guns - 56 cwt. each.

W.H. Shock Engineer U.S.Navy. delt.

H.Adlard. sc.

London: Longman, Brown, Green & Longmans.

51

a Civil List pension of £200.[147] After the Crimean War Brunel reflected that the Admiralty 'had a penchant for bullying and defrauding inventors'. While the Admiralty had never bullied or defrauded him he may have been thinking about Smith, or his own father.[148]

IN RETROSPECT

It should be clear that the 'Brunel' version of the introduction of the screw propeller was heavily influenced by personal and political problems, the difficulty of working with Sir William Symonds, compounded by the hostility of incoming tory ministers in 1841. His object in joining the project had been to advance research and experimental work for his own project, *The Great Britain*, which owed much of her success to his work on *Rattler*. However, such a skilful exploitation of events was hardly going to make edifying reading in the biography of a Victorian hero. He needed a dragon to slay, and Claxton was pleased to cast the 'tory' Admiralty in that role.

After his experience with the screw Brunel had little need to involve himself with government. During the Crimean War he produced a portable hospital, working with his brother in law Benjamin Hawes, then Under-Secretary for War, while Claxton offered his sketch plans for an armoured gunboat, armed with a large, built-up wrought iron cannon, to attack Cronstadt. The Admiralty did not adopt the gunboat plan.[149] However, Brunel was too busy with the *Great Eastern* to develop his sketches. While happy to work with Government departments where he had personal contact, notably Hawes, Brunel generally preferred private work.

Rattler was the world's first screw propeller warship. The claim customarily advanced for John Ericsson's USS *Princeton*, launched in September 1843, is only valid <u>if</u> *Rattler* was a converted paddle-wheel vessel.[150] This chapter has established that she was laid down and built as a screw vessel, using an existing paddle wheel hull form for comparative experimental purposes, not the hull of an existing paddle wheel ship. Furthermore *Princeton* was a typical Ericsson design, conceptually brilliant, but less convincing in execution. She displaced 1046 tons, being 156ft long, 30ft 6in broad and drew 18ft. Although a fine model under sail, *Princeton* was not particularly fast under steam, making no more than 8 knots, way below *Rattler*'s best. In truth she was, like *Rattler*, an excellent steam auxiliary, capable of sailing, steaming and towing. Her Captain insisted that she was not a steam ship. She was broken up in 1849, having been built with unseasoned or inferior timber, another area where *Rattler* proved to be superior.

With the *Rattler* trials Brunel was able to serve the Admiralty, and his own interests, at the Admiralty's expense. Aside from a little personal friction he had nothing to complain about. Unfortunately his delightful stories and Claxton's vitriol provided the raw material for a legend. The self-serving, politically naïve and technologically determinist accounts left by the hagiographers of nineteenth-century engineers, who wished to portray their subjects as high-minded servants of humanity, have been taken at face value for too long. Brunel was, above all, a successful commercial engineer, but such considerations were ignored by Victorian authors in search of noble men and morally edifying causes.

It is important to stress that the Admiralty was clear-sighted, technologically dynamic, and adopted a professional approach to the management of change, which it handled with skill. It was prepared to act ruthlessly, and exploit the commercial sector whenever possible. By hiring Brunel, who had his own agenda, the Admiralty saved time and money, and began the process of breaking down the screw patent and the SPC. By employing Brunel rather than Smith to instal the screw in *Rattler* the Admiralty paid very little for the use of the patent, and ruined the SPC, which had collapsed by mid 1845. At the same time Brunel's own screw project, the *Great Britain*, had reinforced his position at the head of his profession. He owed a good deal to the *Rattler* trials. At this point Brunel's career, and that of his warship, diverged.

4

Iron Shipbuilding

The iron ship was introduced to the world on 14 May 1819, when in front of a disbelieving crowd lining the Monklands Canal at Faskine near Coatbridge, the iron passage boat *Vulcan* was launched and the face of British (and indeed world) shipbuilding was changed for all time. The hilarity and indeed downright hostility of the bystanders, who were well enough educated to know that iron is heavier than water, was to turn to amazement as the beautiful hull floated gently on one of the two Scottish canals where she was to make a substantial living during the subsequent 54 years.

While technically not the first iron vessel in the world, the *Vulcan* can claim to be the best thought-out of all the early designs and certainly the most meticulously crafted. Her construction methods were to impose new methods of production in the shipyards, and the system of manufacture was to be adopted by all iron and later steel shipbuilding companies. It is unquestionable that she had an influence on all subsequent iron shipbuilders, and Brunel must have been aware of her and the construction techniques used.

The coming of iron to industrial practice is a complex matter, and a subject that has its origins first in the development of the two great iron districts, namely Staffordshire in England and the Clyde Valley in Scotland; secondly in the growing problems being encountered in the procurement of timber for United Kingdom shipbuilding and other similar large-scale construction projects.

Wood is one of the most appropriate materials to use for ship construction: it is a living organism, pliant, machineable and with a beautiful texture, feel and smell. It has been used since time immemorial for the building of ships, windmills, dams, mechanical structures and so on. Wood is easily available and within a few years new plantings can be well on the way to replacing felled trees. The massive growth of British overseas interests in the late seventeenth,

eighteenth and early nineteenth centuries placed enormous strains on the Royal Navy, strains that were compounded during the late eighteenth century when the British fleet was forced into fighting wars on international fronts and also had to manage a continental blockade in Western Europe as Napoleon's influence increased. At this time, the Royal Navy had close to 800 ships on the active list and with continual new building the forests of the south of England were becoming denuded of timber. The Royal Navy, conscious of the forthcoming timber famine, had already begun building ships overseas, in North America as well as in India. Within a few years British merchant shipowners were to purchase many vessels from Canada and in some cases from New England, and indeed, several British shipbuilders were to move across the Atlantic and operate in Canada, especially in the Province of Quebec.

In historical terms, timber prices fluctuate in direct proportion to demand for ships, a situation which has parallels with the oil industry of the twentieth century. As forests run-down the first symptom of shortage is the inability to find long and straight timbers. These trunks are needed for the masts and even more for the long lengths of planking required for the shell planking of the wooden ship. To maintain strength in a wooden vessel, all plank butts must be kept well apart which means that planks and timber pieces must be of considerable length – planks should not be less than 12 metres in length, although this figure is having to be revised owing to the great shortage of long timber in the current world market.

It is probable that the building of the first two recorded iron vessels came about more for convenience, than for technical innovation. The very simple iron barge *Trial*, built by John Wilkinson at Coalbrookdale in 1787 was constructed (at least according to the legend) to overcome delays in barge construction brought about by labour shortages in the boatyards of the English canals. The need for raw

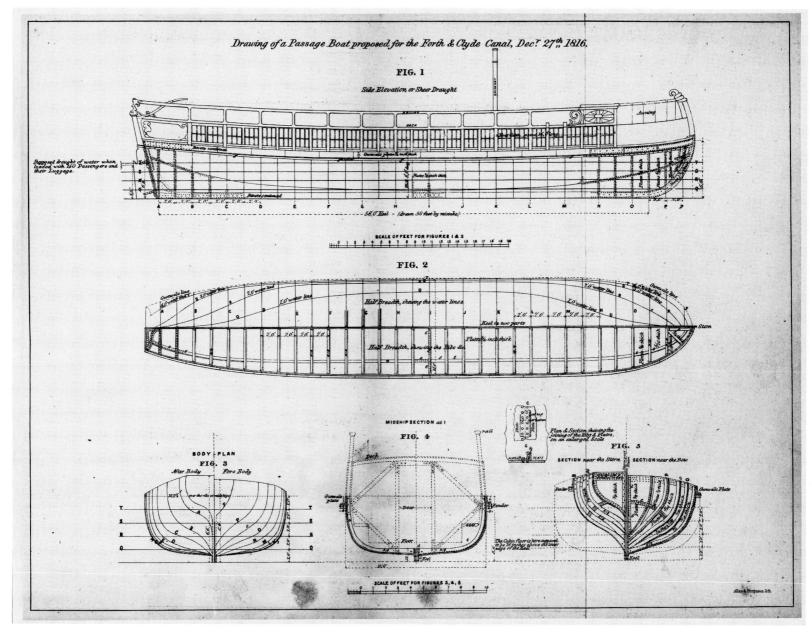

Drawing of the iron passage boat Vulcan, *the world's first practical iron ship.* (By courtesy of Fred M Walker)

materials at the foundries of the Telford area induced Wilkinson to construct a simple timber frame to which cast iron plates were bolted. This original thinking brought about a boxlike structure which in turn was able to lift considerable quantities of ore or scrap and which had a fairly long operational life. With the speeds on the canals being low, the shape was immaterial and the most important factor was the lifting power. It was appreciated within a short time that iron construction gave much greater carrying capacity than a similar-sized timber barge with its bulky keel, keelson, frames and stringers, and, even more impressive, the iron shell thickness was perhaps only 15 per cent of the combined thickness of the frames and the outer shell planking.

The boxlike shape of the barge was to some extent dictated by the use of cast iron. Puddled[1] and wrought iron were such new products on the market that Wilkinson almost certainly used cast plates, and these were simplest if flat or if shaped then with a slight shaped configuration only. Within a few years a series of iron barges were to be constructed in Staffordshire and the surrounding counties, presumably of increasing usefulness as the plate sizes increased and the supply of material became more abundant.

A rather different problem faced the Directors of the Forth and Clyde Canal which was a main transport artery in Central Scotland with passenger and goods services on a highly structured and timetabled basis serving the cities of Glasgow and Edinburgh and the associated seaports on the Rivers Clyde and Forth.[2] The Forth and Clyde was unusual in that it had a deep channel which in addition to the large fleet of barges, lighters and gabbarts also enabled deep-sea vessels and fishing boats of fair size to cross the industrial belt of Scotland in a couple of days. The canal had one very special service, the fleet of passenger barges, some of which were extremely swift and could take passengers from one city to the other in a few hours. These passenger services were fairly sophisticated and the advanced ship design reflected the part of the market at which they were aimed; a well-appointed passage barge was over 20 metres long, had two cabins, catering facilities and separate overboard discharge toilets for men and women. They were horse-drawn and could take one from the outskirts of one city to the other in one day, or sometimes on one overnight passage. Their popularity reflected the pleasantness of the trip with good scenery, smooth motion and (relative to a stage coach) ample space to move around without too much restriction. They supplied food and drink and some were equipped with books and games to while away the passengers' time.

The ultimate in passage barges were the Fly-Boats which pulled by regularly changing teams of horses could take barges at speeds of up to 15mph. The technique was to pull a barge through the enclosed water of the canal thereby generating a massive bow wave, on to which the ship was pulled and then with greatly reduced resistance the barge rolled along on top of this wave – technically called a 'Wave of Translation'.

With heavy traffic, some of it operating at speeds well above that of normal canals, the difficulty became one of avoiding damage to barges and at the end of the eighteenth century, repair costs were becoming significant. The Canal Company appointed a committee to look into the problem and their highly original proposal was for the construction of a fully ship-shaped barge using iron throughout. This task took some years to plan and execute, but when it was delivered in 1819, a new form of shipbuilding had been developed and overnight the requirements of precision engineering had been absorbed into the shipwright's trade. The *Vulcan* was built using a fairly deep bar keel with the normal floors, that is, the frame endings riveted at right angles, stringers around to keep strength although some deck beams were made of wood. The shell plates were relatively small and were riveted to the frames which were spaced 610mm (24in) apart. To the modern shipbuilder, this craft would not seem out of place, the only change being the laying of the shell plates in vertical strakes as distinct from modern practice which is horizontal.

Perhaps the most remarkable part of this whole episode was that Thomas Wilson, the shipbuilder, with his two blacksmiths, did not have the benefit of iron plates delivered from an ironworks nor angle iron or other section purchased from stockists. The industry was at such an early stage of development

Rainbow, *an early iron-built coastal steamer. The visit of the ship to Bristol in October 1838 allowed some of the GWSS Co Technical Committee to evaluate the practicality of iron construction, and to observe at first-hand the compass correction system that iron required.* (National Maritime Museum neg PU6697)

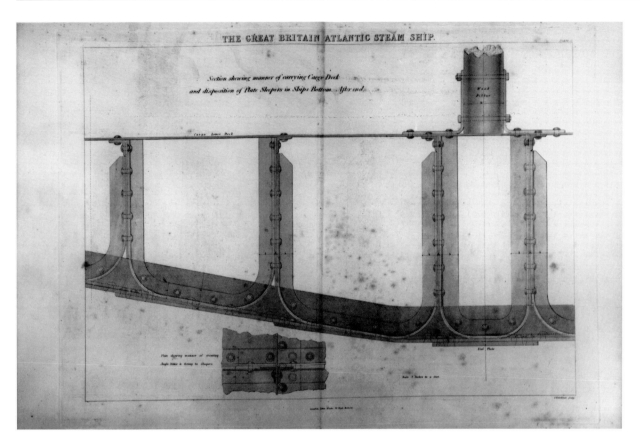

THE GREAT BRITAIN ATLANTIC STEAM SHIP.

Great Britain: '*Section shewing manner of carrying Cargo Deck and disposition of Plate Sleepers in ship's Bottom. After end.*' Some of the early solutions to construction problems with iron were, like this, remarkably modern in concept. (National Maritime Museum neg A8935G)

that the best raw material which came to them was billets of puddled iron, which had to be reheated, cut into suitable sizes and then forged by the hammer on the blacksmith's anvil. Truly the *Vulcan* was built by the sweat of the brow of the Smellie brothers and by the determination and ingenuity of Thomas Wilson. It would be false to say that every part of the *Vulcan* was thought out individually, as it is inconceivable that no other places in Britain were experimenting with riveted iron structures, but we can be sure that this ship was not only the first, but also the grandfather of all iron vessels to follow in the subsequent sixty years.

The preparation for building an iron ship required new skills, the work of the blacksmith, and then a few years later the specialist skill of the plater, the man who cut, shaped and punched the plates and sections making up the complex structure. From the outset, however, there was need for shipwrights, known to this day as loftsmen, who drew the ship out fully and then prepared full-sized wooden templates of each part. This was critical as with riveting, there was need for great accuracy in the jointing of plates and sections with all holes being in exact alignment – a matter of importance when connecting a ship part with curvature in two directions.

This precision had other benefits: the naval architect found he had a stronger hull and one which could be designed for specific tasks. The growth in understanding of naval architecture and the even greater speed in the understanding of structural engineering gave great impetus to this scientific side of the industry. This was aided by the fairly relaxed manner in which engineers and shipbuilders of the earlier years of the nineteenth century were willing to share their knowledge and experience, often by publishing in the journals of learned societies or the Proceedings of the Institution of Civil Engineers.[3]

The inventors of the age were a closer-bound group of people than their counterparts of today. Most would know of each other's work, and without doubt there was considerable cross-fertilisation of ideas amongst the engineers and builders of the time. The development of iron shipbuilding had two other unexpected benefits, both of which directly or indirectly led to the building of the *Great Britain* only eighteen years after the *Vulcan* had been launched. The first was the ability of an iron ship to carry a far bulkier cargo than the timber counterpart with the same overall dimensions. This comes through the thinner shell plating, and the vastly reduced size and thickness of frames, beams and stringers. Taking two identical ships, one iron and the

Great Britain: *'Section at After end of Vessel, shewing Sleepers and Lower Cargo Deck.'* (National Maritime Museum neg A89351)

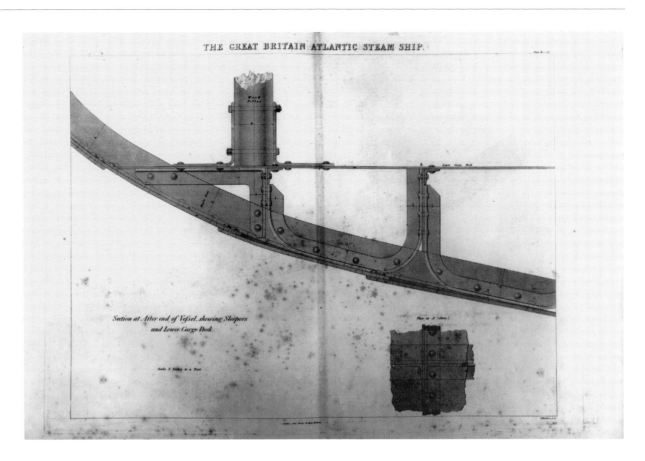

THE GREAT BRITAIN ATLANTIC STEAM SHIP.

Section at After end of Vessel, shewing Sleepers and Lower Cargo Deck.

other timber, it is possible to have an increase in cargo space of the region of 20 per cent, which in other words means that the space available within the wooden ship could be as low as 80 per cent of the measured gross amount while that of an iron (and in later years steel) ship could be as high as 96 per cent.

The greatest benefit was the ability to build ships of greater length and to be assured that they could withstand much more abuse and stress, and that they would be less affected by poor loading of cargo. By and large the longest wooden ships in Europe up till the end of the eighteenth century were about 75 metres at most. Admittedly towards the end of the nineteenth century wooden ships had become longer with one or two exceptionally large examples coming from the shipyards of the United States of America. Currently it is claimed that the longest wooden ship hull in the world is that of the San Francisco Bay paddle steamer *Eureka* (now over 100 years old and in the keeping of the San Francisco Maritime Museum) which is just over 92 metres. However, such craft were by far the exception and with the coming of iron, shipbuilders, particularly in Britain were quick to appreciate the advantages of building longer ships. Length confers many benefits: increased speed for the same power output, greater cargo-carrying capacity rising by the cube of the

length, better sea-keeping in the long swells of the oceans and, subject to good design, better handling qualities in rough conditions.

From 1820 onwards, more and more iron hulls were constructed, although none of great size until the *Great Britain* was built in Bristol. Despite their efficiency, problems were to arise with the iron hulls, some of which in a much more limited extent continue to this day. First it was important that the hull of an iron ship did not have dissimilar metals on the hull and in close proximity to salt water. The effect of galvanic action leads to one of the metals being eroded or corroded owing to the tiny electrical current flow set up by the steel of the ship's hull in sea water. Initially, with copper and other metals in close proximity to iron, this was a serious problem, but with experience and also with improved painting this problem receded, and later in the century was finally defeated by the introduction of sacrificial anodes, blocks of metal such as zinc which were designed to be eaten and to protect the ship's hull.

Another problem, which had been unexpected, was the surprisingly quick growth of algae on iron underwater hulls. As early as the mid-1820s considerable efforts were being made to find a way round this problem, and many patent concoctions were tried with the triple objectives of keeping the ship's

hull smooth, free of plant growth and protected from corrosion. The vast number of papers to learned societies indicates the importance attached to this matter and also the riches to be won by the success- ful chemist or paint manufacturer. The mixtures included some very unlikely materials including various tars, horse hair, manure, oils and so on. One really effective remedy was found for ships that had to lie at anchor for long periods like the Trinity House and the Northern Lighthouse Board Lightships, or to remain hove-to off coasts in tropical conditions, like the Royal Naval sloops on anti-slavery patrols off East Africa – on completion of the iron hull, the vessel would be further sheathed with a fairly thin shell of timber, usually teak in those days of ease of supply, and on top of that a further shell of either copper sheeting or of some closely- related alloy like Muntz metal. This final sheathing, usually of the order of 1mm thick, would protect the

ship from growth and the timber and iron under from corrosion. Examples of this can be seen on the occasional old vessel and prove the efficacy of the system, despite the high cost.

The most serious problem encountered by the iron ship, and in some cases an alarming one is the phenomenon known as 'magnetic deviation'. In a nutshell this is the result of inherent magnetic effect built into the iron hull during construction. The ship while lying on the building berth and subject to hammering and vibration, picks up magnetism from the earth's magnetic field and retains it on a fairly permanent basis. With any magnetic field whatsoever in a ship, the normal seafarers' compasses are made inaccurate, in some cases to a severe degree. One of the first fully-recorded instances of this is in 1831 when the *Lord Dundas* built by Sir William Fairbairn at Manchester was delivered to the Clyde, found that instead of sailing to the Isle of Man, the ship had

In the forty years following the Vulcan *the size of structures that could be fabricated in iron increased astronomically; even so, Great Eastern herself represented a quantum leap in dimensions over anything that had gone before. The size of the ship is demonstrated by the figures in the foreground. (By courtesy of Denis Griffiths)*

reached the coast of Cumberland which was many degrees off course.

Many methods of rectifying this problem were tried, ranging from the workmanlike to the ridiculous. A case of the former was the installation of a wooden mast on the quarter-deck of large iron sailing vessels, upon which a magnetic compass was fitted high enough to be out of the range of the magnetic influences; the compass could be read by the officer of the watch by looking up a prefocussed monocular. This system was used aboard the four-masted full rigged *County* ships sailing from Glasgow in the 1880s. A less practical solution was that of having a copper lifeboat which was towed behind an iron ship. It was manned by an experienced seaman and equipped with a compass. The ship's course could be read at all times and signalled back to the officer of the watch by semaphore!

This problem was attacked with vigour at two old and renowned academic establishments, the Royal Observatory, Greenwich and the University of Glasgow. The two men most involved (and not especially good friends) were Sir George Airy, the Astronomer Royal for England and Sir William Thomson (later Lord Kelvin) the Professor of Natural Philosophy at Glasgow. On the face of it Kelvin seemed to have come out the winner as his new compass design became the basis for the Admiralty Standard Compass, but the contribution of Airy and of Captain Matthew Flinders (1774-1814) all added to this problem being solved well before the end of the nineteenth century. It is standard practice for magnetic compasses to be 'swung' or adjusted prior to any important voyage, and at least once every few months. While magnetic compasses are still required in the outfit of a ship, their importance has declined in real terms, and indeed it is possible that some day they may be relegated to history.

PRACTICAL CONSIDERATIONS GOVERNING THE CONSTRUCTION OF SHIPS

The building of ships is a skill which goes back over thousands of years, and is a craft which is remarkably international with conventions that are accepted worldwide. These traditions are important in that they assure the shipowner of standards of equipment and practice which are understood by seagoing and shipbuilding personnel from any part of the world and with differing languages. The most obvious example of this is the layout of running rigging on a sailing ship, which varies little from ship to ship or from nation to nation. It is worth looking at the main criteria in the building of wooden ships, as this in turn helps us understand the fantastic revolution brought about by the introduction of iron, and in later years steel which is effectively an alloy of iron with many better and a few lesser qualities.

The main, indeed the only, ship construction material until the early nineteenth century was timber, which to this day is in plentiful supply in many parts of the world. Timber comes in many species, each with differing qualities of resistance to abrasion, work- ability, strength, compressibility and so on. In some parts of the world, timber can be cut down and used almost immediately in construction projects, whilst elsewhere it is advisable to allow it to dry and mature before being incorporated in a hull under construction.

Examples of building ships from green timber are to be found nowadays in South East Asia where many yards use tropical woods with both strength and longevity, an example being Belian or Borneo Ironwood (*Eusideroxylon Zwageri*) for construction. Once this material is cut, it is taken straight to the yard and planks are laid out to form the bottom of the ship, with the plank edges being doweled together with timber pegs and the space between the planks being caulked with the bark of the tree. This is the eastern form of construction, with the hull being formed prior to the frames (often called the ribs), which are added later to give the hull both strength and rigidity.

The western tradition, which has been used in the United Kingdom and most of western Europe for the best part of 500 years is to build a skeletal structure based on a backbone or keel with frames and beams to form the cage round which the ship is planked. It was usual for the timbers to be indigenous, and it was always regarded as an advantage if the timbers had lain airing under cover for a month or two prior to construction. In the case of small ships built in Britain the choice of timber could be oak for keel and frames, larch or pine for planking, pine for decks and fir for the masts and spars. Another well-used timber was elm for the keel until the outbreaks of Dutch elm disease in the past few decades made this uneconomical.

The most important aspect of wooden hull construction is that the shipbuilder must attempt to use the largest pieces of wood available as this cuts down the number of joints and thereby the sources of potential weakness in the structure. The jointing by tradition uses iron bolts, iron dumps or treenails which theoretically should make the joint almost as strong as the surrounding timber, but in reality weaken the ship by the introduction of holes and stress points and in the long term by the corrosive effects of the iron. Except in dinghies and very small boats, the frames which girth the ship are so large that they cannot be made in single pieces and therefore are fabricated from a series of sawn timbers bolted together to form either one side of the frame or in some cases the complete unit port and starboard. This is an example of prefabrication which predates by centuries the system 'invented' in American and British shipyards in the twentieth century!

To enable a wooden ship to be built in the western tradition, the shape of the frames is critical to the whole undertaking as they govern the shape of the hull and their shape relative to one another governs the smoothness of the hull. The building of a ship 'by eye' indicates that it is built without formal plans and using the judgement, experience and local tradition available to the shipwright in charge. Wood is a fairly forgiving material and should one frame be slightly proud or uneven in a build-by-eye construction, then efforts can be made to rectify the situation.

All ships' hulls have structural stress points. Almost all hulls of whatever material tend to 'hog', that is, droop at the bow and the stern through the large concentrations of weight there and at a point of the hull with least buoyancy and therefore least support. To overcome this the wooden hull has massive timber constructions at the ends known as deadwoods which increase the hull strength and reduce the likelihood of serious hogging. In some very large

This superbly detailed diorama model of John Scott Russell's yard shows the Great Eastern *under construction. Despite the size of the project, the yard is not equipped with much in the way of obvious machinery or cranes, most of the work being done from stages over the side of the hull. Iron construction at this time still involved much hand-crafted work.* (National Maritime Museum neg C3440)

and strong ships (an example being the wooden exploration ship *Discovery*) these timbers are known as Fortifications!

The greatest drawback in a timber ship is the reduced space available for cargo and stores. To take an extreme case the volume of a ship up to the waterline could be $500m^4$ made up of the construction material and empty stowage space. In the wooden ship the timber could account for over $100m^4$ leaving less than $400m^4$ for cargo, living space, etc. In the case of a modern steel ship this figure could be as little as $20m^4$ for steelwork leaving $480m^4$ for working space, or in naval architect's parlance the permeability of the wooden ship is less than 80 per cent while that of the steel ship is over 96 per cent. These figures vary throughout the ship and vary according to the waterline at which it is computed, but the overall effect is clear and unambiguous.

Finally, the length of time that a ship can remain operational is affected by the material used. Some of the oldest ships in the world are of course timber, an example being the former Royal Navy frigate *Trincomalee* built of teak in India in 1816, and now after a massive refit as good as new. The choice of teak and the limited duties of the *Trincomalee* assured her survival with less than 40 per cent of her timbers replaced. However, some wooden ships last very short periods, examples being the vast fleet of merchant trading vessels built in North America in the late nineteenth and early twentieth centuries, often hastily assembled from unseasoned softwoods. The ships of the Russian fleet assembled in the eighteenth century often had lives as short as seven years, having been built during summers periods only and then remaining laid up for many months each year in the inhospitable conditions of the Russian coastline.[4] Finally, lack of maintenance and lack of funding in periods of peace ensured their early demise.

Today, a general rule of thumb is that a steel ship (on average) can last between fifteen and twenty-five years depending on its service, maintenance and original standards of construction. An iron ship, which is less prone to corrosion, may be in good condition 100 years after construction, an example being the four masted ship *Munoz Gamero* of the Chilean Navy stationed at Punta Arenas, formerly the *County of Peebles* built in Glasgow in 1875. Here care, coupled with the low ambient and water temperatures of the Straits of Magellan have contributed to her longevity.

The final drawback of timber as mentioned earlier is the inability of timber hulls to remain strong and without distortion once the 75m barrier is reached. While the earliest iron ships were fairly small, it was not long before the iron ship had become a large ocean carrier, and as carrying capacity rises not in proportion to the length of a ship, but by a factor similar to the cube of the length, then it was not long before the benefit of building in iron became abundantly clear.

THE PROBLEMS FACING EARLY IRON SHIPBUILDERS

The first difficulty facing any shipwright on changing from wood to iron was the recruitment of suitable workmen. Few shipwrights had any training in using iron or any other metals, and the only metal craftsmen in yards were the blacksmiths who handled forged iron up to at most one or two tons, for anchors and the few hanging and lodging knees fitted into the structure. In the case of the *Vulcan*, the building was supervised by a shipwright of the highest competence with the vast bulk of the work being carried out by two blacksmiths. They had puddled iron delivered and from this they forged the plates, angles and all parts of the iron structure. On completion of each part it had to be drilled (by hand!) for holes for the rivets, and each part had to be an exact fit against the next item on the ship. With oxy-propane and oxy-acetylene cutting far in the future, the trimming of plates had to be carried out by hand with chisels and similar hand tools, making the manufacture of each part of the ship a costly and time-consuming process. Overnight, high precision had been introduced to shipbuilding, and this in turn allowed the naval architect (whose profession was gathering momentum), to calculate all matters with an accuracy previously unknown.

The next hurdle to be overcome was the finding of suitable supplies of material, as each yard depended on the delivery of abundant blooms of puddled iron. Here the areas of Britain with coal and iron ore were at an advantage – Yorkshire and the English North East Coast and of course Clydeside with the nearby Lanarkshire pits producing coal and blackband ironstone. It is interesting to note that Clydeside which has produced more ships than any other region of the world only commenced shipbuilding in a serious way in the early nineteenth century and most probably as a result of the success of the *Vulcan* and subsequent iron ships. (Reliable authorities have computed the number of Clyde-built ships as of the order of 30,000 with another 10,000 yachts and small craft – and all since the construction of the *Vulcan*.)

Until the ironworks (which were sprouting up all over Britain) had decided on their main line of produce, the shipyards had to make their own plates and of course iron sections such as angles, channels and joists. These were not forthcoming in the early part of the century as the technology for continuous rolling of sections was in its infancy – but by the 1860s these items had become 'off the peg' items for shipyard consumption and the yards could concentrate on their design and building and not on the manufacture of standard parts. The ship designer was aided by the iron and steel producers' catalogues with an amazing array of angles, bulb angles, channels, girders and other complex geometric sections.

One particular difficulty arose with the sizes of iron plates. In this modern day we are accustomed to steel plates of up to 15m in length, and indeed even more in specialised cases where there is continuous casting at the steelworks. This was not the case in the 1820s, 1830s or even much later, as every plate had to be forged from the puddled bloom, with tremendous manual handling and the continuous likelihood of inherent fracture, interstitial cracks and blowholes. For this reason right up to about 1870 it was difficult to find high-quality plates much longer than 3m, and many yards used smaller ones as standard. A close investigation of the plans of early nineteenth century ships shows the size of plates and the number of vertical butts and horizontal seams far in excess of what is considered normal today, and as has been indicated, additional joints produce potential weak points in the hull structure.

Conventions of building were to change, and some parts of the ship were to have a new form once the shipyards became used to working in this exotic material. With riveting, the effective length of parts like the keel were increased as the joint could (at least in theory) be judged as an integral part of the construction. Frames could be manufacture as single pieces with one long-angle iron being heated in a frame furnace and once red-hot dragged out on to the 'blocks' and hammered into the shape of the ship, and then pegged and allowed to cool in its new form. The skills of the ironworkers increased quickly and they became able not only to shape in one plane but to create double curvatures of the most complex kind.

Iron construction was just past its infancy when work started on the *Great Britain* at Bristol, but it was well developed when work commenced on the *Great Eastern* at the Isle of Dogs. The early development of iron shipbuilding is apparent on the *Great Britain*, with the ship having been built almost as material became available; the ship's frames (which are normally spaced in a regular fashion, say at 600mm apart) are in this case at varying widths brought about by having to space them to allow for the optimum arrangements of ship side plates to be incorporated

THE TECHNICAL BENEFITS OF BUILDING IN IRON

With hindsight it is clear that the early struggles of the iron shipbuilders were to pay great dividends to the shipyards not only of Britain but the world. Once the method of construction had been ascertained, it was a fairly straightforward matter to build to standard methods and in turn for the designers to develop in their plans conventions which were to be understood worldwide. A simple example is the fact that all ship plans are drawn with the ship 'steaming' to the right-hand side of the paper, or in an outboard profile the starboard side is in view. This is far from childish convention, it is vital that every plan from an office can be understood and the co-ordinates appreciated from the beginning.

During the nineteenth century, the science of ship design took great steps forward, aided by the ever-improving understanding of mathematics, natural philosophy and structural engineering. The ship designer was given more and more tools and by the end of the century, few tasks were beyond the ability of a properly-trained naval architect.

5 The GWSS Company Works

With the *Great Western* in service and operating successfully the owners looked towards a second ship and to that end purchased a cargo of African oak, sufficient to construct two vessels. There had always been an intention to construct further ships and it is evident that the second ship would have been similar to the *Great Western,* namely a wooden paddle steamer but possibly slightly larger. In September 1838 one of the local newspapers announced, 'The Great Western Steamship Company are about to build another vessel of equal size to the *Great Western*; she will be called the *City of New York*. A large cargo of African oak timber has been purchased for this and further ships'.[1]

Although the second vessel was originally intended to be constructed from wood a change of mind quickly took place, resulting in the first of many delays which were to plague the ship. At the annual general meeting of the company held on 7 March 1839 the directors stated:

> Your Directors hoped that long before this your second vessel would have been in a state of forwardness, but the same feeling which led to unusual caution in the construction of the *Great Western*, an increased conviction that the nearest possible approach to perfection must be kept in view, retarded their conclusions. After, however, the most ample investigation, they finally determined to build your next vessel of iron, and are now far advanced in their preparation for her construction, which will be carried out under the most skilful superintendence.[2]

It is easy to see Brunel's influence in these changes but he could not have forced any decision on the directors. The *Great Western* was working well and had a successful season on the Atlantic, so there must have been a strong inclination towards building the same again. The decision to build the next ship from iron, taken at the end of 1838, was a major step, for no ship of the intended size had been built from iron to that time and there was no iron shipbuilding expertise in the area. In a letter dated 27 November 1838 Claxton wrote to Charles Babbage, 'We have settled to build an iron ship and mean to construct her ourselves . . . If you wish for full particulars it must be on the clear understanding that they are not to be given to the Enemy'. The 'Enemy' was the British and American Steam Navigation Company, owners of the *British Queen*, a direct competitor to the *Great Western* on the Atlantic. Earlier in the letter to Babbage Claxton had said, '. . . if I recollect right you expressed yourself as connected or intimate with some of the Directors of the British Queen Company with who we are unhappily at issue.'[3]

Brunel, Claxton and Guppy, the Technical Committee established to oversee development of the new ship, first seem to have considered the idea of using iron in October 1838 and the fortuitous visit of the iron steam coasting vessel *Rainbow* to Bristol that month gave ample opportunity for investigation. Guppy, Claxton and Patterson made a number of trips on the ship in order to examine the problems of rusting, fouling, sea-keeping, and the impact on compasses. Claxton was particularly interested in the influence of iron on the ship's compass and during his trip aboard *Rainbow* he had the opportunity of seeing in operation the compass correction system devised by Professor Airy, the Astronomer Royal. In his letter to Babbage, Claxton commented:

> I made a voyage in the *Rainbow* took the bearings and distance – worked the courses – and perfectly satisfied myself of the perfect adjustment of Professor Airy's compasses. Took some of my own on board and made many interesting experiments – Found my

compasses correct in his Binnacles which goes to prove their adjustments will suit ordinary cards . . . The Professor explained cheerfully to me and so satisfied am I of his having confirmed a vast benefit to Science that I would have no hesitation in crossing any sea or latitude with his correctors.

Amongst the advantages claimed for iron construction was an increase in capacity of about 600 tons and comparative safety in ice. A detailed report was prepared for submission to the directors and this recommended that iron be used for construction of the second vessel.[4] Brunel added other advantages which could be accrued from the use of iron, namely the freedom from dry rot, avoidance of vermin and the absence of unpleasant odours due to bilge water. Whilst there may have been advantages such as these when compared with timber, the use of iron itself posed new problems and did not eliminate the likes of vermin. Brunel was, obviously, being selective in his advocacy of iron construction.

The directors agreed with the proposal and authorised Brunel, Claxton, and Guppy to act as a

Building Committee, but these men had no experience of iron shipbuilding themselves so they had to learn quickly. Brunel appears to have looked upon such matters as a challenge but the whole idea was going to be a costly exercise as the company had to build the ship itself, there being no suitable facilities available in Bristol. The company was already committed to erecting its own workshops for the repair of the machinery fitted in the *Great Western* and it is likely that the construction of a dry dock was also under consideration; at the end of 1838 the *Great Western* had to use the Admiralty dry dock at Pater, Pembroke.[5] Workshop machinery was being purchased during the latter part of 1838, much of this coming from Nasmyths.[6] In deciding to built their next vessel of iron itself the GWSS Co would also have needed to make a decision on construction in a dock or on a slip. Construction in a dock was considered to be the most appropriate and the dock was dug to a depth sufficient to allow the ship to float in her lightest condition. Delays and changes in the size and propulsion system resulted in a rethink and in 1842 the dock was '. . . floored by an inverted arch in the most economical but secure manner, so as to be

One of the main rivals of the GWSS Co was the British and American Steam Navigation Company whose British Queen is seen here leaving Spithead for New York on 12 July 1839. (National Maritime Museum neg X1201)

prepared to receive her as a dry dock'.[7] At the same time a decision was taken to install the engines and boilers in the dock, through an aperture left in the ship's side, as that would avoid the heavy expense associated with installation whilst afloat.

It is surprising that nobody had considered the problems associated with dry-docking the ship, and the *Great Western*, until that time. There were few facilities available anywhere able to take the *Great Western*, let alone the much larger new ship, but dry-docking was an essential part of ship operation. At that time the lower portions of the paddle wheels had to be removed whenever the *Great Western* was brought into the Floating Harbour and the entrance at the Cumberland Basin was too small to accommodate the new ship. There seems to have been considerable optimism that problems of access would be overcome by time the new ship was ready for sea and such optimism appears to have characterised the company's operations throughout. The problem of dry-docking also appears not to have entered the minds of those building the ship and it is still surprising that a competent engineer like Brunel

The trunk engine of Humphrys design proposed for the second GWSS Co ship while a paddle-steamer was still under consideration. (Drawing by Denis Griffiths)

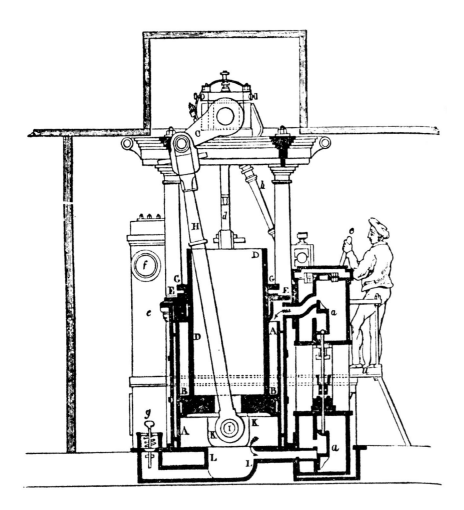

did not raise the matter when proposing a larger ship and iron construction.

In March 1839 the directors were able to report:

The erection of the requisite Workshops and Machinery is rapidly advancing at your Yard, on the banks of the Floating Harbour, the proportions of the vessel are determined upon, and your Directors are availing themselves of the highest professional skill, as well as their own practical experience, in determining on the vital point of the construction of the engines.[8]

In a letter written shortly after the decision had been made in favour of iron construction Claxton stated that the proposed dimensions were to be: length of keel 254 feet, beam not less than 40 feet and depth of hold about 23 feet. By the end of January 1839 the size of the ship had been increased: length of keel 260 feet, breadth at paddle shaft 41 feet and depth of hold 24 feet.[9]

Brunel would have been closely involved in the discussions relating to the new ship and was certainly influential in many of the changes which subsequently took place. The Science Museum holds a number of tender drawings produced by Maudslay, Sons & Field and these give some indications of the changes which were taking place. Maudslays must have had confidence in their ability to win the contract for machinery for the new ship due to the success of the first venture. These drawings indicate arrangements for oscillating paddle engines and there was a requirement for higher power than had been provided for the *Great Western*. In November 1838 Brunel wrote to Claxton concerning the power of the new ship and he expressed the need for greater speed, but he was confident that the ship would be ready by early 1841: '. . . There is not much time to spare if the Vessel is to be as I hope she will be ready to start with the spring of the season of 1841, If these points [on size of cylinder, boiler capacity, etc., to submit for tenders] are well considered we will secure the superiority of the Bristol line for the next 5 years at least . . .'[10]

Despite the decision to build the ship itself the company had no similar intentions with respect to the machinery, at least not initially. While the new ship was still a wooden paddle steamer tenders were sought for the supply of suitable machinery and

The steamer Wilberforce *was fitted with Humphrys machinery, the valve system being of particular interest to Brunel.*
(National Maritime Museum neg 696)

Maudslays proposed a two-cylinder oscillating engine arrangement, whilst a trunk engine arrangement was submitted by Francis Humphrys. The Maudslay involvement at the time can be judged from the drawings at the Science Museum and Humphrys' association from a letter, dated 22 October 1838, sent by Brunel to the engineer Bryan Donkin asking the latter to inspect the engine and valves in the steamboat *Wilberforce*. '... Mr Humphries [*sic*] is the inventor of them and strongly recommends them to us. I am prepared to give the directors my opinion of them but I cannot get down to the vessel to see them. It is necessary, therefore, to obtain a report from such an authority as yourself . . . if you can so arrange it to see them working and try an indicator on them . . . and to report on the advisability of their use on an Atlantic run.'[11] The report was favourable.[12]

Both engine arrangements offered an advantage over the side lever type in that they were much shorter, and lighter; thus they occupied less space in the ship, therefore giving a greater cargo-carrying potential. Steam force on a piston acts to rotate the paddle shaft through the connecting rod and cranks on that shaft. A long connecting rod means that the horizontal component of the force in the rod when acting on the cranks is small, so there is only a small horizontal force acting on the paddle shaft and connecting rod bearings. With a short connecting rod the opposite is the case and large horizontal forces act on these bearings, such forces being potentially damaging. The side lever engine can have very long connecting rods as the side levers are placed low down in the ship but the length of these levers results in a long engine. Placing cylinders directly below the paddle shaft results in a short engine, but such an arrangement also means that the connecting rod will, of necessity, be short with resultant problems at the paddle shaft bearings. There will also be high side forces at the crosshead where the piston rod attaches to the connecting rod. The Maudslay oscillating engine design overcame the problem of high side thrust forces as the cylinders were pivoted and there was no need for a crosshead; the piston rod attached directly to the crankpin and thus acting as a long connecting rod. The main problem with the oscillating engine was that steam passed through the cylinder pivots and these had to be kept steam tight in order to avoid energy loss.

The Humphrys engine had fixed vertical cylinders

but the connecting rod of each cylinder attached to a gudgeon pin at the lower end of its piston; movement of the connecting rod as the piston reciprocated was allowed for by the fitting of a trunk to the upper part of the piston.

In November 1838 Brunel estimated that engines having cylinders of 88 inches diameter would be required and he had details sent to Maudslays, Messrs Hall of Dartford (holder of the rights to the Humphrys trunk engine), and to Messrs Seaward. Maudslays declined to tender this time but, in April 1839, they were again asked to tender, together with Halls, Seawards, Fawcett & Preston, and Bush & Beddoes, for engines having 100-inch bore by 7-foot stroke.

Whether they all submitted tenders is not known but only Messrs Maudslays and Messrs Hall remained in contention and Brunel asked both concerns to submit tenders for larger engines with cylinders of 120 inches diameter. The Maudslay company was developing its double cylinder or 'Siamese' engine at the time and Brunel appears to have had great faith in this compared with the oscillating design for he twice asked the directors to postpone coming to a decision in order that Maudslays could complete development work on the engine.[13]

For each of the two cranks on the paddle shaft the Siamese engine had two cylinders, arranged in a fore and aft manner, with the piston rods of the cylinders attached by means of an open yoke. The centre of the yoke projected downwards and at its lower end was a pin to which the lower end of the connecting rod attached. This system allowed for a short engine but avoided the need for cylinder pivots or trunks. Maudslays initially proposed the use of four 75-inch diameter cylinders which were considered to be the equivalent of a pair of 106-inch diameter cylinders. Brunel subsequently suggested an increase in bore to 77.75 inches which he concluded would be equivalent to the pair of 110-inch diameter cylinders proposed for the Humphrys (Messrs Hall) trunk piston engine. He estimated that the Maudslay engines could be fitted for about £45,500 but this compared unfavourably with the Humphrys' quote of £30,700.[14] Brunel appears to have estimated costs for a larger Siamese engine himself based upon the Maudslay earlier tender. This would seem to indicate that he was very keen to have the Maudslay machinery.

SIDE LEVER ENGINE,
PARALLEL MOTION
MECHANISM © D GRIFFITHS 1980

Radius bar H-F
Side rod   P-D
Conn' link   F-G
Main beam C-D

Parallel
motion bar F-Q

Brunel twice had the Humphrys' tender returned as he doubted that it could be built for the price quoted. When tendering Messrs Hall had stated that if they tendered large tools would have to be purchased by them and charged to the single order for the one pair of engines. They strongly recommended that the GWSS Co make its own engines.[15] In view of this it would seem likely that Humphrys then took over negotiations and tendered himself on the basis of construction of parts by a number of engineering companies or the GWSS Co itself. Brunel is likely to have disputed the costings and hence the return of the tender document for reworking of the costing.

After careful consideration Brunel reported to the directors on 12 June 1839. He was not at all happy with the recosted Humphrys proposal nor with the concept of the company having the engines built piecemeal in Bristol. The idea of having the engine

The general layout of a side lever engine, which was less favoured because of its bulk. (Drawing by Denis Griffiths)

built in such a manner was, he considered, hopeless and this meant that the company would have to build the engines itself. This he was very much against and he then went on to assert that the responsibility of taking such a step rested on the Directors alone, and that they took the responsibility upon themselves in opposition to Mr Brunel's advice.[16]

In the report Brunel does not cast doubt upon the technical merit of the Humphrys engine, although he obviously favoured the Maudslay design, but he was very much concerned that the company would be overstretching itself thereby increasing the risk of failure.

I should not act rightly if I did not communicate that opinion to you, that the first outlay will be fully as large and probably larger by adopting the plan of making our own engines than by employing a manufacturer. It is true we shall have some valuable and costly tools and shops included in this outlay, and a fine establishment formed, which may be rendered fully competent in point of means to continue the manufacture of engines for others, and to keep up the repairs of any number of engines which the Company are likely to have at work. My only fear would be that of the risk of the undertaking being too great for a newly formed establishment. The making of the vessel itself is no mean effort, and to superadd the construction of the largest pair of engines and boilers yet made, and upon a new plan, is calculating very much upon every effort being successful . . . I should have much preferred that it had been adopted gradually, that we had commenced with a vessel, and then proceeded with boilers and repairs; and, as our establishment became formed and matured – we might then have ventured upon making the

Maudslay's design of double cylinder or 'Siamese' engine, as fitted in the steam frigate HMS Terrible. *Brunel seemed very keen on this form of machinery for the new ship.* (By courtesy of Denis Griffiths)

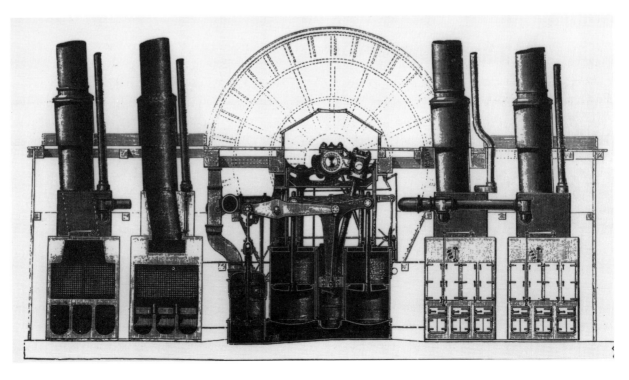

engines perhaps for the third vessel . . . I think advantages are fully counterbalanced by that of the experience in all the details which is brought into operation in an old-established factory, and the great relief from responsibility and risk obtained by contracting for the whole work.[17]

This was sound advice and was somewhat optimistic as later events showed that the company, due to its legal constitution, could not act as a general manufacturer for other parties.[18] The directors, however, failed to heed Brunel's advice and decided that the company would itself construct Humphrys engines for the new ship.

Brunel's close relationship with Maudslay and Field was not shared by all members of the GWSS Co Board of Directors and some may have remembered an earlier dispute between the two companies. When engines for the *Great Western* were being built an argument arose about the practice of charging for extras. What constituted extras resulted in much correspondence between the parties, but at that time the charging of extras, such as additional pipes, fittings and tools, on top of the contract price was the usual practice. In early correspondence between the companies it had been mentioned that the usual practice of charging for extras would be set aside,[19] but this had not been stated in the contract. Brunel did not agree with the engine builder that the paddle wheels and changing water apparatus constituted extras, as he believed that these were actual parts of the propulsion plant for which the contract had been made.[20] Eventually agreement was reached which must have been below the expectation of the builder, for Brunel later stated that Maudslays '. . . could not afford to make a second order as low as the first'.[21]

There was also another contentious matter between the two parties at that time related to personnel. It has generally been thought that Francis Humphrys became an employee of the GWSS Co when his engine was adopted to propel the new ship, but this appears not to have been the case. Having decided to construct its own engine works during 1838 the company sought an experienced engineer to superintend the factory which was established to maintain the machinery of the *Great Western*. It would appear that Francis Humphrys was appointed to the position sometime towards the end of 1838 and certainly prior to January 1839, before a decision had been made to actually adopt the Humphrys

trunk engine for the new ship. The fact that their resident works engineer had devised an engine which the company could use, possibly free from royalties or at a reduced royalty, may well have influenced some of the directors to opt for that design in preference to the Maudslay engine.

It is evident from a letter sent by Brunel to Guppy on 15 January 1839 that Humphrys occupied a position of responsibility in the engine works as a dispute had arisen over the employment of a young engineer who had previously been in the employ of Maudslay, Sons & Field. The charge seems to be that Humphrys enticed the young engineer, H S Harman, from his previous employers.

> In the absence of Claxton I must ask your assistance in enabling me to make some enquiries which I must satisfy my own mind on a subject connected with the Steam Ship.
>
> Messrs Maudslay have made a representation respecting a young man enjoying their confidence and as they consider engaged to them having been induced to leave their employment and enter that of the Steam Ship Company. Mr Humphrys explanation of the terms and circumstances connected with the engagement of this young man are not quite satisfactory to me – I have always maintained a position with manufacturers and my brother engineers by which I enjoyed their confidence and maintained a position agreeable to myself and advantageous to those for whom I act professionally; now one of the rules I have always strictly adhered to has been never to allow persons to be engaged except with the knowledge of the parties with whom they may be – in the present case I think Messrs Maudslays have some ground of complaint and I am anxious to satisfy myself as to the real state of the case that I may either most decidedly exculpate the company's agents or at least clear myself or propose some arrangement satisfactory to all parties – I should like to see the young man himself and then talk to Humphries [*sic*] about it this evening.[22]

Brunel had obviously been approached by Maudslays on the matter and he must have felt that he was in a very difficult position due to his friendship and professional relationship with them. The letter indicates his honesty and fairness for he was not prepared to judge the issue until he had spoken to the parties concerned. This he did that day and then contacted Guppy two days later.

When I parted from Humphrys the other evening we agreed that he should not write to Maudslays till I had thought over the business we had talked of – I have done so and I am sorry to say that I can come to no conclusion but this – that whether Humphrys did or did not act directly and although the young man may have been quite as culpable as any body and may have acted very improperly yet [illegible] he was applyed to and induced by somebody on our part to leave Messrs Maudslays' employment when he filled a confidential situation without their previous knowledge and very much against their wishes – now I think this discreditable to the company and likely to be very injurious to their interests in their peculiar position of manufacturers and if you and the other directors come to the same conclusion I think you have no alternative but to discountenance strongly such a proceeding in the [illegible] and to show to manufacturers that you intend to do so by refusing to ratify or to rescind any confirmation of the appointment made by Humphrey [sic] whatever may be the consequences – I should be the last person to carry my notions of propriety to an [illegible] and I would never separate myself from a party with whom I acted because I entertained different opinions but in this case if the directors do not come to the conclusion I have referred to I must to retain that position with manufacturers necessary to me in business and without which I could not be acceptable to my employers – I must separate myself from the manufacturing part of this concern. If my opinion or advice should at any time be thought valuable I shall be only too happy to give it on points of general construction of the engines or any other points which might have arisen had we been manufacturers, but it must be known that I do not approve of conduct which would deprive me of that confidence which I now enjoy and which gives me free access to all the manufactories where I am known. I think however that you must see that the interests of the concern require as strong a mark of disapproval as I think their credit does.

If you wish to talk the matter over with me again before you mention it to the directors I shall be in Bristol this evening. [23]

Brunel was jealous of the reputation he enjoyed with all of the major engine builders and engineering manufacturing companies and was, obviously, angry after the meeting with Humphrys during which, it would appear, he had obtained little or no satisfaction. There may well have been a clash of personalities, with Humphrys wishing to exert his authority as superintendent of the engineering works, possibly feeling that Brunel, as the company's unpaid consulting engineer, had no right to interfere. Certainly the directors appear to have sided with Humphrys as Harman was retained and subsequently became Chief Engineer aboard the *Great Britain*.

This incident may well have set some of the directors against Maudslays when it came to choosing between an engine from that concern or one designed by its own works engineer, who had been seen to act in the interest of the company by trying to attract the best engineers. It may also have coloured Brunel's views with respect to Humphrys and at the end of his report of 12 June 1839 regarding the choice of suitable engine he appears to cast doubt on the ability of the company's workshops to construct the engines by emphasising the experience of Maudslay, Sons & Field:

I have thus reduced the question to the state in which I can offer no further opinion or advice; it is now for you to determine. The question is one which has frequently to be decided upon by the Directors of public works; it is very much a matter of feeling, but it is simplified in the present instance by the circumstance that the expense in either case will be, to my view at least, about the same, and the work equally good in either case.

Upon this point, as perhaps upon the subject of cost, I have no doubt there will be some difference of opinion. It will be said that the work done under our own superintendence can be more relied upon than the work of a manufacturer, and that even in the engines of the *Great Western* steam-ship, coming from one of the most experienced manufacturers, many defects may be pointed out.

I should fully agree with both these arguments, but I think these advantages are fully counterbalanced by that of the experience in all the details which is brought into operation in an old established manufactory, and the great relief from responsibility and risk obtained by contracting for the whole work.[24]

The directors decided that the GWSS Co should build its own engines in the new works and these would be to the trunk design of Francis Humphrys. In announcing this step to the shareholders the directors were not strictly honest; '... after the closest investigation [the directors] were gradually brought to a conviction that the Company must be its own manufacturers, as many of the most successful Steam Navigation Companies already are; and that the description of engine known by the name of Trunk Engine, was preferable to any other for your purposes.'[25] There certainly were at liberty to come to the conclusion that the trunk engine was preferable, but to state that most of the successful steam navigation companies constructed their own engines was certainly a distortion of the truth. Probably the most successful and extensive operator of steamships was the Admiralty and commercial engineering companies constructed their machinery. All commercial steamship companies with mail contracts employed engine builders, neither P&O, Cunard nor the Royal Mail Steam Packet Company possessing any engine-building establishments.

Brunel lost the argument concerning the choice of engine and over the retention of Harman but he does not appear to have carried out his threat to separate himself from the manufacturing part of the company. On 18 June 1839 Nasmyth, Gaskell & Co wrote to Humphrys about workshop tools stating 'Your name has been mentioned to us by Mr Brunel.'[26] Brunel also suggested that Humphrys contact James Nasmyth with regards to the forging of the large paddle shaft for the new ship.[27] It was this contact which resulted in the invention of the steam forging hammer.

Although Brunel may have mellowed, this appears to have been more towards the interests of the GWSS Co rather that towards Humphrys. There remained a degree of animosity between the pair. In a letter to Guppy, dated 20 December 1839, Brunel discussed the paddle wheels for the new ship and

suggested that no decision be taken until the results of tests with new paddle wheels on the *Great Western* were known. '...Yet I think we must reconsider the question of diameter of wheel as compared with cylinder – I think the former too great or as Humphrys would put it, the latter too small.'[28]

Early in 1840 Brunel was questioning the effectiveness of a scheme proposed by Humphrys for the repair of the cracked engine frames in the *Great Western*. 'I cannot say how useless yet mischievous I consider Humphrys' scheme for breaking the tops of the columns into bits for these I believe would be the only effect. I agree perfectly in all you say of it and I can't refrain from expressing much more to you, however, you might be disposed to quote my opinion to him I will state it more mildly.'[29] It would appear that the two were not then on speaking terms as Guppy would seem to have been delegated to act as intermediary.

Brunel then went on to express his opinions as to how the repair should be executed: '... it is a general union of the extremities that is required and nothing but a bandage embracing the whole will be of any use – the binding the heads would only make the frame weak elsewhere but you cannot bind the heads – the rivetting would break them rather than bend them – pray don't think of it.' A little later there was another letter to Guppy and Brunel was still not happy with Humphrys' work:

> Claxton has described to me Humphrys' new scheme – I confess myself very obstinate . . . I don't like it. I cannot for the life of me see the advantage, it will require much more fitting & cobbling at the place than the large straps, yet this viz the interference with other work I understand is a main objection. However as you may remember in the Clifton Bridge – between the two gothic parties we settled amicably into the Egyptian so I now propose an entirely new plan – I have been to Fields and referred to the drawings etc. – we have schemed a new & I think good plan he is to prepare a drawing and send it me in time for the mail.[30]

The Field/Brunel scheme seems to have been adopted as wrought iron brackets and braces were fitted around the fractured sections.[31] These were still in place when the ship was surveyed for sale in

1947 and the report indicated that the frames did not appear to have moved for some time and that they would probably last as long as the hull without being taken out.[32] Brunel could, obviously, not separate himself from the engineering affairs of the company or more particularly from the ships, and he did not let disagreements with others in the company's employ divert him from the task of ensuring that the ships would possess the best quality engineering which could be obtained.

The antagonism between Brunel and Humphrys continued. A private diary entry for 3 March 1840 mentions a visit to the shipyard and a later meeting. 'Claxton and I went down to steam ship yard . . . Guppy with us . . . I dined at Claxtons in the evening . . . Guppy came discussed engine drawings – Humphrys came.'[33] Matters came to a head later in the year.

The screw steamer *Archimedes* visited Bristol at the end of May 1840 and on 18 June Brunel advised the directors to consider screw propulsion for the new ship. A resolution was passed delaying further work on the engines and on those parts of the ship which might be altered if screw propulsion was adopted. Guppy made a number of trips on the *Archimedes* and reports were also requested from Patterson, Humphrys and Claxton. These reports were not in favour of change but Brunel persisted in his views.[34] He knew of Humphrys' opposition to the screw and had written to Guppy after a visit he made with Claxton to the *Archimedes* when she was in London:

> Claxton and I went up to town this morning to try the *Archimedes* . . . Patterson and Humphries [*sic*] were both in town as I requested that they should be required to see such experiments as I might make . . . I found Humphries [*sic*] was going to report or rather to hit away at it and I had hard work to persuade Godwin and to compel Scott, [presumably Henry Godwin and Robert Scott, directors of the GWSS Co] two directors who attended last Monday, that they had no right to allow Patterson and Humphries [*sic*] to record their prejudices which they could have no means of judging.[35]

Over the summer months of 1840 Brunel continued with experiments aboard *Archimedes*, on drums and straps in the company's yard, and on board the *Great Western*.[36] Berkeley Claxton, son of Christopher Claxton, sailed on board *Great Western* during three of her trips in 1840, conducting tests on engine performance and the effects of the use of expansion valves on speed as well as making observations of rolling and pitching, particularly with respect to the effects on paddle-wheel immersion.[37] At the company's works Brunel instigated a series of tests involving rope power transmission systems, the hope being to use ropes running around drums on the engine crankshaft and screw propeller shafts as a means of increasing the relatively slow speed of the engine to a higher speed for turning the propeller. It would appear that Humphrys was supervising some of these tests when failure occurred. Unfortunately there are no details of the affair but a letter written by Brunel to Humphrys on 8 October gives some indication and incident seems to have finally broken the relationship between the two men.

> I will answer your inquiry as frankly as you desire & as I have always done.
>
> I have remarked strongly upon the delay and the total absence of good will which has appeared to me to characterise your mode of preparing for the experiments which I have lately wished to make – and I have observed, though I am not aware of having mentioned it to others that you do not even speak or write upon the subject, without having perhaps without knowing it yourself the strong prejudice of your mind your incapacity of judging or reasoning upon it fairly and impartially – I never insinuated or supposed that you could premeditately[*sic*] have broken the lightening riggers or destroyed the rope – but since you refer to such a thing I would have told you what I thought of your version of the accident but that on reading the latter part of your letter which I had not done till I commenced this sheet of my own, I find you using expressions as regards me (my diseased mind) which induces me to close all correspondence with you as quickly as possible.[38]

Matters at the engineering works had, obviously, been strained for a long time and it is difficult to understand how the directors could have let the situation deteriorate the way it had. However, the

managing director, Claxton, was a close friend of Brunel and many of the directors appear to have been easily manipulated. Brunel was an experienced engineer with a good reputation and he was certainly a forceful personality. He liked to get his own way and, as far as the GWSS Co was concerned, in the majority of cases he did, the notable exception being the decision taken by the company to manufacture its own engines. The disenchantment shown by a large body of the shareholders at the worsening financial situation caused by the escalating costs of the engine works is evident from the extraordinary general meeting of shareholders called for 9 February 1841. A resolution was passed calling for a separation of the manufacturing side of the business from the ship-owning side and for all future ships to be built under contract.[39] Subsequent action prevented the company from building engines for any other concern and effectively resulted in a need for the company to rid itself of the works as soon as possible.

During 1841 moves were made to sell the works, first by auction and then by private contract, but no satisfactory offer was received; at the end of 1842 some £44,922 had been spent on the manufacturing facility.[40] Even the Admiralty took an interest.

> . . . there is a yard for sale at Bristol and if this establishment is likely to be wanted or any portion of the machinery for the Navy, inspectors could be sent to inspect the same. Board do not intend to form any establishment at Bristol. Captain Brandreth and Mr Ewart to ascertain if any portion of the works can be advantageously purchased for naval yards.[41]

The company wanted to sell the entire works, not just part of the equipment: 'Factory of the Great Western Steam Ship Company, Messrs Ewart and Lloyd have examined the Factory and report that nothing they have is required by the Naval Service and that the whole premises is to be disposed of in one lot.'[42]

Overall the directors seem to have behaved in something of schizophrenic way and they were not at all consistent in their approach to the running of

Two pages from Brunel's notebooks, which probably date from the period in which the second ship was under discussion. The sketches show a number of large paddle-steamers, one with two sets of paddles. The date '1845' appears to be a later addition. The original is in the Bristol University Library. (By courtesy of Denis Griffiths)

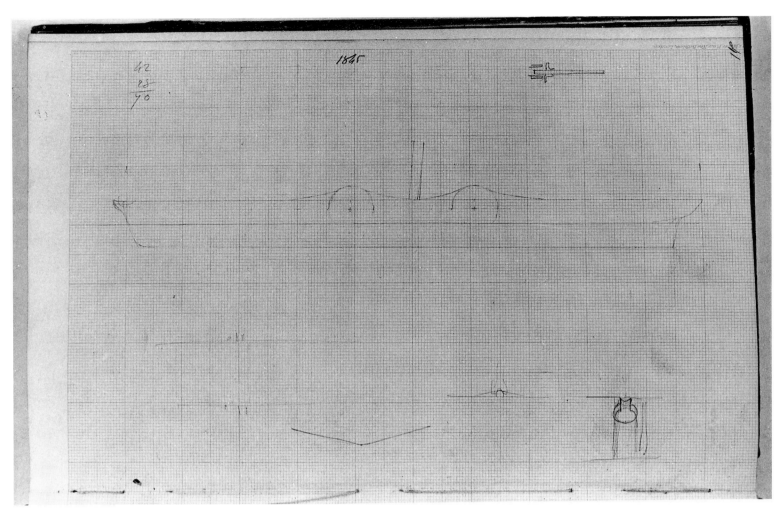

the company. They readily accepted Brunel's advice on enlarging the second ship, changing to iron construction and subsequently to screw propulsion, but they disregarded his valuable, and cost saving recommendation, to purchase engines from an established manufacturer and to avoid moving into the new venture of engine building.

Brunel presented his screw propeller report to the company on 10 October 1840; this long, complex and very detailed thesis on screw propulsion must have confused most of those who or read it or later listened to his oral presentation. The report made some assumptions which were subsequently shown to be incorrect as the science of naval architecture developed, but it was thorough in its approach to and treatment of the subject, a facet of the Brunel character which was to be found in all of his engineering work. Copies of the report were widely circulated at the time and it was subsequently printed in the biography of Brunel written by his son.[43] A detailed discussion of the report can be found in Ewan Corlett's classic work about the *Great Britain*.[44] At a special meeting in December 1840 a

resolution was passed adopting screw propulsion for the new ship. At first Brunel thought that it might be possible to retain the trunk engine and convert it for screw propulsion; that would unquestionably have saved time and money, but it was soon evident that different form of engine would have to be employed. Humphrys resigned as superintendent of the works and, upon Brunel's suggestion, Guppy was appointed to control the manufacturing establishment with Harman as his assistant.[45] Brunel now had a friend in charge of the works. It is a sad reflection on the attitude of those running the company that Humphrys did not receive any recognition for his efforts, even after his untimely death shortly after resigning. The annual report for 1840 merely states, 'When the late Mr Humphrys quitted the service of the company . . .' but at the end it provides a much more glowing tribute to the auditor who was retiring.[46]

6 The *Great Britain* and the end of the GWSS Company

The Great Britain *finally floated from her building dock on 19 July 1843. The local enthusiasm for the event is well captured in this print by J Walter.* (National Maritime Museum neg 4548)

Even at the time of the change to screw propulsion the new ship still did not have an official name, although an assortment of semi-official names had been given, including *City of New York* and *Mammoth*. The name *Great Britain* was chosen during 1842 and the Directors' Report for the year 1842 is the first report to use the name[1] although the *Mechanics Magazine* for 19 March 1842 announced, 'The *Mammoth* steam-vessel, which has been so long building at Bristol, by the Great Western Company, but which is now, it seems, to be called the *Great Britain*, is expected to be ready to be launched in March 1843'. Not surprisingly, the timing was wrong and the *Great Britain* was not launched, or rather floated from her building dock, until 19 July 1843.

Between adoption of screw propulsion and the floating-out Brunel was not idle, although he had much work to do elsewhere on railway business and other matters. He was very involved with screw propeller trials for the Admiralty, as detailed in Chapter 3. The hull was essentially complete at that time, at least in terms of the design work, but the stern area had had to be modified in order to accommodate the change to screw propulsion. He did not work alone in this matter as Guppy was closely involved, the works manufacturing all necessary parts. Design of the semi-balanced rudder and its actuating mechanism has been attributed to Brunel.[2] Initially Brunel persisted with the idea of using rope straps to transmit the drive from the engine crankshaft to the propeller shaft and at the end of October 1840 he wrote on the matter to Francis Pettit Smith, patentee of the screw propeller system adopted for the *Great Britain*:

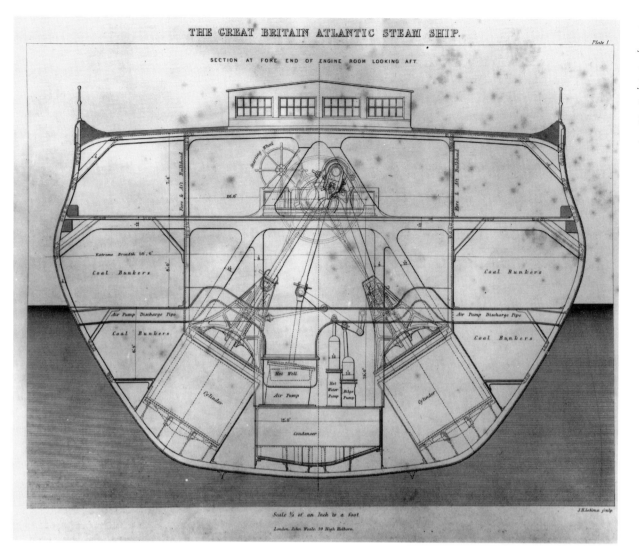

THE GREAT BRITAIN ATLANTIC STEAM SHIP.

SECTION AT FORE END OF ENGINE ROOM LOOKING AFT.

Scale ¼ of an Inch to a Foot

London, John Weale, 59 High Holborn.

Great Britain: 'Section at fore end of engine room looking aft.' The triangular form of the engine is apparent. (National Maritime Museum neg A8935K)

. . . a report to the Directors of the Great Western Steam Ship Company [which he had just submitted] gives the results of experiments I had made on the working of rope straps and results of which actually working in our own shops and under my own inspection proved most satisfactorily the perfect practicability of transmitting even our proposed large powers through very moderately sized rope straps, working not in V grooves, but on smooth drums – the loss of power by friction and wear & tear of the rope in V grooves is considerable – on the flat drum they work beautifully – I should like to see it applied to the *Archimedes*.[3]

In December that year he wrote to Captain Chappell, RN, appointed by the Government to conduct screw propeller tests during 1840, 'We have latterly and for some time worked all our machinery with rope straps and the result is most satisfactory and such as cannot leave the slightest doubt of that

being the right way.'[4] As late as July 1841 Brunel was still expressing optimism for the rope strap power transmission system as can be seen from a letter sent to Joseph Maudslay, '. . . but the flat hemp strap does I assure you appear to me the best – I know you will excuse my expressing my objections so freely [to Maudslay's idea of an endless rope] and will suppose that I think myself infallible or that my opinion is to influence yours more than you may think it worth.'[5] The *Archimedes* was fitted with a geared transmission system but Brunel was not impressed with it, considering the noise to be a major impediment as far as a passenger ship was concerned. His optimism over rope straps proved to be short-lived when faced with the reality of transmitting high powers and by time the new screw engine was taking shape a chain transmission system had been adopted.

In order to obtain sufficient power and at the same time use as little revenue-earning space as possible, Brunel decided to adopt a triangular form of engine, an arrangement which had been patented by

Great Britain: *'Section through centre part of engine room looking forward.' The upper gear wheel of the chain drive system dominates the drawing.* (National Maritime Museum neg A8935B)

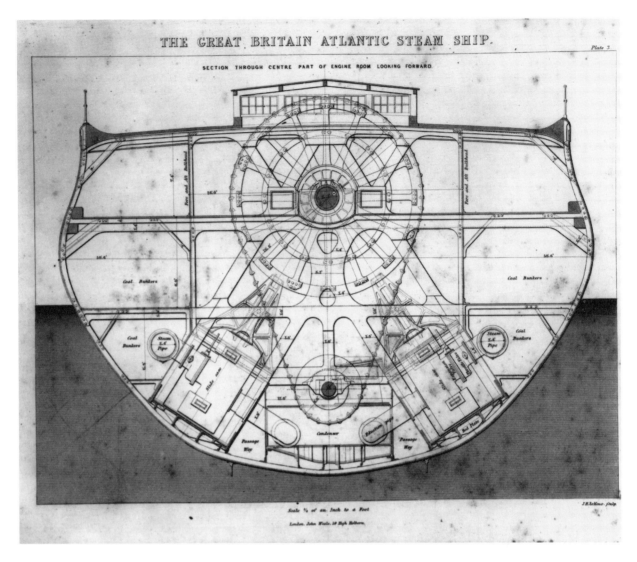

THE GREAT BRITAIN ATLANTIC STEAM SHIP.

SECTION THROUGH CENTRE PART OF ENGINE ROOM LOOKING FORWARD.

his father, Sir Marc Brunel, in 1822 (Patent No 4683). By arranging pairs of cylinders across the engine room space width could be fully used and length saved; four cylinders could provide sufficient power, each opposing transverse pair being connected to the same crank. It is highly likely that Guppy was responsible for the detailed design of the engine but the concept will have originated with Brunel.

With screw propulsion the reaction of the rotating propeller acts along the length of the screw shaft and the force from that shaft then has to be transmitted to the hull in order to drive the ship through the water. A thrust block is needed and a rather ingenious system was devised, probably a modified form of arrangements used on other screw steamers but much larger in order to deal with the powers involved. At the forward end of the screw shaft was fitted a 2-foot diameter gunmetal plate and this pressed against a steel plate, of the same diameter, supported on a block which attached to the engine bed and hence to the ship's structure. Water under

high pressure – up to 200 pounds per square inch for full power operation – was fed between the two plates in order to keep them apart and provide effective lubrication.[6] The concept was clever and simple.

The power transmission system was located between the two sets of transverse cylinders, with a large-diameter drive wheel attached to the crankshaft and a smaller-diameter driven wheel fitted to the screw shaft; the gear ratio was 2.95:1 giving a propeller speed of 53 revolutions per minute (rpm) from an engine speed of 18rpm. The chain design almost certainly originated with Brunel for it is certain that as soon as he realised that rope straps were insufficient for the task he set about designing a replacement rather than leave somebody else to do the work. This was his nature. As can be seen from his letter to Maudslay concerning the rope drive, he was well aware that some people might believe that he thought himself to be infallible and the sole means by which the project could progress. In recognising that problem he also accepted that oth-

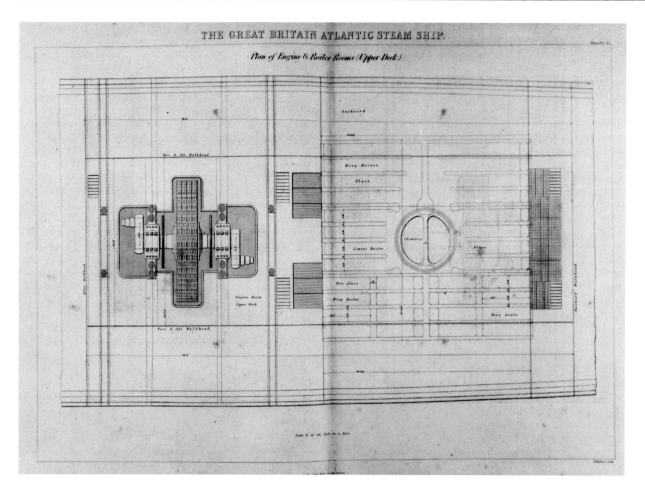

THE GREAT BRITAIN ATLANTIC STEAM SHIP.

Plan of Engine & Boiler Rooms (Upper Deck.)

ers could also make a valuable contribution. However, Brunel had considerable experience in many branches of engineering and he could readily see how solutions to problems in one area could be modified and transferred to solve problems in other areas. This was part of his genius.

The chain drive system when it came was a prime example of his ingenuity. There were four separate chains placed alongside each other and they were of the inverted tooth type, then generally used in engineering practice as they were self-compensating for stretch. The links did not stretch in the manner of elastic, but over a period of time wear at the pins and bushes of the chain results in a gradual increase in length, commonly referred to as stretch. The chain links had wedge-shaped teeth at each end and these teeth engaged with flat-faced teeth on the drive and driven drums. As the chain stretched the pitch of the links increased slightly resulting in the teeth engaging with the drum teeth at a slightly greater radius thus maintaining the desired tension in the chain. The main, or drive, drum had a pitch circle of 18 feet and teak teeth. The 6-foot diameter driven drum on the screw shaft had

lignum vitae teeth in order to reduce the need for lubrication. The system worked well and was relatively quiet in operation. 'The motion is remarkably smooth and noiseless.'[7]

Although the Great Britain had been floated from her building dock in July 1843, she remained at a berth in the Floating Harbour whilst cabins and apartments were completed. Delays were the product of a cash-flow problem caused by the reduction in revenue from the Great Western, due to competition from the Cunard ships, and the company was reluctant to increase the calls on shareholders. There was another major problem which the company had hoped would be solved before Great Britain was ready for sea; but it was not, and the ship was effectively trapped in the Floating Harbour. With the increase in size of the Great Britain it became clear to Brunel and the directors that she was too wide to pass through the locks from the Floating Harbour into the Cumberland Basin and through the locks from there into the River Avon. The GWSS Co directors were, however, optimistic that by time the company's second ship was ready for sea the locks into the Avon would be widened as part of a general upgrading of facilities in the Port of Bristol. Initially it was the intention to fit the machinery when the *Great Britain* was afloat in the Cumberland Basin, so only the lock gates from there into the river would need attention. Due to the shape of the hull the shallower draught would have allowed easy passage from the Floating Harbour. Why the directors were so optimistic is difficult to understand for there had been much trouble with the Dock Company over harbour dues levied on the *Great Western* even though no facilities were provided at the dock.

When the *Great Britain* was floated out of her building dock it was necessary to remove the remainder of the river bank between the Floating Harbour and building dock caisson, the entrance to the dock had been finished in 1842.[8] In order to minimise the expense of this operation the directors applied to the Dock Company for the water to be let out of the lower part of the Floating Harbour – at that time there was a caisson at Prince's Street bridge which effectively divided the floating harbour in two sections. The Dock Company would not agree to this but intimated that the level could be lowered by 6 feet and Brunel prepared a coffer dam at the building dock entrance to allow for the resulting water depth. Because of problems with the Prince's Street caisson the water in the Floating Harbour remained at its usual level on three successive tides. Brunel complained and without the knowledge of the directors the Dock Company lowered the water level way below the 6 feet agreed in order to allow for the bank to be removed. Six months later the GWSS Co received a letter from solicitors acting for the Dock Company requesting payment of some £312 for repairs to the vessel *Augusta* which had been damaged by grounding when the water level was reduced in the Floating Harbour. The GWSS Co denied liability and refused to pay, but the directors were aware that there could be consequences: 'Their not acceding to this demand, your Directors have reason to fear, has operated injuriously upon the consent of the Dock Board to the passage of the *Great Britain* through the locks.'[9]

Brunel suggested that the ship could get through the locks into the Cumberland Basin if a few courses of stone were removed from the upper sections of the lock together with the lock gates. The intention was that the ship would pass into the Cumberland Basin on 21 March 1844 and into the Avon on 4 April. With the approval of the directors he wrote to the Dock Company on 6 February 1844 detailing his plans together with alternatives. Six days later the Dock Company wrote agreeing to the proposal, provided that the owners of the *Great Britain* would make good the stonework, repair, strengthen and replace the gates, and indemnify the Dock Company against any subsequent action by shipowners or others, all work was to be completed by 30 March 1844. Dispute arose regarding the repairs and indemnities required, preventing agreement from being reached and thus the intended dates being met. The *Great Britain* effectively remained imprisoned.[10]

Brunel's mind turned towards ways in which the ship might pass through the locks without removing stonework and gates and the only way of doing this was to raise the ship sufficiently so that the narrower beam of her lower section was level with the upper part of the lock. In May he wrote to Claxton,

> I deferred replying to your letter of the 25 Ult. till I had again seen Mr Guppy – and my engagements have been very pressing. I saw Mr Guppy yesterday and he will send the tracings of the proposed floating apparatus, I can state generally however at present that I approve entirely of the plan of forming one large floating vessel under the bottom of the *Great Britain* and although it may be more expensive than the plan I proposed of air vessels, it will unquestionably be a more certain, a more easily managed and a more safe mode of preceding.[11]

Such measures were not required and agreement was reached with the Dock Company for alterations to the locks at the Cumberland Basin; in October 1844 the *Bristol Mirror* reported that work at the locks was proceeding and the ship would enter the Cumberland Basin on or about 26 October and thence into the River Avon on the highest tide in the early part of November.[12] Again this was optimistic.

The ship was moved into the Cumberland Basin in late October, but there she stayed until the lock gates between the basin and the Floating Harbour had been replaced and the tide was right to allow her to proceed through the final lock gates into the Avon. On 10 December all was ready for the move, and a steam tug commenced towing her at high water. However, before half of the ship was through

the lock it was evident to Claxton, on board the tug, that she was stuck between the copings. An order was made to pull her back into the Cumberland Basin before she became jammed with the falling tide. In order not to lose the next spring tide it was important that the lock be widened by removing the upper part of the stonework. Brunel superintended this work throughout the day despite having an important engagement in Wales. In his letter of 11 December, apologising, he expressed his feeling with regards to the ship:

> We had an unexpected difficulty with the *Great Britain* this morning. She stuck in the lock; we did get her back. I have been hard at work all day altering the masonry of the lock. Tonight, our last tide, we have succeeded in getting her through; but, being dark, we have

been obliged to ground her outside, and I confess I cannot leave her till I see her afloat again, and all clear of her difficulties. I have, as you will admit, much at stake here, and I am too anxious about it to leave her.[13]

Brunel was, obviously, extremely concerned; this was his ship, his child. He had invested much of his time and his reputation and was certainly correct in saying that he had much at stake. The fact that he devoted so much of his pressing time to this ship, and to the *Great Western*, is indicative of the feel he had for all of his major engineering projects and particularly his ships. Liberal use of 'we' in the letter indicates that Brunel felt himself very much part of a team; he may have been one of the country's most eminent engineers but in many ways he relied upon others as much as they relied upon him.

Great Britain *lying in the Basin, 1844. This plate, by Fox Talbot, is thought to be the earliest photograph of a ship.* (National Maritime Museum neg c5373)

RIGHT *The original propeller and stern frame of the* Great Britain. (City Museum, Bristol)

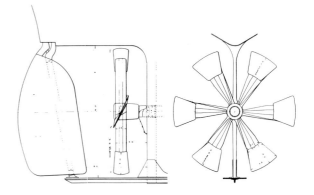

Great Britain underwent sea trials prior to visiting London, from where she headed to Liverpool and her entry into service as an Atlantic liner. So much time was spent in London that the ship did not reach Liverpool until July 1845 and her maiden voyage to New York commenced on 26 July. Why there was such a protracted stay in London is difficult to imagine as the company was urgently in need of funds, but it would seem that the directors and others associated with the ship enjoyed the partying and praise which constituted the major part of the sojourn. In view of the lateness of the first trip there was only time for two round voyages to New York that year and they did show up some defects which required attention when *Great Britain* was laid up in October. The steering of the ship was not as expected when she got into the Atlantic and that was attributed to the semi-balanced rudder, stern frame aperture.[14] Re-rigging of the ship was carried out to improve handling and this was also expected to help the steering. Iron wire was replaced by rope and the third mast, immediately aft of the funnel, was removed, the fourth mast being brought forward and re-rigged to carry square sails just like the mainmast. The two remaining masts aft of the funnel, which had originally been hinged, were replaced by masts which passed through the 'tween decks; these masts were also arranged to carry trysails. During the Atlantic voyages difficulty had been experienced in maintaining steam and it was decided to modify the boilers. One major change was, however, forced upon the company, as on the final Atlantic crossing of the season *Great Britain* had lost all of the blades from her propeller.

Brunel had worked on a second propeller design when the ship was in Bristol and this spare now became the new propeller. It was a four-bladed solid unit and at 7 tons it was heavier than the original; being of solid construction there was optimism that it would last longer than the first propeller. The directors were probably disappointed that their new ship had encountered so much trouble after the sanguine reports during the trials, and they seem to have sought the advice of outsiders when considering what should be done. Brunel was not at all happy with this. In December he wrote to Claxton:

I am afraid I must object more clearly than I before did to Grantham's having anything to do with the alterations in the *Great Britain*.

Field came to me this morning to say that he had heard of Grantham's engagement & the possibility of his having anything to do with the work & we both agreed that it would be dreadful – no power on earth will prevent its being generally reported in newspapers in all old women's gossip in papers to the Institution of Civil Engineers – in every possible shipping channel that by the advice & assistance of the eminent Lt Grantham – such improvement were effected as ensured the success of the *Great Britain* which was before a total failure – I know the man. Field was in a fever at the thought of it and I couldn't stand it. We must send our own people & I must beg that G–m is specially excluded. Guppy if poor fellow he is getting to work & the more he has to do the better – must for his own sake take especial care that nobody has anything to do with it. I will rather take it in hand myself I will really without any joking or exaggerating . . . .[15]

This ship was his baby and he was not going to let an outsider interfere. He was also concerned that the directors would send the ship to sea before the alterations had been properly completed, and he worried that another failure would ruin all prospects for the ship. In April 1846, shortly before the first scheduled voyage of the season, he again wrote to Claxton:

I am much grieved to receive your report confirmed by Guppy . . . as to the state of unreadiness of the *Great Britain* – it seems from Guppy's letter that the boilers are not likely to be ready before the engines & that it will be sharp work to get the engines ready for the 27th. Now if this is her state I must strongly urge upon the Directors the propriety of at

once making up their minds to postpone the day of sailing – However painful it may be however annoying. No one I think will deny that it could be much more injurious to their interests – for the Company to send the vessel again imperfect than to delay for a short time her first voyage this season for in all probability it would only affect her first – No risk ought to be run of another bad voyage – she is ruined in character and would remain on your hands unsaleable. I cannot myself conceive that there can be a doubt as to the necessity of any cost of delay of trying her . . . the success of [the next voyage] depends little less than her whole value hangs upon the result. If you look at it in this simple light – the question of her sailing on the day advertised is not worth consideration for a moment surely in comparison with such a sum and as regards feeings and credit everything is in favour of delaying her sailing until we feel sure of her success – if we can get a trial say by the first – and if everything is right – she might either sail from the river without coming into Dock or come in on the 9th & sail on the 16th – but in the meantime you ought to write to America postponing the day. I trust the Directors will do this I am convinced it is right and therefore may as well be done at once.[16]

Brunel's wise counsel seems to have prevailed as *Great Britain* did not leave Liverpool until 9 April 1846.

Apart from failure of the air pump on that out-ward voyage, resulting in the need to proceed under sail alone for a number of days, the second season seemed to offer improvement as passenger bookings steadily increased. Disaster struck at 9.30pm on 23 September when *Great Britain* went aground on the Irish coast in Dundrum Bay.

Brunel could not go to the ship immediately but he was in constant communication with Claxton who had gone to Ireland as soon as the grounding became known. Arrangements were made to try to get the *Great Britain* clear on the next spring tide, 28 September, but a gale the previous day prevented this and it was decided to drive the ship further ashore to a position of greater safety. Patterson, and Alexander Bremner, a salvage expert, attempted to protect the ship by breakwaters but they were soon carried away in gales and a number of the directors appeared to lose hope that the ship might ever be recovered. On 8 December Brunel, free from parliamentary work, went to Dundrum Bay at the request of the directors and underwriters. His feelings at seeing his ship were mixed; from reports received he had expected to see her in a very damaged state but was pleasantly surprised to find that she was 'almost as sound as the day she was launched and ten times stronger and sounder in character.' However, he was very distressed that little seemed to have been done to protect her and she was 'lying unprotected, deserted and abandoned'.[17]

Whilst others may have given up any hope of saving the ship Brunel was an engineer who looked for solutions and not problems; however, immediate action was essential and he knew that little could be

This lithograph after a Joseph Walter original shows Great Britain *proceeding under sail and steam. In the background a sailing line of battle ship, the traditional 'wooden wall' that underpinned British maritime power, makes the contrast with the new elements of iron and steam.* (National Maritime Museum neg PY8916)

done that year apart from securing the ship against the ravages of the coming winter gales. In the absence of any director to sanction the work he ordered Hosken, the ship's master, to start work on the protection scheme he had planned, guaranteeing to pay all immediate expenses himself if the directors would not. He planned a flexible breakwater made of faggots and this worked to prevent further damage from gales; the success of this breakwater, devised after only a short time with the ship, contrasts with the failure of previous breakwaters contrived by maritime men and salvage experts and illustrates the open-minded ingenuity Brunel applied to his work.

On his return to London two days later Brunel penned a strong letter to Claxton giving vent to his feelings and offering advice on what should be done to remove the ship from the shore.[18] 'I have returned from Dundrum with very mixed feelings of satisfaction and pain almost amounting to anger, with who I don't know . . . I was grieved to see this fine ship lying unprotected, deserted and abandoned by all those who ought to know her value and ought to have protected her, instead of being humbugged by schemers and underwriters.' The pain was real, for here was a ship, his ship, left to the elements when with a little thought and care she could have been shielded from the worst of the weather. It is obvious that Brunel had scant regard for most directors – indeed, he seems to have shown little deference to business men as a whole throughout his career. To him they appeared to care only for money and had no regard for the engineering works which made their fortunes; but his life was engineering. 'Don't let me be understood as wishing to read a lecture to our Directors; but the result, whoever is to blame, is, at least in my opinion, that the finest ship in the world, in excellent condition, such that £4,000 or £5,000 would repair all the damage done, has been left, and is lying like a useless saucepan kicking about on the most exposed shore that you can imagine, with no more effort or skill than the said saucepan would have received on the beach at Brighton.' He even went on to castigate his friend Claxton: '. . . the first glimpse of her satisfied me that all the part above her 5 or 6 feet water line is as true as ever. It is beautiful to look at, and really how she can be talked of in the way she has been, even by you, I cannot understand. It is positively cruel; it would be like talking away the character of a young woman without any grounds whatsoever.' This is a sure sign that Brunel could

become very emotional about his works, and particularly his ships.

He had not finished his attacks on the directors or some of their advisors: '...than as pointing out the necessity of precautions if she is to be saved. I say "if", for really when I saw the vessel still in perfect condition left to the tender mercies of an awfully exposed shore for weeks, while a parcel of quacks are amusing you with schemes for getting her off, she in the meantime being left to go to pieces, I could hardly help feeling as if her parents and guardians meant her to die there.' He did not like the scheme proposed for refloating the ship during the winter and moving her across the Irish Sea with the help of camels or floats:

> Why; no man in his senses can dream of calculating upon less than three months for the execution of any rational scheme of getting her off; and no man in his senses, I should think would dream of taking her across the channel in the winter months, even if he had got the camels or floats fast. In this I don't feel so competent to form an opinion, though I think I can judge, and I should consider it a wanton throwing away of my shares if the Directors allowed her to be taken out, even if afloat; but at all events I am competent to judge of the probable time occupied in getting means to float her and I maintain that it would be absurd to calculate upon less than two or three months.

The letter then went on to describe the arrangements he wished to see put in place immediately in order to protect the ship and this letter was followed four days later by a formal report to the directors, this subsequently being printed and distributed amongst the shareholders.[19]

Brunel was nothing if not thorough and he gave full value for money, except in this case he was not getting paid and had actually offered to guarantee money for immediate action. The report reiterated much that had been covered in the letter to Claxton but without the caustic comments about the directors. He repeated in more details his plans for protecting the ship during the winter and expanded upon his ideas for her eventual removal from the beach and movement to a safe harbour. It is evident from the report that views had been expressed by some that

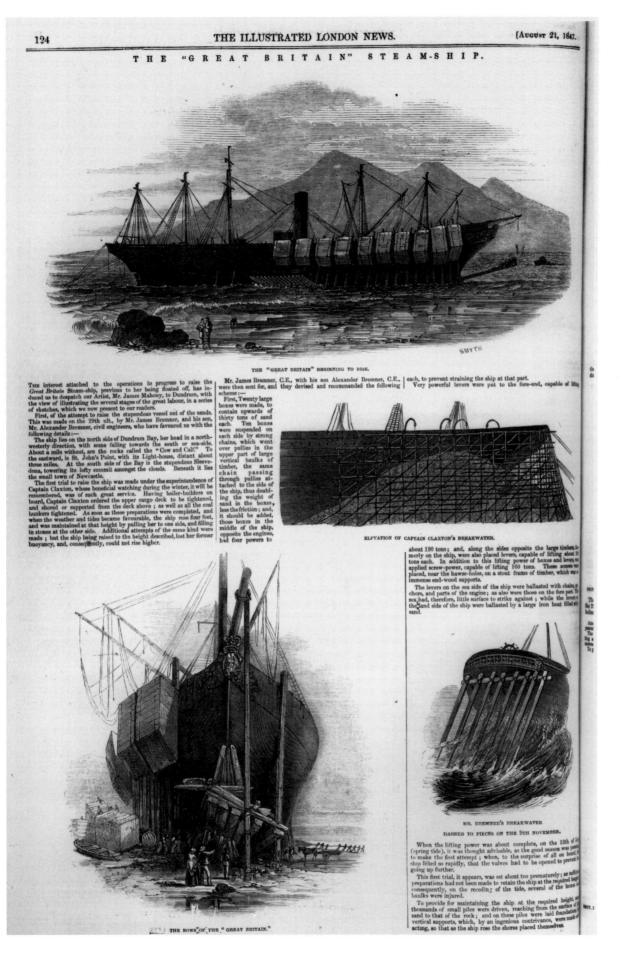

Part of the quite technical coverage by the Illustrated London News *of the salvage attempts in Dundrum Bay, 21 August 1847. There was considerable public appetite for stories of technical achievement in the Victorian era, engineers being the artists of the industrial Renaissance.* (National Maritime Museum neg E0453-4)

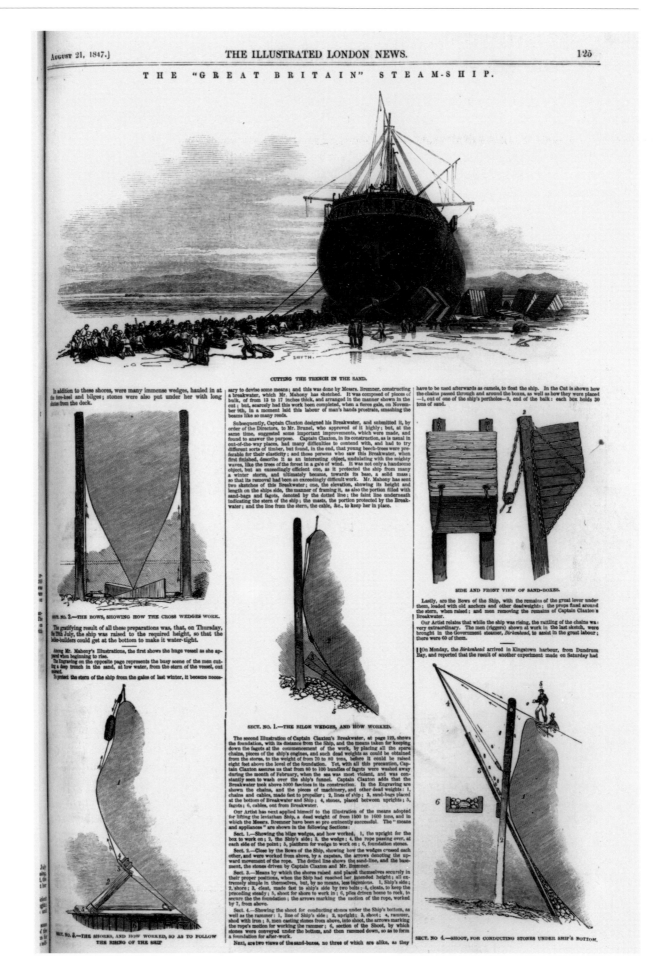

the ship should be scrapped where she lay and Brunel was firmly opposed to this idea. He was, obviously, very attached to the ship and sentiment could have played a part, but he was also a good and imaginative engineer who appeared to relish solving difficult problems. The easy alternative was never an option for him. However, the mercenary directors had a different agenda and Brunel had to be careful to keep them on his side. He was shrewd enough to talk to their wallets:

I can only imagine two alternatives – the one to break her up on the spot and make the most of the materials; the other to get her afloat and into port, and restore her into good condition, or sell her to those who would restore her . . . The first alternative may I think be discarded at once; the plates and ribs of an iron vessel are difficult enough to convert into useful materials for any other purpose, even in the midst of workshops and with tools and appliances at hand. In such a place as Dundrum Bay I do not believe the materials would pay the expense of cutting up . . . probably hundreds would be a safer estimate of the amount to be realised clear of all expenses. To remove the vessel and take her into port and either restore her or sell her, is then the only means of recovering any part of the whole of the capital invested in this ship. If she is brought into port she may be worth, unrepaired £40,000, £50,000 or £60,000.

He was wide of the mark in terms of the selling price for the ship fetched only £18,000 when sold to Gibbs, Bright & Co in 1850.[20]

The directors agreed with Brunel's plans for salvaging the ship and the work was undertaken under Claxton's direction. The salvage started in March 1847 and proceeded well but Brunel became concerned that it had not been possible to raise the ship as much as he had hoped with the methods he proposed. At this point he did not hesitate to acknowledge that fact and suggested that the directors approach a specialist in such matters. He recommended that James and Alexander Bremner be called

in.[21] Such action indicates an absence of arrogance as it shows that Brunel was more than willing to acknowledge the superior skills of others even when it came to projects in which he had deep involvement. The ingenious lifting arrangement devised by the Bremners worked, and the ship was raised enough to allow the hull to be repaired and the major leaks stopped. The correspondence between Brunel, Claxton and the GWSS Co directors was published in 1847 and makes fascinating reading, the event being one of the most spectacular marine salvage events to that time.[22] The *Great Britain* was refloated in August and, after a call at Belfast Lough for more repairs, was towed to Liverpool. The Great Western Steam Ship Company had underinsured both of its ships and with the sale of *Great Britain* it was wound up – the *Great Western* had been sold in 1847 to fund the salvage.

Although the company which built and owned Brunel's first two ships failed to make a lasting impact on the maritime world, the ships were a success and Brunel made a valuable contribution to the shipping and marine industries of Britain. He was an engineer who took time and trouble to see that things were done correctly, and he experimented to ensure that the best methods were selected. In his reports he left a valuable legacy which indicate his devotion to scientific investigation. There must have been considerable frustration dealing with company directors who did not appreciate the need for such investigation but the strength of his personality generally won through. In retrospect it is easy to criticise Brunel for insisting upon the change from wood to iron and then from paddle propulsion to screw, but it was not his fault that the company was under-capitalised and that, against his advice, a decision was made to set up the engine manufactory. Advances in engineering science cost money, but progress is not made without spending that money. Brunel did his job, and he gave his service without payment, but others betrayed his efforts and the confidence of the GWSS Co shareholders. Subsequent generations of marine engineers and naval architects, not to mention historians, have much for which to thank Brunel.

PART II: The Ships

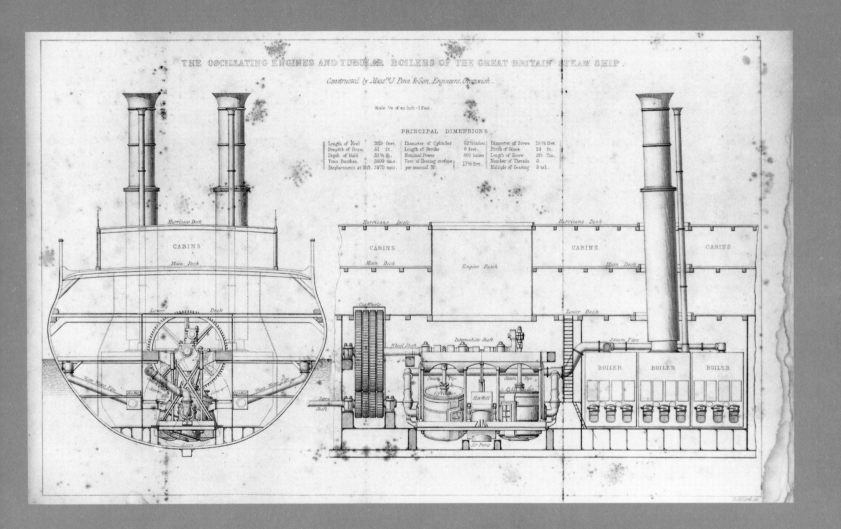

The revised machinery of 1852: oscillating engines and tubular boilers, with twin funnels abreast. From A Treatise on the Screw Propeller, *by John Bourne.* (National Maritime Museum neg E445)

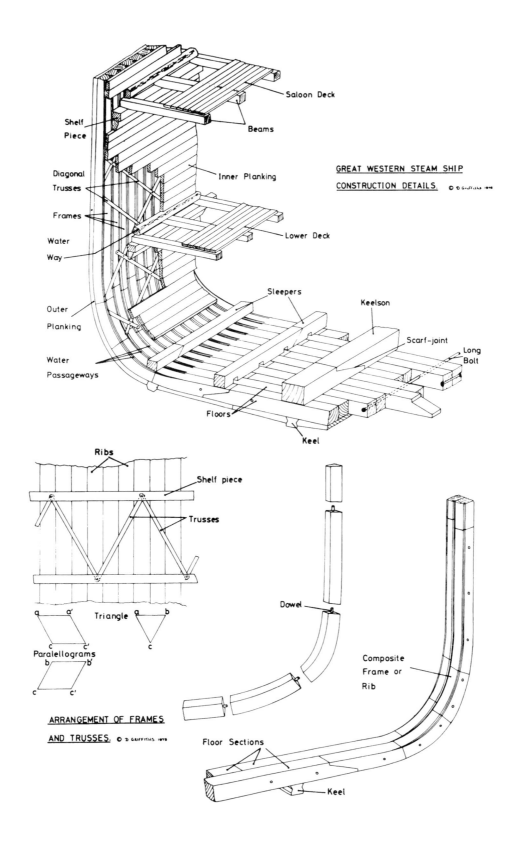

Saloon Deck

Shelf
Piece

Beams

Diagonal
Trusses

Inner Planking

GREAT WESTERN STEAM SHIP
CONSTRUCTION DETAILS. © D GRIFFITHS 1978

Frames

Water
Way

Lower Deck

Outer
Planking

Sleepers

Keelson

Scarf-joint

Long
Bolt

Water
Passageways

Floors

Keel

Ribs

Shelf piece

Trusses

Dowel

a   a'

Triangle   a   b

c   c'

c

Paralellograms
b   b'

Composite
Frame or
Rib

c   c'

ARRANGEMENT OF FRAMES
AND TRUSSES. © D GRIFFITHS 1978

Floor Sections

Keel

7

The Steamship *Great Western*

STRUCTURE

Brunel was not a naval architect or shipbuilder but he understood that a high-strength hull was needed to withstand the rigors of an Atlantic crossing and he knew where to go for advice, The Admiralty. The contacts established by Brunel, and Christopher Claxton who was a half-pay naval officer, allowed plans, drawings and calculations relating to naval steam vessels to be put at the disposal of the GWSS Co. Sir William Symons and Oliver Lang both offered practical suggestions and Claxton acknowledged the help given in the 1838 publication *The Logs of the First Voyage of the Great Western*.[1] In 1820 Sir Robert Seppings, then Chief Surveyor to the Admiralty, advocated a new method for constructing merchant ships, based upon recent naval practice, which produced stronger structures and actually saved timber. The method proposed used shorter sections of timber joined by dowels to form complete frames; these frames were then placed close together and diagonal trusses employed to give greater strength and rigidity.[2]

No single individual can be said to be responsible for the design of *Great Western* but William Patterson, in whose shipyard the vessel would be built, was the practical shipbuilder and he drew the lines and must have done much of the design work; a signed copy of the lines is preserved at Bristol Museum. Brunel's knowledge of structures must have been valuable, particularly as the ship was to be larger than any merchant steam ship built to that date. There are no drawings of the actual construction but a description was given in the Directors' Report in 1838.[3]

Her floors are of great length and over-run each other, they are firmly doweled and bolted, first in pairs, and then together by means of 1.5 inch bolts, about 24 feet in length, driven in four parallel rows, scarfing about 4 feet. The Scantling is equal in size to our line-of-battle ships, it is filled in solid, and was caulked to the first Futtock Heads, previously to planking, and to all above this height of English Oak. She is most firmly trussed with iron and wooden diagonals and shelf pieces, which, with the whole of her upper works, are fastened with screws and nuts, to a much greater extent that was hitherto been put in practice …

The method of construction employed provided an exceptionally strong hull which answered in every way the demands of the North Atlantic weather. As a protection for the timber against dry rot Brunel had all susceptible wood treated by Kyan's patent corrosive sublimate process.[4] Brunel had found this wood preservative to be effective from his work at the Monkwearmouth Dock, Sunderland. To protect the outer timber from the ravages of Teredo Navalis and other worms, the whole of the underwater section of the hull had copper sheeting firmly applied. Between each adjacent pair of frames a shallow channel was left at the joint in order to allow any leaking water to fall to the bottom of the ship from where it could be regularly pumped overboard. It is unlikely that inner planking was applied throughout the ship. In passenger areas such treatment would be essential but certainly not in the cargo and bunker spaces. As a protective measure the coal bunker spaces were encased in iron sheeting to prevent the coal from damaging the internal timber work and this was known as 'tanking'. The use of the term 'tanking', however, appeared to have resulted in many erroneous statements in the newspapers of the day, probably all copied from the same source. The popular misconception was that the bunker 'tanks' would be filled with seawater ballast as quickly as the coal was used.[5] Certainly the available log books make no mention of such an important task as ballasting at sea. The log books do, however, indicate a draft change during the Atlantic crossing. This change corresponded to the amount of coal consumed, illustrating that no ballast can have been taken during the passage.[6]

Details of the structure of the Great Western, *including the arrangement of frames.* (Drawing by Denis Griffiths)

The annual surveys conducted by the local surveyor to Lloyd's Register of Shipping, Mr George Bayley, confirms that the *Great Western* was truly a sound ship. In February 1841, after seventeen round trips to New York, he reported: '. . . In these places [the bottom outer planking] I found the caulking to be hard and sound, and the pitch in the butts and seams to be unbroken . . . The wood trussing being free from movement or strain I directed my attention particularly to the state of the suspension truss bars, and selected a point where the strain is the greatest, and requested that two bolts might be driven out – they proved to be in perfect state . . . The holding down bolts do not show the slightest indication of movement, nor is there any appearance of straining in the scarphs of the keelsons or of the sleepers. She is, as far as can be seen, in a perfectly sound state, and free from the slightest indication of decay in all parts to which access was had'.[7]

The following year he wrote: 'We found no appearance of straining or working in any of the Butts or Seams of the bottom, the caulking was remarkably sound and hard, and had the appearance of having been done last year, instead of five years since . . . A yellow metal bolt driven out of the scarph of the keelson immediately abaft the Engine Room, it was quite perfect and free from corrosion . . .The scarphs of the Keelson, Engine Sleepers, Butts in the Bilge Planks, and the lower ends of the Trussing, are all quite close, firm and in a very sound state. The wood and iron trussing is all firm, shews no appearance of yielding or movement at its ends'.[8]

During the winter of 1842-3 no dry-docking took place and so Bayley examined the ship whilst aground on the mud at Kingroad, at the mouth of the Avon. His report was as glowing as in previous years; particular attention being directed in his survey to dry-rot: '. . . we could not discover the slightest trace of its existence, excepting a little fungus by the side of one timber on the starboard side forward. I recommend the fungus to be removed and the rooms (or spaces) between the timbers on each side filled with salt to some height above the point referred to. She has now been running five seasons, cross the Atlantic fifty-four times, and (as per log) traversed 166,687 nautical miles without requiring any material repair to the hull or to the machinery . . . she is still in a most efficient state'. In a postscript to the report Bayley wrote: 'To shew that no movement has taken place, I may just mention that in one

of the store rooms, forward, a movement had taken place about three years since. The place was lime washed about two years since, and the last wash is still unbroken, shewing the ridge produced by the movement referred to'. An interesting sentence in the report gives an insight into the actual materials used in the frame construction. The original statement from the company report of 1838 indicated that only English oak was to be found in the framework below the first futtock heads but Bayley stated: 'Her frame consists of one set of English oak timbers, fayed close with felt between them, and, I am informed, are coaked and bolted together, and one set of Danzig fir timbers, fitted and secured the same as the oak timbers'.[9]

For the hull alone some 36,702 cubic feet of oak, elm, hard pine (Danzig fir) and soft fir were used and the paddle beams were made with '. . . four pieces of timber 12 or 13 inches, confined together at their ends and separated by a distance of 6 or 7 inches at the middle length'.[10] This form of construction provided strength for transferring the paddle wheel thrust to the hull of the ship but it also allowed for elasticity in order to dampen out any sudden loading. Some 40 tons of permanent iron ballast were provided together with 60 tons of copper sheathing for the lower portion of the hull.[11]

Great Western was rigged as a four-masted topsail schooner and this remained the same throughout her operating life. The fore mast was placed in front of the funnel and this was the only mast fitted with square sails; studding sails were carried during periods of favourable light winds. Main, mizzen and jigger masts were placed abaft the funnel. All masts could carry spencer sails and trysails whilst jib and stay sails could be rigged when required.

Originally *Great Western* was provided with a short poop but this was extended between the second and third voyages in order to provided six additional cabins. At the end of the first season a completely new poop was erected and this extended as far as the mizzen mast. At the end of the second season the poop was extended by a further 16 feet, bringing the poop to the paddle boxes, and a deck added at the fore part of the ship, almost reaching the funnel. The ship remained like this until 1847 when she was sold to the Royal Mail Company for service to the West Indies. The two sections of the spar or upper deck were then joined to form a complete upper deck extending from the bow to the stern.

The sail plan of the Great Western. (Drawing by Denis Griffiths)

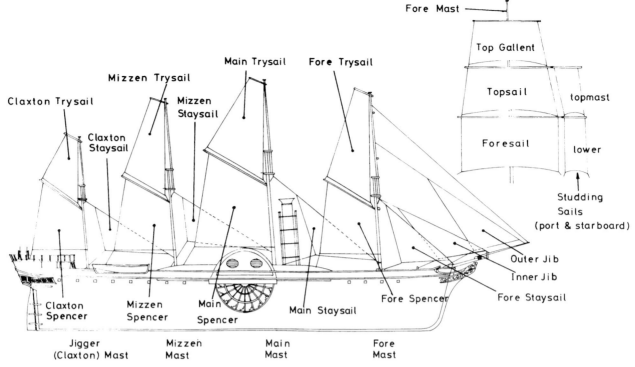

A print showing the ship as modified with an extended poop. (National Maritime Museum neg B9320)

Great Western *in Royal Mail service with extended upper deck.* (By courtesy of Denis Griffiths)

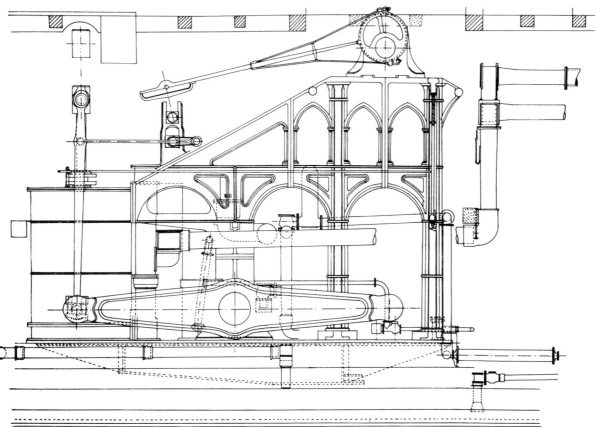

The side lever engines – elevation. (Drawing by Denis Griffiths after an original in the Science Museum)

This was the final change in the profile of *Great Western*.

MACHINERY

The side lever engine was a derivative of the Watt beam engine but, as its name implies, the large overhead beam was replaced by two smaller beams, or levers, positioned as low as possible alongside the cylinder. A bearing pin placed at mid-length provided a fulcrum about which the relevant lever could pivot. The piston rod connected with the side levers by means of a crosshead and two side rods. At the other ends of the levers a similar crossbar, called a crosstail, attached the side levers to the paddle crank via a long rod called the connecting rod. In most cases, a number of pump drives were taken from the side levers. The steam cylinder of a side lever engine was double-acting; that is, steam pressure alternately forced the piston downwards when given access to the top of the cylinder and upwards when allowed into the lower part, and *Great Western* had two such cylinders. So as to maximise the effect of the steam on the piston, and hence gain more useful work, the side of the piston not subjected to steam pressure was maintained at a very low pressure. The use of a condenser made very low pressures possible. A slide valve, placed alongside the cylinder, controlled with the correct timing, allowed admission of steam to one side of the piston and connection of the opposite side to the condenser. An eccentric on the paddle shaft operated the slide valve drive. The condenser chamber converted the steam back into water, thereby reducing its volume by about 1700 times. Thus the pressure within the condenser fell considerably. The condenser was of the jet type in which a spray of cold seawater was directed into the chamber where it came into contact with the exhaust steam.

The seawater supply for the condenser spray came directly from the sea through a valve in the ship's side; correct regulation of the seawater quantity being of supreme importance. If too little seawater was used all of the steam in the condenser did not

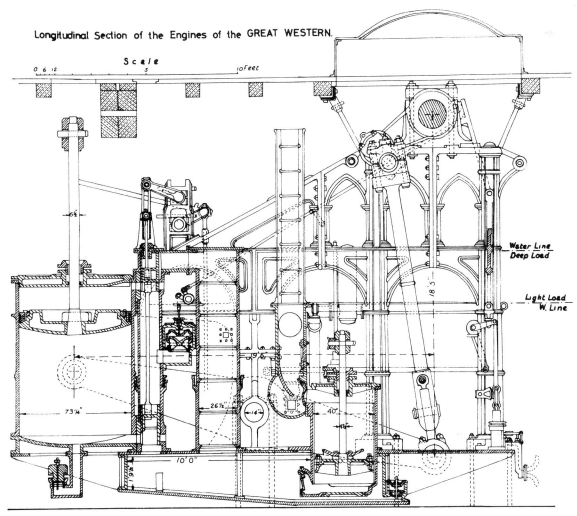

The side lever engines — longitudinal section.

(Drawing by Denis Griffiths)

200 Horse Marine Engines 1837

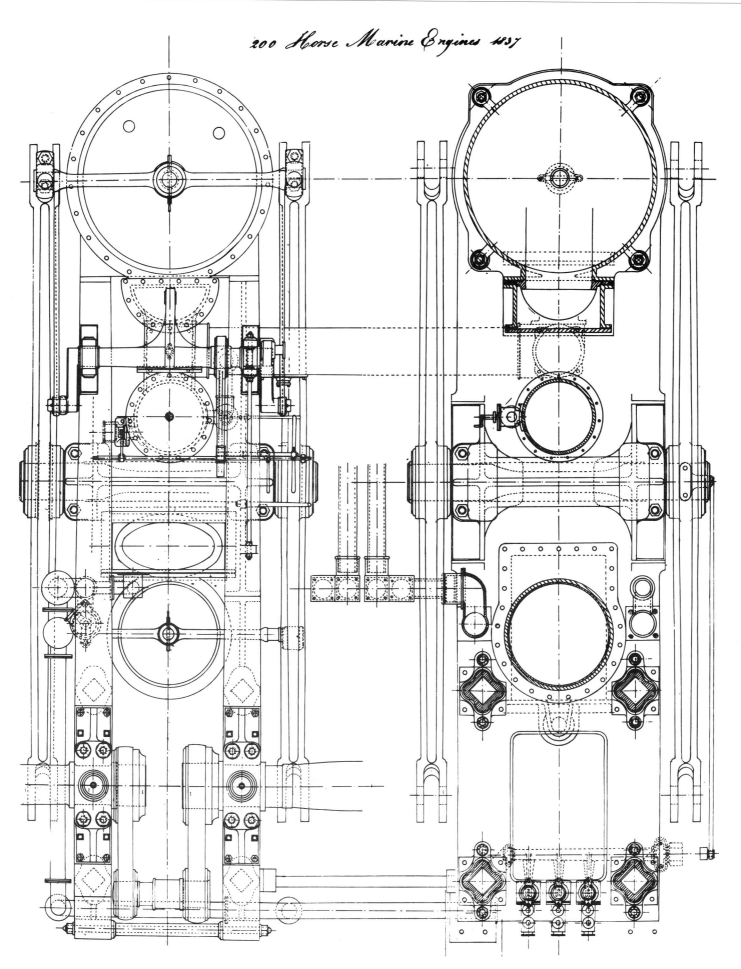

RIGHT *The side lever engines – end view.* (Drawing by Denis Griffiths)

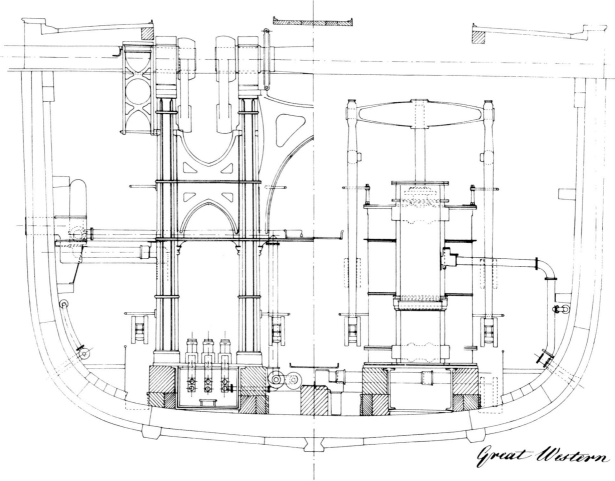

Great Western

LEFT *The side lever engines – plan view.* (Drawing by Denis Griffiths)

turn back to water and so the back pressure on the piston rose. With boiler steam pressures being, generally, below 5 psi even a slight increase in condenser pressure would produce a considerable loss in power. Too much seawater spray would flood the condenser and cylinder causing the engine to stall, possibly resulting in damage. At that time all jet condensers were equipped with a pipe connecting the bilge with the water spray box on the condenser. The idea was that in the event of the bilge pumps failing to remove sufficient water from the bilge, due to mechanical breakdown or hull damage, the low pressure in the condenser would draw in bilge water. This pipe and its connection to the condenser were known as the 'bilge injection', a term still used in ships today to describe the largest direct bilge pipe connection to the bilge pump.

Seawater contained dissolved gases and these would be liberated when the water was boiled but these gases passed with the steam to the engine and as they were not condensed in the condenser they would soon destroy the vacuum if not removed. For this purpose an air pump was used, such a pump being operated by the side levers. The air pump drew gases and water from the condenser and discharged them to the open topped hot-well from where water was taken by the feed pump to supply the boiler. The gases escaped to atmosphere from the open top of the hot-well whilst the excess water was discharged overboard via a ship's side connection.

As the piston reciprocated it rocked the side levers and these in turn rotated the paddle shaft through the action of the connecting rod and crank. Bearings had to be provided where moving parts connected with stationary or other moving parts. All required careful lubrication and, for most engines, were a major source of trouble. Paddle steamers had insufficient headroom to allow for the fitting of piston rod guides above the cylinder and so a parallel motion mechanism was used to ensure that the piston and its rod moved with a motion parallel to the axis of the cylinder.

The above is a description of a typical side lever engine and the engines fitted in *Great Western* were typical of the period but they were provided with a system which allowed the cylinder steam to be cut-off at some part of the piston stroke rather than have steam supplied for the entire piston stroke. Such an arrangement allowed for expansive working of the steam and this reduced steam consumption, and

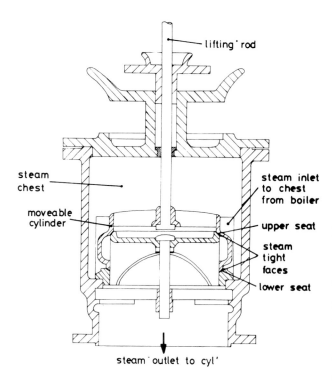

Expansion valve. (Drawing by Denis Griffiths)

hence coal consumption, although it did reduce cylinder power slightly. Steam supply and exhaust from the engine cylinders was controlled by means of a slide valve as was usual for all steam engines, but the engines fitted in *Great Western* also had an expansion valve fitted in the steam supply line to the cylinders. This balanced valve was actuated by a linkage driven by a cam, or rather system of cams, fitted to the engine crankshaft. By moving a circular cam follower, attached to the actuating linkage, to one of ten cams the engineer could adjust the period for which steam was supplied to the engine cylinders. During the first crossing of the ship to New York the Chief Engineer conducted tests which involved adjusting the expansion cams, taking indicator cards to determine power and weighing the coal in order to determine fuel consumption. The engine room log book for that trip also show that the expansion was continually being changed to suit prevailing wind conditions.[12] Results of the tests confirmed that considerable savings in coal were possible by expansive working.[13]

Steam Consumption	Grade No.	Engine rpm	Speed mph	Coal cwt/hr
Full Steam at 3.5 psi	0	15.5	12.75	28
0.8 full steam	2	15	12.5	27
0.7 full steam	3	14	12.25	26
0.5 full steam	5	13	11	23

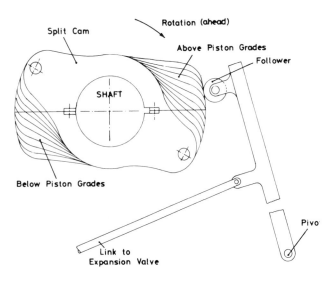

Expansion cam. (Drawing by Denis Griffiths)

Operating at full steam pressure of 5 psi the 73.5-inch bore by 7-foot stroke cylinders could develop about 750 indicated horsepower and the engines appear to have given very little trouble throughout the life of the ship, apart from the cracking of the frames already mentioned. There were bearing failures at times but these were common amongst most large marine engines of the period. Shortly after the ship left New York for Bristol on her first voyage the crank bearing on the port engine began to overheat and the usual practice of cooling the bearing with water only served to fracture the upper of the two bearing brasses. It took the engineers some 16 hours to reassemble the damaged unit which gave problems for the remainder of the passage.[14] Just after the start of the twenty-third voyage, for which the log book survives, on 2 April 1842, an unscheduled stop took place in order to cool a connecting rod bearing on the port engine and during this work the

Cycloidal paddle wheel.

(Drawing by Denis Griffiths)

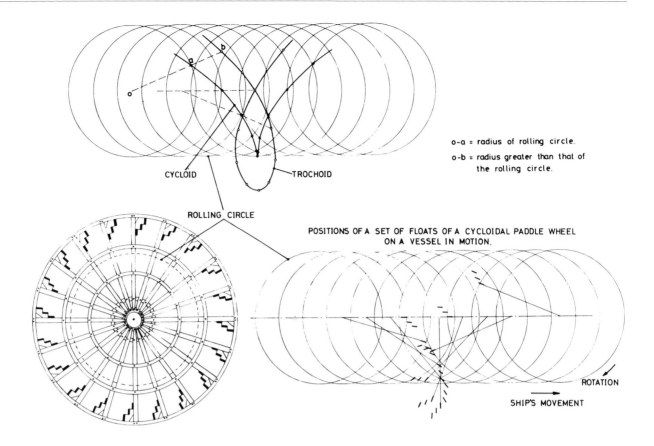

second engineer suffered an injury.[15]

The paddle wheels fitted initially were of the cycloidal type, an arrangement devised by Joshua Field in 1833 but patented by Elijah Galloway in 1835. Instead of a single paddle board on each arm of the wheel Field and Galloway fitted a number of shallow boards arranged in a step fashion. A single board entered the water with considerable shock which lost power and caused vibration but with a cycloidal wheel the shallow sections of board followed the first section into the water at the same position thus reducing shock. The sections of the boards described a cycloid as the paddle wheel rotated hence the name. *Great Western* had four shallow sections of paddle board fitted to each arm, there being 20 arms to the 28-foot 9-inch diameter wheels.[16] Maudslays provided the paddle wheels and the outer or first section of each board was 4.5 inch–es deep and made of iron, in order to resist the heavy shock of impact with the water, the other sections of the boards were made from wood. From the first voyage the boards presented problems and constant adjustment and reconnection was necessary. At the end of 1843 Guppy reported that they were too far gone to be of further service and advised replacement.[17] For the start of the 1844 season new paddle wheels were fitted, these being of conventional

design with 28 boards.[18]

As part of the machinery package for the ship Maudslays constructed four flue-type boilers which were the type most commonly fitted in ships of the period. Each boiler had three furnaces and they supplied steam at a pressure of 5 psi. Coal consumption varied but under full engine power with expansive working amounted to about 6.25 lbs of coal per horsepower per hour. Seawater was supplied to the boilers which meant that salt scale formed on the inner surfaces but as the steam pressure was low and the flue type of boiler was relatively inefficient anyway such scale did not present any particular problems. In many respects the layer of scale actually helped as it reduced internal corrosion, boiler water treatment not being used as the mechanism of boiler corrosion was not then understood. Below the water level there was generally little corrosion because of the protective salt scale but in the steam space there was often severe corrosion due to the oxygen liberated from the feed water as it was heated. Steam space corrosion usually limited boiler life to about five or six years.[19] The outer surfaces of the boilers were insulated in order to reduce heat loss and it was the felt lagging on the upper part of the boilers which caught fire during the passage from London to Bristol.

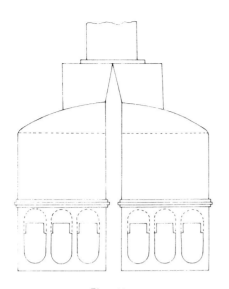

Boiler arrangement.
(Drawing by Denis Griffiths)

Elevation.　　　　　Section through furnace.　　　Sectional elevation　Sectional elevation
　　　　　　　　　　　　　　　　　　　　　　　　　　　through middle.　　through furnace.

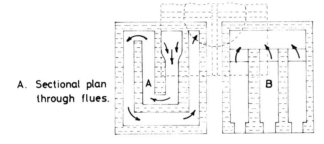

A. Sectional plan　　　　　　　　　　　　　B. Sectional plan
　 through flues.　　　　　　　　　　　　　　 through furnaces.

Each of the four boilers had three furnaces, and all boilers connected to a single funnel. Within each boiler all three furnaces connected at the rear to a passageway which gave into a rectangular flue system arranged above the furnaces, the hot combustion gases passing to the funnel uptake through this flue system. Flues were about 15 inches wide and about 3 feet high and were thus subjected to high pressure force even though the maximum steam pressure was only 5 psi. Flat surfaces did not support high pressures as well as curved surfaces and flue boilers were not suitable for high steam pressures. Even with steam pressures as low as 5 psi the flues had to be supported in some way and the boilers had flues connected to each other and to the shell plating by a large number of stays. A drawing of the boilers in *Practical Mechanic's and Engineer's Magazine* for November 1842 shows the positioning of these stays. The flues had to be cleaned of soot periodically in order maintain boiler efficiency and this had to be done manually by sending the smallest engine room

hands into the flue spaces.

Water level was maintained about 12 inches above the tops of the flues in order to prevent over-heating of the flues, the water acting as a coolant. A large-volume steam space existed at the top of each boiler, this providing a steam reservoir which had capacity to meet changes in demand without allowing adverse changes in steam pressure. The flue uptake passed through the steam space thus providing a drying effect on the steam. Water level in the boilers had to be maintained within strict limits and this would be done manually by regulating the feed water supply, checks being made on the water gauge glass. At least one drawing of the boilers shows a gauge glass arrangement. Drawings of the boilers in the Science Museum show floats in the boilers at about the water level and each of these connects, via a system of linkages, with a handle or pointer at the front of the boiler. This could well have been a water level indicating device. Dead weight safety valves, located in the steam space of each boiler prevented

Furnace end of the boilers.
(Drawing by Denis Griffiths)

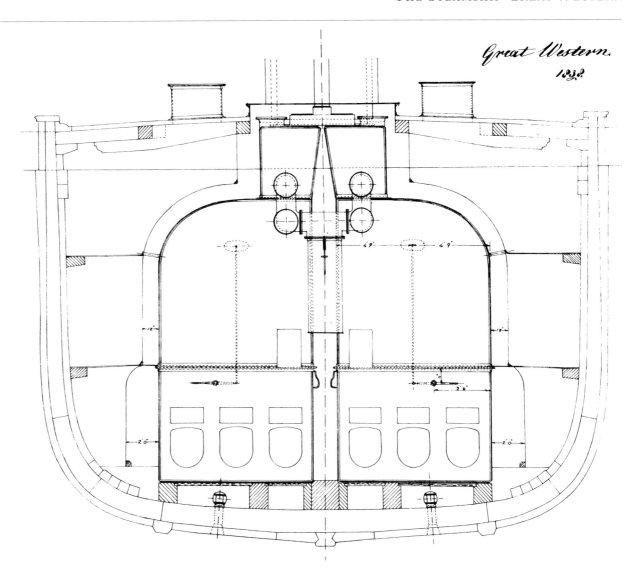

Great Western.
1838.

over pressure; steam passing through these valves when they lifted discharged into waste pipes, one forward and one aft of the funnel.[20]

Each boiler unit had a height of 16 feet 9 inches, length 11 feet 6 inches and width 9 feet 6 inches; each weighed 22.5 tons and could hold 20 tons of water. Boilers were positioned, in pairs, back-to-back with passageways between them and at each side allowing for movement between the stokeholds. Movement was essential not only for tending of the boilers by the firemen and supervision by the watch-keeping engineer but also to allow coal to brought to the boilers. Bunkers were arranged in the lower spaces alongside the boilers as well as at the forward and after parts of the ship. It was also essential to dispose of ash and after this was raked from the bottoms of the furnaces it would be cooled by water spray and then bagged, hauled up on deck and tipped overboard.

In September 1843 Thomas Guppy reported on the state of the boilers and informed the directors that they could be made to operate efficiently for another year or two for the outlay of £1000. He did, however, recommend that they be replaced and this was accepted. Guppy designed a new tubular boiler which would operate at a pressure of 12 psi and would occupy little more than half the space of the originals, the space saved being available to extra cargo. The cost was estimated at £3000.[21] Guppy's recommendation on the new boilers was accepted and they was manufactured in the company's work-shop.

The new boilers comprised essentially of one single unit, 24 feet wide, 12 feet deep and 18 feet 6 inches tall, with three separate sections. The outer section contained three furnaces whilst the inner section had two. Furnaces remained separate until the back of the boilers where those for each boiler combined into a smoke box. Iron tubes, 3 inches internal diameter and 8 feet long, carried the gases from the rear smoke box to the front smoke box which acted as a bend and returned the gases to the

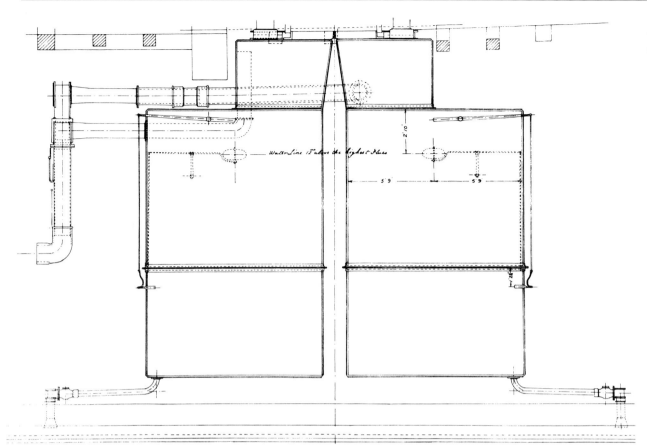

Boilers – side view.
(Drawing by Denis Griffiths)

back of the boiler through an upper set of identical tubes. From the only available drawing and description of the boiler[22] there appears to have been a total of 750 tubes, 258 on each of the outer boilers and 234 on the centre. It would also seem that more tubes existed in the lower bank than the upper, the upper bank containing six rows to the lower's ten. The tube heating area of 5900 square feet would have been provided by the 750 tubes if the thickness of the tube walls measured 0.375 inch; a not unreasonable figure. No indication has been made available as to the arrangement of the boilers within the ship. Certainly space saving could only have been accomplished with the 24-foot width athwartships. Whether the furnaces faced forward or aft is unknown. Positioning the furnaces facing the engine would not only allow the engineers to watch both engines and boilers more conveniently, but also enable shorter steam and feed water pipe runs to be used. The usual boiler mountings had to be connected as for the earlier steam generating plant.

Not only were the tubular units smaller and lighter than the flue boilers but they consumed less fuel per horsepower output, the important factor as far as the owners were concerned. Efficiency of operation was not matched by steaming capability, a fact that Guppy readily admitted.[23] This scarcity of steam gave an excuse for the government surveyor to reject the ship when a sale to the P & O Company had been arranged soon after the new boilers were placed on board. How great an influence the steam shortage had on the service speed is not known but it did have some influence as passage times across the Atlantic were one or two days longer than before the boiler replacement. Although the increase in passage time may have caused concern there was a reduction in the fuel bill and an increased cargo capacity. The poor steaming was due to the high heat transfer surface area which resulted in the combustion gases being cooled too much, resulting in a low funnel gas velocity and consequent poor air draught through the boiler furnaces. The ratio of actual heating surface area to fire grate area of the new boilers was 49.5:1 compared with 19.2:1 for the original boilers and it is hardly surprising that the funnel gas temperature was low. Solutions were sought and Brunel suggested a steam blast up the funnel in the same manner as a steam locomotive and he also advocated the use of a more lively coal.[24] Both were discounted because of the higher fuel costs involved. John Bourne (author of *a Treatise on the Steam Engine*) agreed that the problem lay in the large heating surface area to grate area and he also advocated a steam blast up the funnel. The solution eventually adopted was to cut a hole in the water box, which separated the rear smokeboxes for the upper and lower tube banks, thus allowing some of the hot combustion gas to bye-pass the tubes. This resulted in an increased funnel gas temperature, and velocity, which induced better air flow through the furnaces. Although this may have alleviated the problem it did not overcome the steaming difficulties and when the *Great Western* was sold to the Royal Mail Steam Packet Company in 1847 the engine surveyor commented, 'The boilers are Tubular and defective in form.'[25]

After a few voyages in the service of the RMSP Co. during 1847 *Great Western* was taken out of service for a refit and her boilers were replaced. Four flue type boilers, working at a pressure of 5 psi, were installed, there being a single stokehold so the boilers must have been arranged in pairs with their

furnaces facing. They were constructed by the Southampton firm of Smith & Ashby, Engineers and Boilermakers. No further mention is made of any other boiler replacement so it is likely that these remained in the ship until she was broken up in 1856.

OPERATION

Great Western was launched on 19 July 1837 and left Bristol, under sail, for London on 18 August. She arrived at the East India Dock four days later and remained there until March 1838 having machinery installed and accommodation fitted out. It is probable that a decision to delay the maiden voyage until spring 1838 was taken before the hull was launched, most likely on the grounds that the ship would not be ready for sea until the latter part of the year 1837 and a voyage in the winter months was likely to meet with bad weather and be poorly supported.

Great Western, *with extended poop, at anchor in the Avon*. (By courtesy of Denis Griffiths)

Great Western was always taken out of service during the winter months. The argument that Atlantic crossings are more difficult during the winter than in the summer is certainly valid but spring on the Atlantic can also be very rough.

The maiden voyage commenced on 8 April, *Great Western* having to take on her cargo and passengers at the mouth of the Avon rather than in Bristol. She was actually too wide to pass through the locks without removing the lower parts of her paddle wheels and, despite promises from the harbour authorities that the lock entrances would be widened, *Great Western* always had to lie at anchor when loading and discharging. During the maiden crossing there were problems with the machinery in that difficulty was experienced in maintaining steam pressure. This was due to problems in moving coal from the bunkers to the boilers; as the trip progressed coal had to be fetched from the extreme ends of the ship and the coal trimmers only had wheelbarrows to assist. In addition ash had to be removed from the stokeholds and seamen had to be drafted in to assist in this as the trimmers were fully occupied moving the coal. At one stage steam pressure fell to such a level that *Great Western* barely made any headway.

No problems were experienced with the engines but several stops were made in order to resecure loose paddle floats. *Great Western* arrived in New York with over 100 tons of coal still in her bunkers, 445 tons having been consumed on the outward passage. At New York George Pearne, the Chief Engineer was scalded when blowing down the boilers and subsequently died as a result of his injuries. Apart from problems with an overheated bearing the return crossing was made without incident and *Great Western* proved that an Atlantic steamship service was practicable. Over the years she also illustrated that such a service was also profitable, returning working profits in each of her service years, 1838-46, despite the fact that she never sailed in the winter months.

When sailing from Bristol *Great Western* used an anchorage at the mouth of the Avon and this always presented inconvenience for passengers and the handling of cargo but despite many promises the harbour company made no efforts to widen the locks. Liverpool offered enclosed dock facilities as well as good rail communications with other parts of the country and so a decision was taken that for the 1842 season the ship would operate alternately from Bristol and Liverpool. This move was a success and from 1843 Liverpool became the British terminal port. From Liverpool the company was in direct competition with Cunard, although that concern sailed to Boston and not New York. Whenever a Cunard ship sailed at the same time as the *Great Western* Cunard habitually reduced fares and freight rates in order to attract trade. The *Great Western* was able to maintain her share of the market and generally could offer faster passages.[26] The Cunard mail ships were, however, subsidised and profits from the ship were not as high as they had been before the Cunard services commenced. Money was also required to complete the *Great Britain* and in 1844 the company attempted to sell *Great Western* to P&O. A purchase price of £32,000 was agreed but the sale fell through due to a dispute about the boilers and surveys.[27]

Great Western remained in service with the GWSS Co. until withdrawn at the end of the 1846 season and sold to the West Indies Royal Mail Steam Packet Company. She was a successful and profitable ship but had to be sold in order finance salvage of the *Great Britain* from Dundrum Bay. She was finally sold for scrapping in August 1856 and Brunel went to visit her whilst she was being scrapped at Castle's yard, Millbank, near the site now occupied by the Tate Gallery. 'Among those who went there to take a farewell of her before she finally disappeared was Mr Brunel; thus he saw the last of his famous ship.'[28]

HMS *Rattler*: Brunel's Warship in Service, 1845-56.

By late 1844 *Rattler* had completed Brunel's trials, which made a vital contribution to the development of screw propulsion for the Royal Navy, and the Great Western Steamship Company. These trials established efficient screw forms both for the Navy, which sought an auxiliary power, and for Brunel, who required a full-powered solution. The remaining twelve years of *Rattler's* life would be one long trial, first of the screw as a practical sea-going propeller, and then a sustained test to destruction of the machinery and fabric of the ship in years of hard service on distant stations.

IN COMMISSION

On 11 December 1844 *Rattler* was docked at Woolwich to repair the copper on her keel. The following day she was ordered to be commissioned

for general service. On the 14th Commander Henry Smith read his commission, and was joined by Lieutenants Robert Robertson and Henry D Blankley. Henry Smith had entered the Navy in 1810, serving in Sir George Cockburn's flagship the *Northumberland* in 1815-16, and served with Sir George again between 1832 and 1834 in the *Vernon* and *President*. He was promoted Commander in November 1841, only two months after Cockburn took office as First Sea Lord, and was employed on particular service on board *Rattler* until promoted Captain by the outgoing Tory Board on 27 June 1846. Clearly he was a favourite with Cockburn, and several other tory admirals.[1]

On the 21st the Admiralty ordered the Steam Department to fit the ship for General Service with Smith's two-bladed screw. Mr Langlands was appointed Chief Engineer. The total cost of building and fitting the ship for sea had been £17,413, of which the machinery accounted for £8376. Her rig cost a further £9400. The ship was un-docked on 27 December, and between 3 and 23 January 1845 a further series of trials was carried out (detailed in Chapter 3).

Having concluded her propeller trials programme *Rattler* left or Portsmouth on 2 February, arriving at Spithead the following day, and coaling in Portsmouth harbour. On the 18th she left for Plymouth on a trial in company with the powerful paddle-wheel Royal Yacht *Victoria and Albert* and the Admiralty Yacht *Black Eagle*, under the command of Captain Lord Adolphus FitzClarence on board the Royal Yacht. The vessels reached Plymouth Sound on the 20th. They set out for Milford Haven from Falmouth on the 23rd, into the teeth of a Force 8 gale, with heavy seas and a swell. All three ships struggled, but the relatively under-powered *Rattler* laboured heavily, and pitched so deep as to show her propeller shaft. She lost much ground to the more powerful paddlers after taking in all sail and striking her topmasts as they passed the Longships lighthouse. The two paddle steamers arrived at Milford Haven eight and ten hours before *Rattler*. The officers conducting the trials concluded that the *Rattler* had been disadvantaged by her low power and would have liked to see one of her paddle wheel half-sisters in the squadron, but still concluded 'we do not think it would it advisable to substitute it [the screw] for the paddles as the sole propelling power, without further and more extensive experiments with vessels of equal power and tonnage under all possible circumstances.'[2] In truth *Rattler* had done well against two of the most powerful paddle steamers afloat, which were equipped with advanced wheels and far greater power per ton. Yet simplistic reports of this apparent 'defeat' by the older system had a significant adverse effect on public opinion, which supposed the screw to be an inferior propeller against a head sea.[3] This adverse publicity may well have prompted the universally famous, but distinctly 'stage-managed' *Rattler-Alecto* trials of the following month, which met the basic experimental criteria of comparing like with like.

After arriving at Milford Haven on the 22nd *Rattler* was docked at Pembroke on 26-27 February 1845 to unship the screw and repair the waste water pipe. She left Milford on the 1st, only to suffer a burst condenser joint the following day, requiring new bolts to be fitted. Despite this mishap she was back at Spithead on the 3rd, and reached her base at Woolwich on the 5th. Here she encountered one of the perennial problems of the new system. After a run down the river on 28 March the screw was hoisted up, and found to be fouled by 24 fathoms of 9-inch hawser and a fishing net.

On the 30th *Rattler* left Woolwich in company with her paddle wheel half-sister HMS *Alecto*. At 5.54am the ships left the Nore and raced to Yarmouth under steam without using any sail. *Rattler* arrived at 2.30pm, *Alecto* 20 minutes and 30 seconds later. *Rattler's* speed of 9.2 knots had been produced by 334.6 indicated horse power (ihp), *Alecto's* 8.8 knots came from only 281.2ihp. The screw showed 10.2 per cent slip. A second trial followed almost immediately, the two ships leaving Yarmouth Roads at 3.32pm, heading north under steam and sail to Cromer. At 6.21pm *Rattler* stopped her engines, *Alecto* rejoined 13 minutes and 30 seconds later. The ships had been running at 11.9 and 11.2 knots respectively.

The third trial followed on the next day, with the ships running north under steam alone to the Humber, from 9.22am, when they were already running under full steam, to 5.17pm, when *Rattler* stopped. *Alecto* rejoined her 39 minutes later, and once again her power, 250ihp, was significantly lower than the 364ihp of *Rattler*.

The fourth, fifth and sixth trials were all run under sail only, with *Alecto* unshipping her lower paddle boards. *Rattler* easily won all three. In the seventh and eighth trials the two ships took turns in towing each other, *Rattler* having the advantage, towing 1 knot faster than she was towed. On 2 April the ships reached Newcastle. On 3 April, off St Abb's Head the ships tried their respective turning circles before being lashed stern to stern at 5.30pm for the famous ninth trial. Although *Alecto* was allowed to start her engines first, and towed *Rattler* at 2 knots, when *Rattler* applied her power she arrested the forward motion of the *Alecto* within 5 minutes and eventually towed her astern, her wheels churning furiously, at 2.8 knots. At 6.00pm the engines were stopped. *Rattler* had developed 300ihp, while *Alecto* only managed 140ihp. However, the slip on the screw reached 66 per cent. That evening *Rattler* was tried on reduced power, with the cut-off being

THE *RATTLER/ALECTO* TRIALS

	Length (ft-in)	Breadth (ft-in)	Tonnage	Power (nominal)	Area of midship section.	Draught (ft-in)		
						Fwd.	Aft.	Mean
Rattler	176-6	32-8½	888	200	281.8	11-9	12-11	12-4
Alecto	164	32-8½	800	200	281.8	12	12-3½	12-7

During the trials the engine power generated was measured by indicators, and the thrust of the *Rattler's* screw shaft was measured by Brunel's thrust meter or dynamometer, which used a system of levers to measure thrust against weight. The main difference in hull forms was that *Rattler* had been lengthened 15 feet by the stern to install the propeller. However, her Maudslay 'Siamese' engines were significantly more powerful than the direct-acting engines installed by

The famous towing trials between Rattler *and* Alecto *in April 1845. At this point* Rattler *still carries her barquentine rig.* (National Maritime Museum neg B1783)

applied at the lowest grade of expansion, and then reduced steam pressure. This experiment ascertained that propeller slip was not affected by the lower speeds.

The ships anchored in Leith Roads on the 4th, leaving on the 7th. After a tenth trial, under steam on 8 April, the two vessels steamed into a strong head wind and a heavy sea for 7 hours on the 10th. This eleventh trial gave a slight advantage to *Alecto*, although this could be attributed to the *Rattler* having to close her engine room hatches, to keep out the sea, thereby losing draft to the stokehold. The ships arrived back at Yarmouth on the 12th and conducted the twelfth and final trial as a run under steam from Yarmouth Roads to Woolwich the following day, but due to interruptions and navigational hazards the results were imprecise, although *Rattler* had a decided advantage.[4]

The results of the 'trial' were by no means as clear-cut as later accounts would suggest. Even Francis Pettit Smith's leading publicist John Bourne recognised that the experiments demonstrated that the paddle was the most efficient propeller when towing, or in a head sea, and that in other conditions the two were generally equal. In view of the superior power applied to the screw throughout the trials, any claim that they 'proved' the superiority of the propeller could only have related to the superior

sailing of the screw ship, and the greater ease with which she could make sail. The screw proved better suited to meeting variable loads and speeds, hence her success in the stern-to-stern trial of strength. In truth the manner in which the trials were reported may have been intended to justify the decision to adopt the system more widely, a decision which had already been taken.[5]

The trials had also revealed another problem, this time caused by the application of the screw to a sharp paddle wheel form. Without the roll-damping effect of the wheels and sponsons the *Rattler* was an uneasy ship. She was ordered to be docked at Woolwich to have bilge pieces fitted 'with a view to check her excessive rolling', while any defects were made good. Before going into dock Henry Smith's patron, and the key professional figure in the early and successful application of the screw, Admiral Sir George Cockburn, the First Sea Lord, came on board to witnesses the unshipping of the propeller on 24 April. Cockburn had been intimately involved in the adoption of the screw from the formation of the Tory Admiralty in 1841. He was a convert:

The proofs we have lately had [the *Alecto* trial] of the efficiency of the screw as a propeller on board the *Rattler* convince me, that it will be

in future generally adopted and we are now adapting those building for that description of propeller. . . . The French I believe have only one or two with screw propellers. We are therefore taking the lead in this important change of getting rid of the cumbersome paddle wheels.[6]

The ship was docked at Woolwich on the 30th, and came out on 5 May with a new false keel, repaired engines, a new screw and shaft bearings.[7] On 6 May Lieutenant Blankley was replaced by Lieutenant Joseph Nourse. On the 9th *Rattler* outran the paddle wheel steamer HMS *Vesuvius* during a run down the river.

FRANKLIN'S LAST VOYAGE

On 16 May *Rattler* and the old paddle wheel tug *Monkey* were ordered to accompany Captain Sir John Franklin's ill-fated Arctic expedition in the ex-bomb vessels HMS *Erebus* and *Terror*, as far north as Pentland Firth. The selection of *Rattler* reflected the fact that the two exploration vessels had been fitted with small screw propeller steam plants, in fact ex London-Greenwich railway locomotives with the shaft emerging on one side of the keel. The following day Commander George Smith, who had been commanding the Woolwich dockyard steamer HMS

Sulphur, was temporarily detailed to supersede Henry Smith while *Rattler* escorted the Arctic ships. George Woodberry Smith had entered the Navy in 1812. He began a steam career in 1833, joining HMS *Dee* and then *Phoenix*. In 1838 he took command of the *Meteor* and then the *Tartarus* in the West Indies. From 1841 to late 1846 he was an additional Commander of the yacht *William and Mary* at Woolwich.[8] His extensive steam experience may have included commanding *Rattler* during the Brunel trials.

The expedition set off from Woolwich on the 19th, with the Arctic ships in tow. They were cast off on 4 June, having been taken out beyond the Orkneys and given three rousing cheers as they left. By the 9th *Rattler* was back at Woolwich, and two days later Henry Smith resumed command. After repairing minor engine defects while alongside at Woolwich (cost £1212), she left on the 21st for Portsmouth, where she would join the Evolutionary Squadron under Admiral Hyde Parker.

JOINING THE FLEET

By this stage the future of the screw propeller in the Royal Navy appeared assured. On 9 June Sir George Cockburn provided his First Lord, the Earl of Haddington, with a report of the latest debate in House of Commons. In reply to a question from

This eyewitness sketch shows the Rattler *(far left) and* Monkey *(foreground).* Rattler *is towing the ex-bomb vessels the* Erebus *and* Terror *of Franklin's Arctic expedition, May 1845.* (National Maritime Museum neg PX8143)

Captain Sir Charles Napier, the leading liberal proponent of steam warships, Cockburn had stated that he was convinced *Rattler* had proven the screw concept, and proposed to proceed gradually, increasing the size of ships to which it was applied. The next would be the small frigate HMS *Amphion*, before going on to try the system in battleships.[9]

After a brief stay at Spithead, punctuated by the loss of a boatkeeper, who fell overboard and was drowned on 14 July, the Squadron left on the 17th. Francis Pettit Smith was on board, although the cruise was generally under sail. After eight days *Rattler* was detached to Cork with the Squadron mail, raising steam for first time. After discharging F P Smith at Plymouth on 21 August, *Rattler* proceeded to Portsmouth, flying Admiral Hyde Parker's flag. Shortly after arriving she was ordered to be docked to make good defects and then flushed to get rid of vermin.[10] For the latter task the crew took three days to clear the ship, and she was 'smoked' for 12 hours on the 27th.

Rattler steamed out of Portsmouth on 19 October, and rejoined the squadron at sea two days later. On the 24th and 25th she was employed towing the large two-decker sailing battleships *Rodney*, *Albion* and *Canopus*. She returned to Portsmouth with the squadron on 3 November, and was prepared for a further docking, this time to repair her copper and fit a trunk for shipping and unshipping the screw, on a plan proposed by John Fincham, the Master Shipwright at Portsmouth. In addition the dockyard was instructed move *Rattler*'s mainmast aft, and alter her rig.[11] She would spend December in dock, and January alongside at a total cost of £3011. When she went out of harbour on 27 January for steam trials, with Woodcroft's propeller, the Commander-in-Chief, Admiral Sir Charles Ogle was on board. After a cruise to Plymouth and back in mid February she was inspected on the 14th by the new First Lord, the Earl of Ellenborough, and Junior Sea Lord Rear-Admiral Sir William Bowles who, like Cockburn before them, watched the screw being unshipped and shipped. The following day she took Ellenborough and Bowles out of harbour to board the two-decker HMS *Superb*. It is worth noting that in

The first screw frigate HMS Amphion (foreground) under sail with ships of the Baltic Fleet in 1854. (National Maritime Museum neg PY8326)

early 1846 the introduction of the screw propeller was considered almost inevitable, but the proper form for a sailing battleship was matter of profound political controversy. Ellenborough and Bowles had come to see the *Superb*, one of Symonds' controversial 80-gun ships, which had lately been re-coppered, at Bowles' insistence, and recovered all her speed.[12] After their inspection *Rattler* returned the two Lords of Admiralty to the dockyard.

On the 23rd *Rattler* went up to Southampton and back with Lord Cochrane's experimental paddle wheel steamer HMS *Janus*, which was observed to

give off unusual quantities of steam. *Janus* was a case study in how not to conduct experiments in an empirical age. She was built with a novel hull form, experimental engines and advanced boilers. The failure of the engine, which could not use all the steam produced by the boilers, effectively condemned the hull form and the steam plant. The contrast with the careful process employed with *Rattler* is particularly significant. Thereafter *Rattler* was treated like any other small steamer while waiting for the 1846 Squadron of Evolution to assemble, carrying a detachment of Royal Marines and their families to

Symonds' controversial two-decker Superb, *with the royal yacht and vessels of the Royal Yacht Squadron in the Solent. Since Symonds originally made his reputation as a yacht designer the battleship is in appropriate company.* (National Maritime Museum neg 777)

Cork, and towing the *Calcutta* out of Plymouth harbour on 17 April. In May the Admiralty instructed the Surveyor that all screw steam vessels were to have a passage from the engine room along the shaft to stuffing box, to allow the Engineer to attend to the shaft and bearings while at sea.[13]

On 12 May Captain Francis Liardet joined the ship for the cruise. Liardet had commanded the *Powerful* on the coast of Syria in 1840, including the bombardment of Acre. He was there to witness the trial of his ball signals, which proved unsuccessful. The following day *Rattler* joined the squadron. On this cruise, lasting between 13 and 28 May, *Rattler* proved the screw as a naval propeller. In his report Commodore Sir Francis Collier declared:

> The performances of the *Rattler* have far surpassed my most sanguine expectations under sail, whatever might be the weather, either light winds, or strong, smooth water, or heavy sea, she has been at all times in her station. And in a trial between her and the *Brilliant* [an old 36-gun frigate of 1814, lately reduced to a 22-gun corvette], on being ordered to look out to windward on the 24th Inst. In a moderate breeze and smooth water, the Captain of the *Brilliant* has admitted that the *Rattler* beat her 2 miles to windward in 4 hours.

Unlike *Rattler*, paddle wheel vessels were unable to sail with the fleet, being 'run out of sight in a few hours' in a topsail breeze.[14] *Rattler* was also a capable tug, towing *Superb* and *Rodney* out of Cork harbour on 11 June, as the Squadron made sail for Oporto, where they arrived on the 15th, before turning round and heading back to Cork. Here, on 13 June Admiral Sir William Parker arrived to take command of the Squadron. Parker, the leading sea-officer of his generation, had been appointed to resolve the sailing ship question, and consider the screw. He would report to a new Liberal Board, under Lord Auckland, the Tory ministry having been defeated in the summer. In a memorandum prepared for his successor Lord Ellenborough reported that the screw was superior to paddles, but 'as yet the screw could not be used for 20 days without requiring repair on account of the effect of friction on its bearing. The farther discoveries of science may obviate this defect'.[15] *Rattler* would spend the rest of her short life acting as the practical test-bed for this process –

her outstanding engineering installation being subjected to an unprecedented trial.

After proceeding to sea at the end of July Parker went on board the *Rattler* on 3 August and proceeded round the squadron to collect his captains. *Rattler* was then secured stern-to-stern with her paddle wheel half-sister *Polyphemus*. After ordering the paddle wheel ship to tow *Rattler* she was quickly brought up and then towed astern at 3 knots when the screw was applied. Parker and his Captains left the ship after this convincing, if highly misleading, experiment. As with the *Alecto* the *Polyphemus* produced significantly less power than the screw vessel. However, her exploits had persuaded an important group of officers that the screw was a powerful tug.[16] Clearly Parker was convinced. He told Admiral Bowles:

> We have also tried the powers of *Rattler* and *Polyphemus*, in which the *former prevailed* when stern to stern, and she had also a decided advantage in a steam run of eighteen miles in a calm; but when it came to a *stern-board* the *Polyphemus*'s paddles had the best of it. The *Rattler* performs to admiration, and keeps company like a frigate, under canvas only. *Polyphemus* also does well with her *floats* unshipped, and, with some addition in her rig might still be improved.

The new First Lord, Auckland, was highly satisfied with the results, telling Parker:

> What you say of the performance of the *Rattler* is very satisfactory and important. Immense sums have been expended in the construction of steamers and machinery and (necessarily so) long before the best forms and sizes of vessels and the best description of propulsion could be satisfactorily determined, but I think we are beginning to learn something definite by experience, and I am led to believe that very shortly the screw will supersede the paddle, that steamers of very large dimensions will not be found useful in proportion to their expense, and that we shall not again be persuaded to build an iron vessel.[17]

As the cruise turned into a prolonged intervention in Portuguese politics Parker reflected on the experience:

It has been to me a great satisfaction that the steamers sail well enough with their floats unshipped, to keep company with the fleet *under sail only*; but I have no doubt the screw will eventually supersede all others, and the *Rattler* has proved an admirable specimen of this description of steam vessel.[18]

However, there were still important lessons to be learnt, and in early October the Admiralty ordered that work on all duplicate screw vessels then building should be suspended until further notice.[19]

During this time *Rattler* was running between Lisbon, Gibraltar, Cadiz and the coast of Morocco, carrying mail and provisions, a task she shared with the other small steamers (Commander's commands) in the fleet. While anchored at Lisbon on 10 November stoker William Patterson died, and although he was buried ashore Patterson's effects were still sold in the traditional manner at the main-mast on the following day.

On the 17th Commander Richard Moorman was ordered to ordered to replace Henry Smith, who had been promoted Captain by the outgoing tory board on 27 June. Born in Cornwall, at Falmouth, in 1810 Moorman had commanded packets, and merchant ships in the 1830s before attending the Gunnery Training Ship HMS *Excellent* in 1838, and the attached Royal Naval College in 1839. He was promoted to lieutenant on the recommendation of Sir Thos Hastings, Captain of the *Excellent*, to indicate the Admiralty's support for improved gunnery. Moorman served briefly on HMS *Calcutta* during the Syrian Crisis of 1840-1, but then went back to *Excellent* as First Gunnery Officer until promoted Commander in 1845. Since September 1847 he had been in command of the paddle steamer HMS *Hecate*.[20]

WAR AND DIPLOMACY

Commander Moorman joined his new ship on 3 December, just in time to welcome the Dutch Admiral Prince Willem of Nassau on board at Gibraltar for the usual demonstration of shifting the screw. At the end of the month Parker sent *Rattler* from Lisbon to Oporto and England with dispatches announcing a victory that he expected would bring the latest Portuguese Civil War to an end.[21] After being docked at Devonport between 11 and 15

January 1847 to repair copper, *Rattler* went to Portsmouth, where February was taken up repairing her engine. While there she was selected for an important diplomatic mission, conveying the new Minister to Brazil, Lord Howden to the River Plate, where he would try to resolve the long-running crisis over Montevideo. The mission was also a severe test of *Rattler* as an auxiliary steam ship. In late February Howden's luggage was stowed, and on 9 March Lord Auckland, his old friend, the First Lord when the *Rattler* project began, Lord Minto, the First Sea Lord, Admiral Sir Charles Adam, and the Commander-in-Chief, Sir Charles Ogle, visited the ship.

Before leaving Portsmouth Moorman had to change his officers, Lieutenant Augustus Hampden Hobart was arrested and discharged from the ship, while Lieutenant Nourse was discharged sick. Hobart, who had a chronic inability to accept a subordinate situation, would be one of the most unusual nineteenth-century officers, commanding a blockade-runner in the American Civil War, becoming Commander-in-Chief of the Turkish Navy in the 1870s, and then retiring to compose a set of highly questionable memoirs. On the 16th Lieutenants Henry T Hire and Samuel T Dickens joined the ship.

On 27 March Howden and his suite came on board and the *Rattler* steamed out of harbour. She proceeded, calling for fuel, water and provisions at Funchal, Tenerife, Porto Praya, Bahia, Rio de Janeiro and Montevideo before landing Howden at Buenos Aires on 11 May. During this cruise the crew were more prone to drunkenness, leading to increased punishment, disrating of petty officers and flogging than had been the case under Smith's command. After reaching Buenos Aires *Rattler* went on a round-trip back to Rio carrying Mr Ousley, the British Minister at Montevideo, for negotiations. Howden left Argentina in early July, for his Embassy in Brazil, *Rattler* then proceeded home.[22] On the ocean passage from Rio to Fayal in mid-August she ran short of coal and was forced to burn coal sacks, spare wood, tar, empty barrels and a spar picked up from the sea. After dropping the mail at Falmouth she steamed round to the Thames and landed her powder at Purfleet. Once at Woolwich she was inspected by the Board of Admiralty, landed her guns, took out her masts and finally paid off on 13 September 1847. After the crew had left the ship was docked in late

September and December 1847 to refit, repair the copper, and overhaul the engine and boilers (total cost £2006). She would not return to commission until February 1849. More significantly she had passed the test posed by this mission with flying colours. The steam auxiliary with a screw propeller was ideal for that peculiar combination of long ocean passages and intricate riverine navigation that made up so much of the Royal Navy's operational existence. The concept had been proved.

Rattler provided vital experience to refine new designs for a screw steam navy. When the Surveyor proposed building new a vessel of her class at Sheerness under the 1847/48 programme Lord Auckland minuted:

> I presume that with the several vessels which are building or projected to be built after the *Rattler* great care will be taken to guard against any defects, which may have been obvious in the *Rattler*. I believe her at present to be the most handy and useful vessel of her class, and that she is the best model that we could follow,

but nevertheless we have latterly learned much upon the adaptation & fitting of the screw. The *Rattler* is at the moment subject to a very severe test and it is probable that improvements (certain, and not experimental) may be introduced. Capt. Smith might be consulted on this subject, and above all things the specification of these vessels should be submitted to the Steam Department, and the Surveyor of the Navy & Comptroller of Steam should act together.[23]

In the event the new vessels were enlarged to carry a heavier armament, and adopted a new hull form after the retirement of Symonds.[24] At the end of the year a ship to this improved design was ordered at Sheerness, as the *Miranda*.[25] However, the decision to adopt screw propulsion was not without infrastructure implications. In mid-1849 the Admiralty paid £200 for a large lathe, specifically designed for turning screw propellers, which was supplied to Woolwich Dockyard by Joseph Whitworth, the Manchester machine tool manufacturer.[26] In the constant search for more durable bearings Joshua

Miranda, an improved design built after the retirement of Symonds, seen here off Reval (Tallinn), in early 1854, while operating in advance of the Baltic Fleet. Ice navigation would have been impossible in a paddle-wheel vessel. (National Maritime Museum neg PW4903)

Woods' white metal type were tried experimentally in *Rattler* when she was refitted in 1849.[27]

In April 1848 *Rattler* was discussed by the Select Committee on Naval Estimates. Sir James Graham, a once and future First Lord, expressed some doubt of her success, basing himself on the adverse opinion given by Captain FitzClarence, but Captain Alexander Ellice, the Controller of Steam, declared her 'a very successful experiment, when you consider the shape of the ship'. This was a sharp retort, for Graham continued to advance the cause of Symonds' hull form, and *Rattler* was a true Symonds' ship, being a paddle wheel vessel with a different propeller. Ellice went on to give his inquisitors a lecture: 'You must recollect the great advantages of the screw: you have every broadside gun; you lose nothing; and every particle of the machinery, boilers and all, are perfectly protected from the fire of the enemy.' He then weighed in with his own heavy-weight referee, Sir William Parker.[28] The screw had passed its final test, *Rattler* had been the test bed.

ON THE ANTI-SLAVERY PATROL

Although out of commission *Rattler* was listed as an Advanced Ship at Sheerness in March-April 1848, meaning her stores and gear were available for a rapid return to service. She later moved to Portsmouth, where she was docked in August-September 1848 to shift two sheets of copper. While there her propeller shaft was damaged when the hook used to hoist the screw gave way. The Steam Department demanded to know why preventers had not been used.[29] She was then moved to Devonport, and an Admiralty Minute of 16 October ordered that she be kept ready for immediate service. She was then fitted for sea at Devonport between January and March 1849. She was commissioned by Lieutenant Godfrey Smith on 4 February, with Commander Arthur Cumming coming on board on the 22nd. The other officers were Lieutenants Peter Godfrey and Richard Dawkins, with Engineer Joshua Chase.

Arthur Cumming had entered the Navy in 1832. He was commissioned as a Lieutenant following gallant service on the Syrian coast in 1840 as a mate on the steam frigate HMS *Cyclops*. He was then an additional Lieutenant on various Mediterranean Fleet Flagships, becoming a Commander 1846, and serving as First Officer of HMS *Albion,* the greatest of all Symondite 'whig' ships.[30]

Following an inspection by Admiral Sir John Louis, the Port Admiral, on 3 March 1849, *Rattler* steamed out of harbour on the 4th under her own power for the first time in nearly two years. She then set course via Madeira to Sierra Leone, arriving on the 25th. Her next two years would be spent on the West Africa anti-slavery patrol. Within days of arriving local Kroomen were hired for the most arduous duties in the harsh climate, especially coaling. Continuing south *Rattler* joined the station Commander, Commodore Arthur Fanshawe, at Ascension Island on 6 April.

The British attack on the Atlantic slave trade had reached an impasse shortly before *Rattler* arrived on station. Under the 1839 'Equipment' Clause, applied against Portuguese ships, the presence of hatches with open gratings, bulkheads within the hold, planks for constructing an additional 'slave deck', shackles and handcuffs, extra water casks, surplus food and cooking equipment was enough to condemn a vessel, even if there were no slaves on board. This clause dramatically increased the success of the naval blockade. However, the effect of this legislation had been largely counter-acted by the 1846 Sugar Act, which reduced the barrier against slave-grown sugar entering Britain, prompting marked increase in Brazilian slaving, from 20,000 a year to nearly 60,000. Fortunately the development of Brazilian politics favoured suppression. The elite 'Portuguese' capitalist faction, who dominated the slave trade, were losing power to the 'nationalist' Brazilian movement. In 1845 the Equipment clause was extended to Brazilian ships, and in early 1850 Lord Palmerston sanctioned a direct attack on slave ships inside Brazilian territorial waters. This prompted Brazil to outlaw the trade, leading to an exodus of capitalists to Portugal. By 1853 the Atlantic slave trade was effectively over. Under Fanshawe's predecessor, Commodore Sir Charles Hotham (1847-9), the anti-slavery patrol had been kept off-shore, both to reduce the human wastage from disease, and as a reflection of Hotham's ambivalence toward the cause.[31] Fanshawe (1849-51) was altogether more dynamic, resuming the inshore patrols and blockade.[32] Almost all the vessels seized in this period were Brazilian schooners.

Although the introduction of paddle wheel steamers had been effective, the arrival of a ship capable of cruising under easy sail, with the appearance of a sailing sloop, but rapidly connecting her screw and pursuing the sailing slaver directly into the wind was calculated to eliminate the last vestiges of this loathsome traffic. *Rattler* quickly proved her worth. Cruising between Porto Novo and Whydah she took the Brazilian schooner *Ardesinha* on 5 July. She was fully equipped as a slaver, but had to be burnt as unsafe to navigate. Like most slavers, she had been hurriedly and crudely built in Brazil to minimise the loss of capital if captured. Her crew were set ashore at one of the Portuguese settlements. On 11 September *Rattler* and *Cyclops* took the Brazilian schooner *Sophia*, also fully equipped for the trade, which was towed into Freetown by *Cyclops* for adjudication. The crew were set ashore at Whydah. On 13 October off Lagos *Rattler* took the Brazilian slave brig *Conquestador* with 317 slaves on board, which was sent to Sierra Leone under a Prize Crew. On the 30th she took the Brazilian slave brig *Alfrede*, which had no slaves, but proved to be fully equipped. She was also sent to Sierra Leone.

However, this success came at a price. Lieutenant Godfrey was arrested for neglect of duty in September, and on 29 December Joshua Chase the Chief Engineer died, and was shortly afterwards buried at sea. The practice of cruising off the coast at night, and closing in to inspect the creeks and rivers where the small slavers tended to hide at day break avoided the feared 'miasma' commonly blamed for the yellow fever and malaria. More significant was the ability of the steamers to distil their own water, rather than relying on the infected supplies to be had on shore. While the ship ranged along the coast from Lagos and Sierra Leone to the Congo Delta she often sent her pinnace off alone.

On 20 February 1850 *Rattler* captured the *Lucy Anne*, a Brazilian vessel with 547 slaves on board, and false papers. She was sent under prize crew to St Helena. By this time the bulk of all sightings were British, Portuguese, American and French warships, along with British, Portuguese and Sardinian merchant ships. *Rattler's* next capture came on 2 July, when she stopped the Brazilian brigantine *Solusia* of the Congo, which was equipped for the slave trade and falsely flying American colours. *Solusia* went off to St Helena with a prize crew, to be followed shortly by another Brazilian brigantine, the *Esmerelda*, seized on the 7th, and also fully equipped.

The next capture, on 27 September, exposed the limits of steamships on this station. Having detained the Brazilian brig *Echo*, which had too much water

Rattler, now carrying the 'foreign service' barque rig, in chase of a Brazilian slaver, probably the Conquestador *as reported in the* Illustrated London News *for 29 December 1849.* (National Maritime Museum neg E0451)

on board for normal trade, *Rattler* was forced to burn the usual emergency fuel, a mixture of wood, coal sacks and barrel staves, to raise steam the following day. She was forced inshore to secure firewood. More fundamental problems would follow. On 30 November the air pipe of the hot well was broken by the working of ship, providing the engineers with a few days work. By January 1851 it was clear that the boilers were failing, the entire structure was breaking up, and much patching was needed to keep them running until she reached home. With the end of the commission in sight discipline and health on board began to give way. Finally in March *Rattler* embarked the defective machinery of the river gunboat HMS *Albert* and headed for England. After picking up supernumeraries at Spithead for passage to the Thames she continued, with the firebars falling out of her fractured, leaking boilers as she steamed up the Channel. Once she reached Woolwich the ship was

stripped, and the steam factory mechanics came on board to dismantle the engines. *Rattler's* second commission ended when her pendant was hauled down on 15 April 1851, but she was not destined to wait long for her third, and final, commission.

THE SECOND BURMA WAR

While at Woolwich *Rattler* was docked in April, June and August 1851 to re-copper her stem, shift the stern post and replace worn sheets of copper on the hull. The engine was overhauled and new boilers fitted. A two-bladed Smith screw was still used. The total cost of the refit was £2600. She could now stow 110 tons coal in her bunkers, and 20 tons elsewhere. Her armament was set at one 8in shell gun and eight 32-pounder 25 cwt 'gunnades'. The crew comprised 21 officers, 26 petty officers, 28 seamen, 13 boys, 20 Royal Marines and 22 stokers (130 all told).

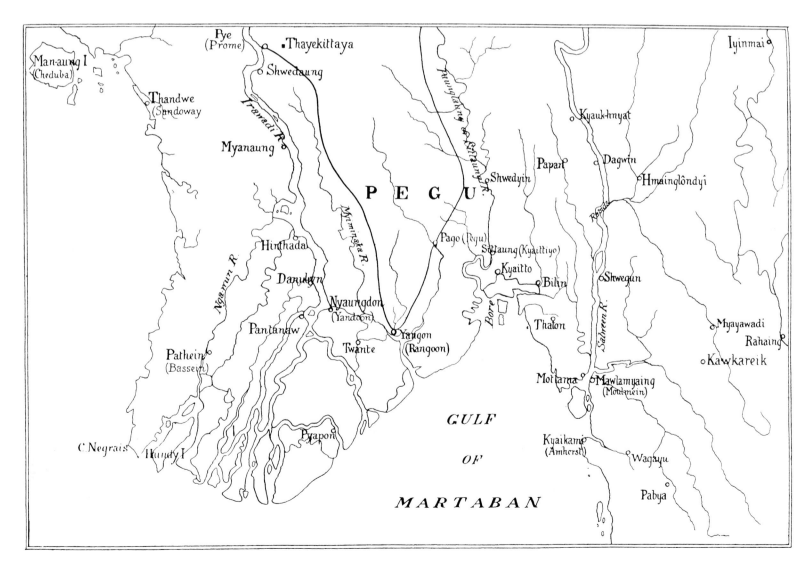

ABOVE *A view of Rangoon about the time of the Second Burma War.* (National Maritime Museum neg PU1830)

On 1 September 1851 *Rattler* was commissioned by Commander Arthur Mellersh, with Lieutenants George A Pidcock and John W Dorville. John Bonney, the Assistant Engineer who had been doing duty as Chief Engineer since Chase's death on the African coast, was confirmed as Engineer. Arthur Mellersh, a lieutenant of 1837, had served aboard the steamer *Phoenix* on the Syrian coast in 1840, and subsequently on various stations, including South America and the East Indies.[33]

On sea trials *Rattler* made 9 knots. She then stopped at Portsmouth for minor defects to be made good between 6 and 11 October 1851. As an experienced seaman, and steam officer Mellersh quickly took the measure of his command.

> She may be said to sail well, especially in light weather. She rolls and pitches easily though deep: she is crank, her angle of inclination when under topgallant sails, Topsails & courses, job & spanker gaff foresail and mainsail being as much as 10 degrees. Her best point of sailing trim 2' by the stern. [Her] Present lower masts longer and lighter than [those fitted] previous[ly], and cannot be set up properly, or used like sailing ship masts as [they are] too light to carry proper canvas.

Map of Lower Burma, from Laird Clowes, The Royal Navy, *Vol VI. The railway had not been built in 1852.*

The basic performance was not untypical of a 'Symondite' ship. On 11 October *Rattler* embarked

Lord Frederick FitzClarence, another of William IV's illegitimate sons, and his suite for a passage to Madeira. After stopping at Lisbon between the 24th and 26th FitzClarence and his party were landed at Funchal on the 30th. *Rattler* then proceeded south via Sierra Leone, Ascension and St Helena to Cape Town. On departing Cape Town in early February 1852 she struck her guns below for a boisterous passage, arriving at Singapore on 22 March. Three days later she joined HMS *Hastings*, the 74-gun flagship of Rear-Admiral Charles Austen, Commander-in-Chief of the East Indies Station, at Penang.

In January the Second Burma War had broken out, and with active operations about to start the *Rattler* would be entering a war zone for the first time. Rear-Admiral Austen, brother of the novelist Jane Austen, then hoisted his flag on board *Rattler* and left for Rangoon. By early April two brigades of British and Indian infantry had assembled at the mouth of the Rangoon river, escorted and supported by a mixed force of Indian and Royal Navy steamers. *Rattler* arrived off Rangoon on 1 April, going into the river to coal. The fleet left for Martaban on the 3rd, where the steamers bombarded the Burmese defences on the 5th. *Rattler* fired 180 rounds of shot, shell and grape at the Martaban stockade. The troops then landed without opposition to occupy the town. On 7 April *Rattler* took 100 men of the 18th Regiment (The Royal Irish) on board at Moulmein and headed for Rangoon. On the 11th

she helped to clear the Burmese stockades and land troops to occupy Rangoon, firing 230 rounds. For this operation she had embarked two extra guns from the sailing frigate HMS *Fox*. Two men were slightly wounded. On the 12th the troops landed under close gunfire support, and quickly secured their positions. Between the 10th and 14th *Rattler* played a leading part in the attack on Rangoon, her crew occupying the stockades on the opposite side of the river at Dalla on the 11th. In his despatch of the 16th written on board *Rattler* at Rangoon Austen praised Lieutenant Dorville, the senior Lieutenant, who had been particularly noticed by the army commander, General Godwin. On the 15th three men died, marking the onset of a cholera epidemic that was to ravage the entire force. *Rattler* would received a battle honour for the Burma War, while Lieutenant Dorville was promoted commander in February 1853 for his services.

On the 22nd *Rattler* was detached to Calcutta with despatches, and the Admiral, who was among the sick. By 7 May *Rattler* was back at Rangoon, going on to Penang, where she towed the *Hastings* out of harbour, and proceeded to Trincomalee, arriving on 27 June for repairs. She returned to Rangoon in early September. Shortly after arriving part of the air pump failed, and bent the connecting rod of the fore engine. She was then in the Bassein River, engaged with dacoits. Austen had returned to

Rangoon with his flagship, and transferred to the steamer HMS *Pluto*. While up the river close to Prome Austen fell ill again, and died on October 7th. On the 14th *Rattler* embarked the Admiral's body from *Pluto* for passage to Trincomalee, where he was buried on the 27th.[34]

After stopping at Madras for provisions *Rattler* returned to Rangoon before sailing for Calcutta, where she was docked and overhauled between 30 December and 11 January 1853 in the Kidderpore Dock. While under refit three men deserted, but were quickly returned by the local police for a £3 reward, which was deducted from their pay. When her refit was completed *Rattler* sailed to Rangoon carrying troops. With the war already far inland, up a river she was too deep to operate in *Rattler* was sent on via Penang, Singapore and Labuan to Hong Kong, arriving on 4 March.

AT WAR WITH THE PIRATES

Within days *Rattler* fell victim to poor charts, striking a rock while entering Amoy harbour on 15 March, losing an anchor and making water. Chinese labourers were hired to pump the ship. After taking considerable trouble to lighten the ship she was put ashore on the 30th to repair her stem and copper. The work was complete by 10 April, and she was hauled off. At this time the local pirates were

The attack on the Dunnoo stockade, 10 January 1852; one of the opening actions of the Burma war. HMS Fox, *42 guns, is in the centre with HEICS* Phlegethon *ahead and* Hermes *astern.*
(National Maritime Museum neg PW4891)

BELOW *The Royal Navy was involved in numerous actions against Chinese 'pirates', this being an earlier action before* Rattler *arrived on the scene in the Gulf of Tonkin, 21 October 1849.*
(National Maritime Museum neg PY8219)

extremely bold, exploiting the Taiping rebellion that broke out in 1850 and lasted until 1864. The Taiping rebels captured several major southern Chinese cities, including Nanking, which was the 'capital' of their leader, Hung Hsiu-Ch'uan. While the British properly remained neutral observers of this civil war, they were forced to take active measures to protect their interests by the activities of the Taipings, together with their seemingly endless war with the Imperial authorities, which interrupted trade at Canton and Shanghai, leading to the collapse of the old customs system at Shanghai. The rebellion also lead to numerous anti-foreign riots, in which the lives and property of western merchants were endangered, and the collapse of central authority in southern China, which led to a dramatic rise in piratical attacks on coastal shipping. As a direct consequence the level of western military intervention increased, to protect their citizens and interests against the threat of violence and disorder.[35] The

British representative, Sir George Bonham, Governor of Hong Kong, refused Imperial requests for aid, advised the Government to remain neutral, and restricted his actions to the defence of commercial interests. It was in response to this emergency that all available vessels that could be spared from Burma had been ordered to China. The new Commander-in-Chief on the China Station, Sir Fleetwood Pellew, was ordered 'to provide adequately for the protection of British subjects and property in Canton, Amoy and Shanghai'.[36] While Canton remained in Imperial hands, although under attack, Amoy and Shanghai were taken by rebel Triad groups, rather than the Taipings.[37]

On 16 April Mellersh noted that the pirates were very active off Amoy harbour. As a result British warships were the preferred mode of transport for valuable cargoes. In late April *Rattler* anchored off the Min river to deliver treasure, and used the voyage to look out for pirates. Then on 5 May, while lying

at Amoy Mellersh learnt that pirates had captured a valuable convoy of junks and driven off the armed British schooner that had been escorting them. *Rattler* left Amoy the following morning, setting course for the mouth of the River Min. On the 10th, after being delayed by bad weather, Mellersh ascertained that the Pirates were still at Namquan, (lat. 27° 15' long. 120° 20') where they were waiting to ransom their prizes. The following morning, under the cover of a fog, *Rattler* steamed right into the middle of their fleet, six junks and one lorcha.[38] The opening shell, fired from *Rattler's* 8in pivot gun, blew up the pirate commander's ship. The other junks ran ashore, where many of the pirates were killed by local people. The ship fired over 120 rounds of shell, grape and shot. It was estimated that some 70 pirates were killed by *Rattler's* fire. The ship's boats were then lowered and the pirate vessels captured. The cutter, commanded by Lieutenant Pidcock, went out of sight in pursuit of a body of pirates who were escaping in a seized junk. When Pidcock and his crew caught up with the pirates and attempted to board, they were overpowered. Pidcock and two men were killed, and seven others were wounded but escaped back to the ship. The next day the Chinese Admiral arrived, and the cutter was found with the bodies of the slain. The three men were buried at sea on the 13th. Mate James Willcox was promoted Lieutenant for this action in January 1854. By the 24th the ship was back at Amoy. On 1 June Lieutenant Dorville was discharged following his promotion.

During her stay at Amoy, protecting British interests, *Rattler* hired Chinese divers who recovered the anchor lost when she ran aground in March. Throughout this time there was serious fighting off the harbour mouth between Imperial junks and the rebel Triad forces who held Amoy. The Imperial campaign, which was largely conducted by naval forces, recaptured the city in November 1853.[39] On 28 August Lieutenant Charles Wrey joined. Between the 17th and 20th of September several shot from Imperial and rebel forces hit the ship. Although there were no casualties, the ship was damaged. In October *Rattler* was relieved, and sailed to Hong Kong, before proceeding to Canton with the *Alligator* in tow. There she saluted Admiral Sir Fleetwood Pellew's flag, and was hauled into Whampoa dock on the 18th to make permanent repairs to her stem. After hauling out of dock on the 31st she returned to Hong Kong, and back to Canton. She was back at Hong Kong on 27 December 1853 when Lieutenant Thomas Greer joined the ship. In January she carried treasure from Hong Kong to Shanghai, on a stormy passage. Here she remained, once again protecting British interests in the rebel-held city, towing her squadron mates up and down the river, and providing landing parties. Two Royal Marines deserted, with their muskets, and although spotted in the Imperial camp outside the city, they could not be recovered. Finally on 22 March *Rattler* weighed and proceeded down river, only to collide with a junk that evening. After punishing a Royal Marine Private with 24 lashes for

A view of Amoy during the British attack of 26 August 1841. (National Maritime Museum neg PY8199)

A map of Hong Kong published in 1844. (National Maritime Museum neg PU0072)

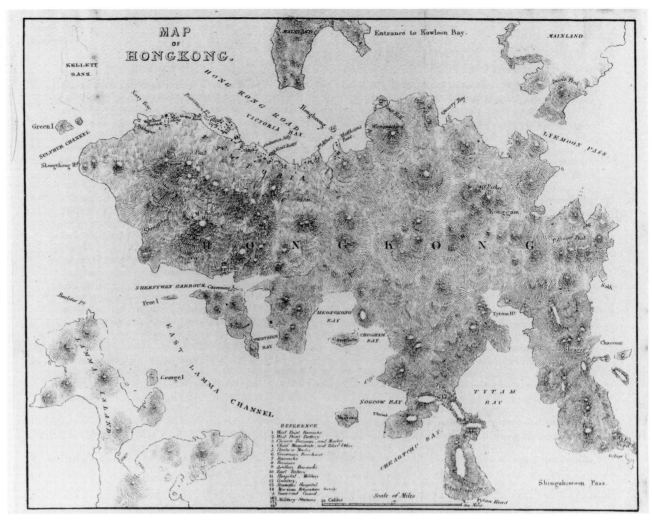

being drunk on duty, and reprimanding Lieutenant Greer for being off the deck, along with the Master, she reached Amoy on the 26th, delivering stores and supplies to *Bittern* and *Styx*.

Rattler delivered treasure at Hong Kong, repaired the collision damage and then steamed to Singapore, where she joined the Flag of the new Commander-in-Chief, Admiral Sir James Stirling, who inspected the ship. In early May she steamed back to Hong Kong, in company with the frigate *Spartan*, which occasionally required a tow. After coaling, and loading $57,900 for merchants at Shanghai she set out again, this time on a mission to Nanking. Sir John Bowring, the newly arrived Governor of Hong Kong and British Minister plenipotentiary in the Far East, had sent her, with HMS *Styx*, to obtain information about the Taipings at their capital, and see if there was any possibility of securing trading rights on the Yangtze. Entering the Woosung River on 17 May *Rattler* collided with another junk, losing her jib and flying boom, tearing off both bow anchors and starting the port side main chains. The mission

confirmed Bowring's low opinion of the Taipings and their prospects.[40] When Stirling hoisted his flag on board on 12 June, for the entry to Shanghai, there were problems connecting the propeller, due the speed the ship was making through the water, and the worn shaft. Three days later she ran aground in the Woosung river, while heading for Nanking. She also ran aground on her way back, and have to be hove off by the *Styx*. While lying off Shanghai in July, repairing the propeller shaft, seaman Charles Augustus received 48 lashes for striking another seaman, and treating Lieutenant Wrey with insolence and contempt. On 2 August stoker John Bryant fell overboard, 'and did not rise'. His body washed up the following day, and was buried ashore.

On 6 August Bowring embarked for a passage to Hong Kong. He had authority to negotiate commercial treaties with China, Siam and Japan, which he fully intended to push through with the support of the Royal Navy. Unfortunately for his plans the Crimean War provided a powerful distraction for Admiral Stirling, depriving Bowring of the naval muscle he was relying on to back up his diplomacy. Anchoring off the Min River, for Bowring to call at Foo-Chow-Foo, *Rattler* struck the ground, splitting her hawse pipe. Bowring then called at Amoy, reaching Hong Kong on the 20th. Mellersh noted that the local coals being used were very poor, having to be burned with wood and coal bags to generate enough steam. The catalogue of disasters continued on the 26th, when she embarked 2 officers and 20 men from *Spartan*, to search for pirates with *Racehorse*, but fouled her buoy and spent 24 hours clearing the screw and searching for her anchor. On the 28th the pirates, who had obligingly waited for their doom, were located in Bias Bay. After opening fire from the ship the boats were sent away under Lieutenant Wrey to destroy the junks. *Rattler* was back in harbour the following day.

THE DIPLOMATIC SHUTTLE

The collapse of central authority in China brought the three major western trading powers, Britain, France and America, into close relations, joining forces to uphold shared interests. Although Britain and France had gone to war with Russia in late March 1854, and the war would spread to the China seas, with the search for the Russian ships at Vladivostok and Petropavlovsk, *Rattler* would not be involved, remaining on the China station to support

British policy. Both the Admiralty and Admiral Stirling appreciated that the real threat to British shipping came from the endemic piracy of the region, not the handful of Russian ships. By early 1854 local trade, and even P&O shipping, was hardly able to operate without escort. With the assistance of the Chinese authorities, the Americans and hired steamers the problem would be largely solved by the end of 1855, although some pirate activity continued until the end of the Taiping rebellion. However, *Rattler's* contribution to this campaign would be interrupted by diplomatic work.

When Bowring's attempts to secure open access to Canton were rebuffed, he elected to head north, in search of superior authority. Consequently in mid-September 1854 a deck house was put up to accommodate the English and French Ministers, who were picked up at Macao, and taken on to Shanghai. After arriving *Rattler's* machinery began to give trouble. The cogs of the spur wheel had worn down ¾ of an inch since fitting. In mid-October Bowring embarked, and proceeded toward Tientsin on the Peiho river, in company with the USS *Powhatan* carrying the American minister. The envoys were seeking improved trading privileges from the Imperial authorities.[41] Further machinery problems followed, with the stern pipe, shaft and the gland of the stuffing box jammed, and boiler tubes failing in steady succession. Mellersh noted that the

The departure of the Bowring mission, the Rattler *under sail.* Illustrated London News, *27 January 1855.* (National Maritime Museum neg E0450)

engines 'require thorough repairs' and estimated their useful life without a thorough overhaul at less than 6 months. In early November Bowring, having been referred back to Canton, returned to Shanghai, and then embarked for Hong Kong. While on passage the funnel set fire to the fore sail. On arrival *Rattler*'s crew set to patching up their tired and battered ship, a task interrupted on 9 December 1854, when they dressed ship overall and fired a salute on receipt of news of the allied victory at the Battle of the Alma, which had occurred 3 months earlier. *Rattler* then took Bowring back to Canton for another attempt to meet Imperial Commissioner Yeh. Bowring was relying on the offer of aid against the nearby rebel forces to secure an audience, but Yeh proved obdurate.[42] For *Rattler* the voyage was punctuated by an outbreak of smallpox, and another grounding. *Rattler* then towed the flagship, *Winchester*, up to Canton, and prepared to go back into Whampoa dock. Her misfortunes continued, grounding at the dock entrance when the tide turned. She was in dock between 6 and 17 February 1855. Six days later *Rattler* and *Spartan* stopped rebel junks from seizing two 'English' lorchas in the river. By mid-March *Rattler* was once again at Hong Kong, embarking Bowring for a passage to Siam (Thailand), in company with HMS *Grecian*, where she arrived in late March. Bowring was hoping to extend the Commercial Treaty he had secured in 1844.[43] On the 30th a Siamese Prince visited the ship, shortly after Boy W J Davies had been administered 24 lashes. After surveying the river and waiting for an official clearance *Rattler* proceeded up the Siam river and eventually anchored off the British factory in Bangkok. Leaving on 26 April *Rattler* had to cast off *Grecian* as the local coal was too poor to allow her to tow the frigate to Singapore. On passage she even had to go inshore to cut wood. While at Singapore seaman James Smith jumped from the mainyard, while the ship's company were bathing, and was not seen again. After Bowring had completed his mission the ship steamed back to Hong Kong with a new Commander, William Abdy Fellows. Fellows, son of a naval Captain, had entered the Navy in 1827, serving in his father's ship at Navarino. He was then 2 years at the Royal Naval College, before returning to sea, again under his father in late 1830s. Promoted Lieutenant in 1840 he had been extensively employed, reflecting his whig connections.[44]

MORE PIRATES

Two days after arriving at Hong Kong *Rattler* set out for Ling-ting, where she captured three junks. On 28 May *Rattler* engaged pirates. Her boats captured and burnt six pirate junks off Sam Chow, and liberated two English lorchas and two junks. Another two pirate lorchas were burnt on 6 June. In late July there were a series of inconclusive engagements with pirates who escaped into coastal waters. After pirates had captured a lorcha and three junks, Fellows located them near Coulan and invited the assistance of the American Navy. *Rattler*, with 100 American seamen and marines manning three of the USS *Powhatan*'s boats and the small hired steamer *Eaglet* left Hong Kong on 3 August. The following morning the boats were towed into position by the *Eaglet*, and then attacked the 34 pirate junks. Ten heavily armed junks were destroyed and 6 prizes released for total loss of 4 killed and 7 wounded from *Rattler*, and 5 dead and 8 wounded from *Powhatan*. Most of the casualties occurred when the seamen boarded junks, which then blew up. In addition to the ten junks destroyed, numerous guns were taken, 500 pirates were killed and 1000 made prisoner.[45] The squadron returned to Hong Kong the following day, calling at the Ladrones Islands. The wounded from both ships were sent on board the hospital ship HMS *Minden*. After a round-trip to Macao with Bowring on board *Rattler* went to the fresh water anchorage at Cambridge Reach, where she was hogged to remove marine growths, loosened by the fresh water.

In early October Chinese carpenters were hired at Hong Kong to help replace the broken and defective cogs and spur wheels. The task was made more difficult by the arrest of the carpenter, John Reid, for drunkenness and insubordination to one of the officers. He was discharged from the ship and the service by order of the Admiral. The same month the Assistant Surgeon, Thomas Wilson, was also arrested for drunkenness. Court-martialled on the 31st, Wilson was mulcted of all pay and prize money, sent to prison for 12 months and dismissed the service in disgrace. A new carpenter, Samuel Nicholls, joined the ship on 4 November just as spur wheel re-toothing was finished and tried. On the 6th *Rattler* went up the Canton River to Cambridge reach, and moved into the Macao passage on the 13th, recovering an English lorcha that had been seized by the Chinese authorities the following day.

Returning to Hong Kong at the end of the month she was present when a salute was fired, on 3 December, in honour of the allied victory in the Crimea.

Finally, on the 8th *Rattler's* time on the China Station came to an end when she steamed out of Hong Kong harbour for the last time. By the 23rd she was anchored in Anjer Roads, before passing through the Sunda Straits en route for Cape Town. This passage was dominated by the leaky state of her hull, and she had to be pumped out every day. On the long haul across the Indian Ocean the ship regularly made 150 to 200 miles a day under sail. On 18 January 1856 a Russian seaman, Ivan Masloff, died, he was buried the following day. Britain and Russia were still at war. John Pine, the gunner, died and was buried on 6 February. Another Russian sailor, Herman Tourman, died on the 11th, the day before *Rattler* anchored in Simon's Bay. Between the 13th and the 24th she was coaled and caulked, with assistance from the Dockyard, and HM ships *Castor*, *Penelope* and *Frolic*. The caulking proved effective, after she steamed out on the 24th there was no further need to pump ship. After a brief call at St

Helena on 5 March, and passing the Equator on the 13th *Rattler* made good progress, only punctuated by the starting of the starboard forward chain-plates five days before she anchored at Spithead, on 10 April.

A LAST HURRAH

On 12 April *Rattler's* crew, who must have expected to pay off, found themselves turned out to clean and paint the ship. While they had been steaming up the coast of Spain, on 30 March, the Peace of Paris had been signed, bringing the Crimean War to an end. Although the war had not provided any dramatic successes at sea, British seapower had strangled the Russian economy, devastated her trade, destroyed key fortresses and threatened the very heart of the empire at St Petersburg.

The force assembled for this last operation was then ordered to conduct great Fleet Review at Spithead, on St George's Day (23 April) 1856, both to celebrate the peace, and to remind the rest of the world of the awesome offensive potential of steam-age naval force. British power rested on the deterrent value of seapower, and this was an ideal opportunity

A view of Hong Kong and the harbour, November 1846. (National Maritime Museum neg A1179)

to restate it. Although *Rattler's* arrival had been entirely fortuitous, she would help to swell the fleet. The review was also the occasion for the Smith Testimonial Fund, with Brunel on the Committee, and John Scott Russell as one of the Secretaries, to press Smith's claims on the nation.[46]

On the day of the review the ship's company cheered the Queen as she passed down the lines in the Royal Yacht *Victoria and Albert* at 1.50pm, before getting under weigh and steaming round the battleship HMS *London*, which provided one of the markers for the movement of a fleet of nearly 300 steam-powered ships and other vessels, at 2.15pm. Fortunately best Welsh steam coal had been loaded, to ensure that the fleet could maintain station, and that the Queen could see her ships. After an afternoon devoted to a mock bombardment of Southsea Castle, standing-in for Cronstadt, Cherbourg and New York, the fleet anchored at 7.45pm and was

then illuminated at 9.00pm. *Rattler's* final contribution was to fire five signal rockets.[47]

With many of the ships from the Review to be prepared for service, paid off, or, in the case of some gunboats, hauled out of the water, it was not until the 30th that *Rattler* steamed into Portsmouth harbour. Here she was lashed alongside the hulk *Dryad*. Captain Drummond of the *Victory* inspected the ship on 9 May, and she steamed out of harbour the following day, heading for Woolwich.

On the 11th and 12th *Rattler* lay at Purfleet, discharging her powder, tying up at Woolwich by the end of the day. On the 13th the crew began dismantling the ship and returning stores. At mid-day on the 16th the ship's company was paid off, and her pendant was hauled down for the last time at sunset. The ship was docked at Woolwich in June-July 1856, and taken to pieces by Mr Fulcher under a contract that allowed the Navy to salvage any useable materials.

Map of the mouth of the Canton River, from Laird Clowes, The Royal Navy, *Vol VI.*

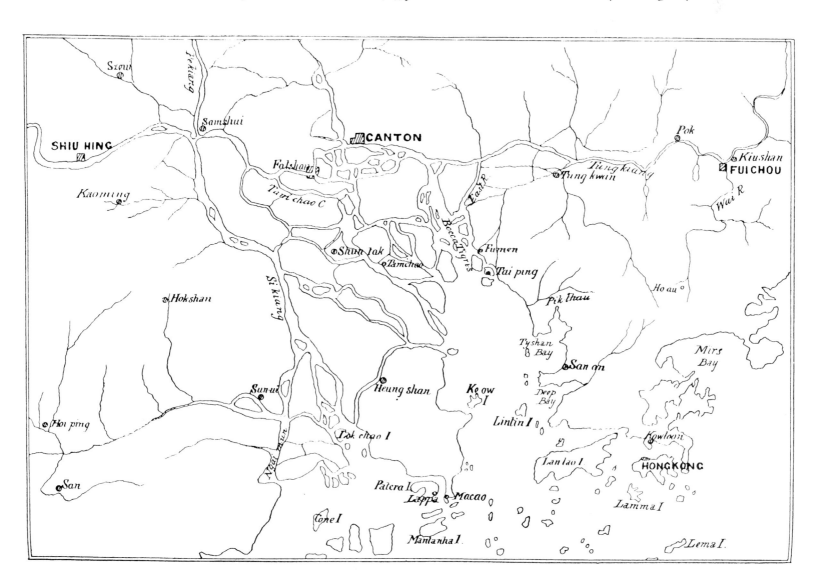

The task was completed on 26 November 1856. Brunel's warship had been demolished not a mile from where his last and greatest ship was taking shape. It is not known if he even noticed her passing.

HMS *Rattler* had two careers. In the first, under Brunel's direction, she demonstrated that the screw was an efficient propeller for auxiliary steamships, introduced the concept into naval service and provided a fundamental input into the development of efficient (as opposed to effective) propeller forms. In her second career, as a naval steam sloop she took part in fleet cruises, carried messages and stores for her sailing squadron-mates, who also looked to her for a tow out of harbour on occasion, carried diplomats to distant stations, helped in the final suppression of the West African Slave trade, fought in the Second Burma War, engaged Chinese pirates and provided a shuttle service for the diplomacy of Imperial trade in the Far East. Throughout this second career her experience continued to influence the design of naval screw steamships.[48] Less obviously her short career, ten or twelve years less than those of her half sisters, aside from the *Polyphemus*, which was wrecked in January 1856, demonstrated that the screw was incompatible with a wooden hull. Brunel could have told the Admiralty that back in 1840, but the introduction of the iron warship in that decade proved to be premature.

A bird's-eye view of the simulated attack on Southsea Castle by the gunboat flotilla, during the royal review of the fleet at Spithead, 23 April 1856. Somewhere in this myriad of ships is the Rattler. *(National Maritime Museum neg PY8275)*

9

The Screw-propelled Iron Steamship
Great Britain

STRUCTURE

The actual structure of *Great Britain* has been described in the classic work *The Iron Ship* by Ewan Corlett, who was instrumental in having the *Great Britain* returned to Bristol where she is undergoing restoration. Brunel worked with Guppy and Patterson on the design of the hull, Patterson having the greatest input in terms of the form. Guppy was responsible for the actual construction and Brunel, the structural engineer, would have considered the strength aspects. In practice there would never have been such strict demarcation of functions as the men

would have worked as a team although those actually on site, Patterson and Guppy, must have dealt with many of the building problems. Brunel would have laid down the ground rules and planned the construction.

Without actual rules the approach to the structural design must have been intuitive but Brunel was an intuitive engineer with a willingness to adopt new concepts in his approach to bridges and other structures. Ten continuous girders provided a platform at the bottom of the hull, this being some 3 feet 3 inches deep at the centre of the ship. The bottom platform

A modern waterline model of the Great Britain *in the National Maritime Museum.* (National Maritime Museum neg C4546-25)

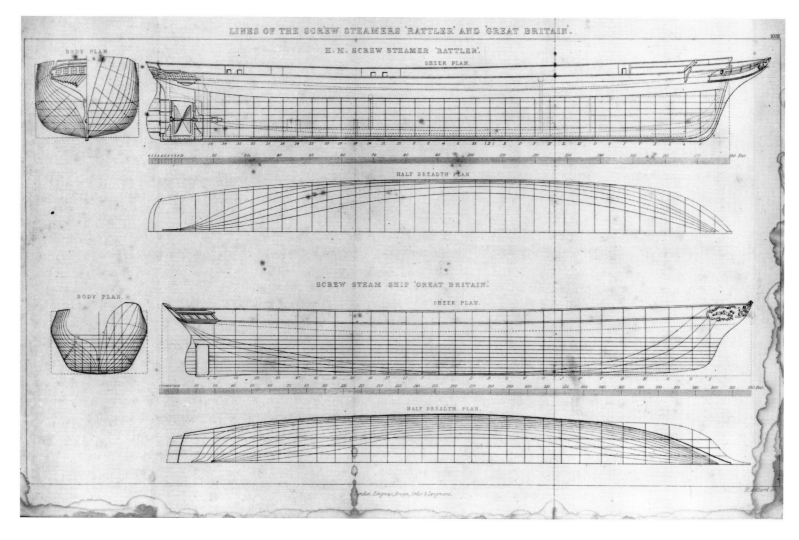

ran the length of the ship and became narrow and shallow at the bow area and at the stern. In the holds, cargo would sit on the platform whilst in the boiler and engine rooms it supported the machinery. Although similar to the double bottom of a modern ship the space between the bottom of the hull and the lower platform was not watertight; when constructing the *Great Eastern* some 15 years later Brunel arranged for a double hull in the lower part of the ship, possibly as a result of experience gained from this ship. Frames were designed to run under the platform to the centreline and so the longitudinal girders had to sit on top of top of the frames. Shell plating attached to the frames directly using rivets whilst the longitudinal girders attached via angle bars. The whole bottom structure was very strong and rigid, testimony to this being the grounding at Dundrum Bay where the hull stood up extremely well to the gales and the rocky shelf on which she sat.

Framing was not regularly spaced, the spacing being arranged to avoid the riveted plate joints.

Double riveting of plates was employed thus greatly increasing the strength of the joint. The actual method of construction is not known and there are two distinct ways in which the frames and plating may have been erected. If the frames were erected first it would have been necessary to determine the exact location of all joints in the plating, from a plating plan, in order to avoid locating frames at the riveted plate connections. Alternatively the plating could have been joined to form a complete hull section and then the frames riveted to the plating. This would have required the hull to be supported on an external cradle prior to fitting the frames. The fitting of the machinery through a hole left in the side of the hull was possible with either method. The bottom plating was fitted in clinker fashion with the seams facing outwards until the turn of the bilge. From there strakes of plating had their seams facing downwards until the point where the hull originally had the white line painted and then the plating was flush. It would seem that construction arrangements did not follow any particular scheme but was chosen

The lines of the Rattler *(top) and the* Great Britain; *they are not to the same scale. From* A Treatise on the Screw Propeller, *by John Bourne.* (National Maritime Museum neg E0448)

to suit ease of erection. It would certainly have been easier to arrange the bottom plating with seams facing outwards as that way, starting from the centreline and working outwards, each plate would be laid on top of the preceding plate. In order to do this, however, no frames would have been present and the lower part of the hull would have rested on an external cradle.

Five watertight bulkheads were provided but these only ran to the deck below the weather deck and in the event of a compartment being flooded water could have overflowed into the adjacent compartment possibly causing the loss of the ship; that was the case for the *Titanic*. The *Great Britain* was provided with considerable longitudinal strength but Brunel well understood that the same degree of strength was not needed in all parts of the ship. He reduced the scantlings (size of components) at the forward and after ends of the ship where high strength was not needed thus reducing the weight of the structure; the structure weight was about 28 per cent of her displacement.

Heavy pillars were used to support the decks in the cargo spaces and these extended up through the dining saloons. However, in the promenade areas the deck was supported on transverse bulkheads positioned in line with the pillars.

In terms of iron ship construction *Great Britain* was a 'one-off'. There were no rules to follow for construction and the designer had something of a free hand, within limits imposed by the materials available. One of these was the maximum size of iron plate which could be obtained. Patterson drew the lines for *Great Britain* but these were greatly changed

as the size of the ship increased, wood gave way to iron and paddle propulsion to screw. Ewan Corlett believes that Brunel had an influence on the lines as drawn by Patterson, due to the interest he had in wave patterns round ships.[1]

Brunel's views were constantly changing, not just for the sake of change but because he gained experience as the ideas progressed. In a letter to Thomas Guppy, written in August 1843 after the hull of the *Great Britain* was complete, he gave his thoughts on the subject.

I have been thinking a great deal of your plans for iron-ship building, and have come to a conclusion which I believe agrees with your ideas; but I will state mine without reference to yours. At bottom and top I would give longitudinal strength and stiffness, gaining the latter from the former so that all the metal used should add to the longitudinal tie, while in the neutral axis and along the sides, and to resist swells from seas, I would have vertical strength by ribs and shelf pieces thus: [he included a drawing with his letter] the black lines being sections of longitudinal pieces, the dotted lines vertical and transverse diagonal plates, throwing the metal as much as possible into the outside bottom plates, and getting the strength inside by form, that is, depth of beams, etc., the former being liable to injury from blows, etc., the latter being protected.[2]

Brunel had gained much experience from the construction of the *Great Britain* and was keen to ensure

Great Britain as originally rigged, from a contemporary print. (By courtesy of Denis Griffiths)

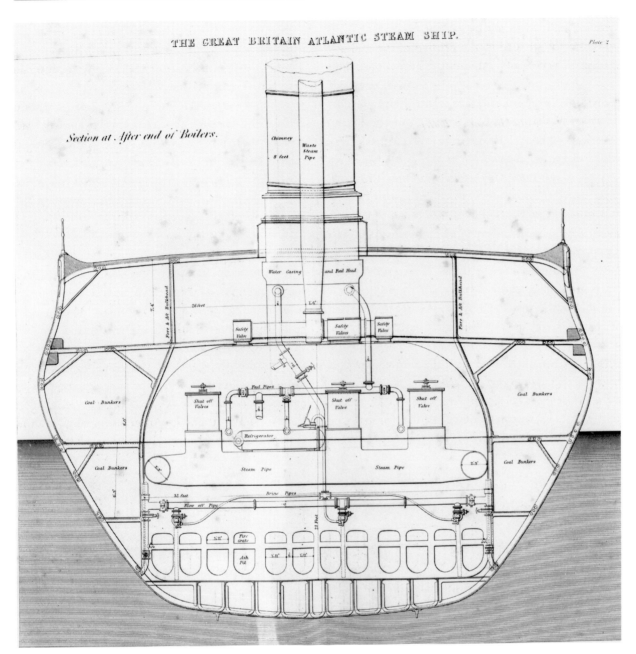

THE GREAT BRITAIN ATLANTIC STEAM SHIP.

Section at After end of Boilers.

Great Britain: 'Section at After end of Boilers.' (National Maritime Museum neg A8935)

that the strength of any future iron ship came not from the amount of metal put into the structure but from the way in which it was disposed; this was good structural engineering.

Great Britain was rigged as a six-masted schooner with the second mast also carrying square sails, the total sail area being 16,000 square feet.[3] Like the *Great Western* studding sails could also be carried. The four after masts were stepped onto the deck using hinges, as they could not be carried down to the bottom of the hull due to the propeller shafting. Claxton, in his description of the ship published in 1845, stated that they were hinged in order that they could be lowered '…when, in the captain's judgement, contrary gales shall appear to have set in'.

This could never have happened as the hinges only allowed a movement of about 40° from the vertical. The rigging of the ship allowed it to be worked with just 20 seamen on a watch, and only the square mainsail required this full complement to furl it.

Wire rigging was employed but no explanation was given as to why this was preferred over conventional hemp rigging. It may have been because it offered less surface resistance to wind when sails were not set and was certainly lighter for the same strength but Ewan Corlett believes that the answer lies in the combination of inelastic wire ropes and hinged masts. The rigid iron hull allowed for a setting of the mast rakes which would remain true almost indefinitely, hemp ropes were elastic and wooden hulls distorted in a seaway. The after masts could not be stepped to the bottom of the hull and the use of hinges offered a solution; the masts, once set to the required rake with the wire ropes, would remain in the set position. This indicated the triumph of Brunel's engineering reasoning over traditional seaman's practice. However, at the first refit the hinges were removed from the after masts, which were stepped through the decks, and hemp replaced wire.

Four iron lifeboats, 30 feet long by 8 feet broad and 5 feet deep, were fitted and in place when *Great Britain* left Bristol, two further boats being fitted in London before the ship entered service. All of these boats were carried on davits, three on each side of the ship, aft of the funnel. There was a wooden boat, similar in size to the iron boats, located in an inverted position on skids forward of the main mast. The iron boats, which could well have been the first iron lifeboats carried by any merchant ship, were constructed following a patent taken out by Guppy (No 9779, 1843). This patent describes the construction of iron boats and iron buoyancy tanks.

MACHINERY

The triangular form of engine fitted in *Great Britain* was based upon a patent taken out by Sir Marc Isambard Brunel, there being four cylinders, two on each side of the ship, driving an overhead crankshaft. Cylinders were inclined at 33° to the vertical and, as with most engines of the period, they operated at slow speed, 18 rpm, and some form of speed increase was needed as the propeller was to rotate at 53 rpm. Brunel eventually selected a chain arrangement, a large diameter chain wheel being fitted to the crankshaft, between fore and aft pairs of cylinders, with a small driven wheel on the screw shaft. Four chains were employed in order to transmit the high power, some 1800ihp, which could be developed by the cylinders. Cylinders were of 88 inches bore and the piston stroke 72 inches; a smaller bore of 80 inches was initially proposed but Brunel increased this in order to ensure that sufficient power could still be generated when working the steam expansively. Pistons employed split cast-iron piston rings and this appears to have been an early form of the piston

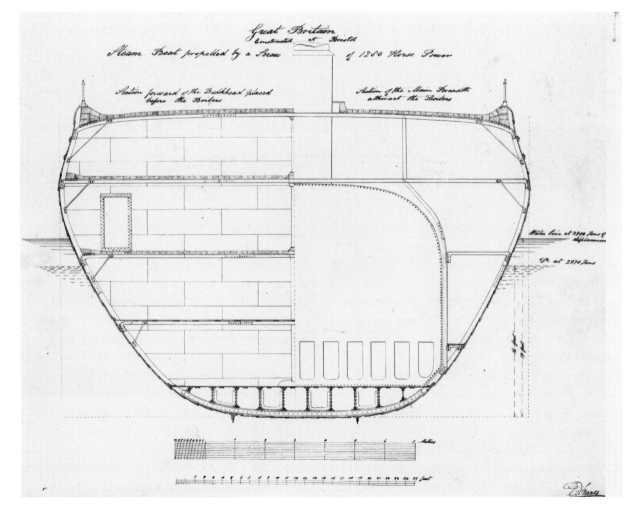

Great Britain: *'Section forward of the Bulkhead placed before the Boilers'* (left), and *'Section of the Main Breadth athwart the Boilers'* (right) (National Maritime Museum neg A8935L)

Great Britain *riding in a gale, 1846* (National Maritime Museum neg B2840)

sealing arrangement subsequently patented by John Ramsbottom.

Cylinder valves were operated by linkages actuated by an eccentric driven from the crankshaft, these valves being of the piston type, obviously an adaptation of the piston valves originally devised by Humphrys which Brunel asked Bryan Donkin to report on.[4] These 20-inch diameter piston valves were worked by a loose eccentric driven from the crankshaft. A butterfly valve, located in the steam line, regulated the steam supply to the cylinders and between that valve and the individual cylinder steam chests, in which the piston valves worked, was the

expansion valve. This was a slide valve which acted against ports cut in the steam chest face; by changing the stroke of the expansion valve the degree of expansion could be varied, maximum expansion being with steam cut-off after 12 inches of the 72-inch stroke, or a 6:1 expansion.

Wrought-iron jet condensers, 12 feet long by 8 feet wide and 5 feet deep, one for the forward pair of cylinders and one for the after pair, were located in the space between the cylinders. The air pumps were driven by cranks from the crankshaft, the axis of the 45.5-inch diameter air pump cylinders being at a slight angle to the vertical. A linkage arrange-

ment ensured that air pump piston rods operated along the axis of the cylinders, this linkage system also having drive connections for boiler feed and bilge pumps via rocking levers.

Although the engines were novel the boilers were not, being of the flue type and essentially out-of-date. It is difficult to imagine why such an old boiler concept was employed when the ship itself was pushing forward the boundaries of marine technology. Maximum boiler pressure was only about 5 psi (some publications quote 12 psi and even 22 psi but these would have been too high for a flue-type boiler of the period). In view of the gravity-feed water supply system employed, a pressure of 5 psi would be reasonable. Feed water was pumped to a casing which surrounded the funnel base and the water was heated in this casing before flowing, by means of gravity, into the boiler. With the top of this feed heater only some 18 feet above the boiler the head of water would only have generated a pressure of about 8 psi and so the boiler pressure must have been lower than this.

The boiler extended across the width of the boiler room; there were two stokeholds, one facing forward and one aft. The single boiler unit, 34 feet long, 31 feet wide and 21 feet 8 inches high, was effectively three boilers in one casing, longitudinal bulkheads separating the three sections. Each of the boilers had eight furnaces, four at each end of the boiler and the combustion gases flowed through a system of rectangular flues before passing to the single funnel uptake. Coal bunkers were provided at each side of the engine room, boilers and stokeholds.

OPERATIONS

After leaving Bristol the *Great Britain* sailed for London where she arrived on 26 January 1845. She then stayed for an amazing 5-month period being opened to the public at certain times and at others being subjected to visits by notable people, including royalty. Why the company, in such dire financial circumstances, allowed its most valuable asset to become a location for social activity rather than earn money at sea is difficult to imagine. Certainly there was publicity to be gained from showing the ship to businessmen and others with money in the capital city but not for 5 months. An Atlantic voyage at that time of year would have been difficult but would certainly have been reasonable by the end of March.

It would appear that some of the directors were more interested in the social status gained from the London stay than the commercial rewards of sailing the ship.

On 12 June *Great Britain* left for Liverpool, calling at Plymouth and Dublin on the way. Upon arrival in Liverpool she was put into dry-dock for inspection and cleaning of the hull but was also thrown open to the public. Departure for New York did not take place until 26 July, only 45 passengers having booked for the voyage. At New York, reached after a passage lasting nearly 15 days, the partying continued, with the ship once more being open to the public. Following a stay of 19 days, during which some 21,000 people visited the ship, she headed back to Liverpool with 53 passengers on board. The boilers gave trouble and difficulty was experienced in maintaining steam whilst the main topmast snapped about half-way down during a sudden squall. On 27 September, after a stay of 12 days, she left Liverpool again for New York. Faulty navigation resulted in the *Great Britain* touching a shoal off Nantucket with the consequent need for dry-docking at New York. Extensive propeller damage was discovered and remedial action taken before she sailed back to Liverpool on 28 October. Within days the propeller failed entirely and the ship had to complete the passage under sail alone. Thus ended the first, and very brief, Atlantic season.

Following a refit *Great Britain* commenced her second season on 9 May 1846 but a few days out the guard on the after air pump fractured and the engines had to be stopped; for 6 days *Great Britain* became a sailing ship. Following engine repairs at New York the ship made a return passage in 13.5 days and all seemed to be, at last, going well. On her next crossing faulty navigation again resulted in he touching ground, this time on the Cape Broil Reef off Newfoundland. Returning from New York she was dry-docked to check for any damage and commenced the next voyage on 22 September. The following day she was aground in Dundrum Bay and her career as a full-time Atlantic liner was over.

Although *Great Britain* seems to have been dogged by misfortune much of it appears to have been self-inflicted. The extensive partying at the expense of commercial reward did not do the company's coffers any good whatsoever and to save money its ships were grossly under-insured.

The First Class dining saloon in the long deckhouse built during the post-Dundrum refit. (National Maritime Museum PU6723)

BELOW LEFT *The refitted ship dropping the pilot, Liverpool Bar, 1852; from an original by Samuel Walters.* (National Maritime Museum neg 4552)

BELOW *The appearance of the ship after 1857, with a single funnel and a full ship rig.* (National Maritime Museum neg 4549)

Hosken had a habit of finding shallow water and his navigation left much to be desired.

Having been released from Dundrum Bay the *Great Britain* was towed to Liverpool and eventually sold, at a knock-down price, to Gibbs, Bright and Company. Fitted with new, and more economic, machinery she was converted for the Australia trade, the engines being auxiliary to her sailing capabilities. Apart from a period as a troopship during the Crimean War, *Great Britain* remained on the Australian run from 1852 until the beginning of 1876, a testament to the quality of her build. Following a long lay-up at Birkenhead she was converted to sail and after two successful voyages to San Francisco she was beached at the Falkland Islands during her third. There she stayed acting as a storage hulk and then a derelict until being brought back to Bristol in 1970 and a restoration berth in the dock in which she was built.

The National Maritime Museum's modern model of Great Eastern. (National Maritime Museum neg C5138)

10 The Steamship *Great Eastern*

Following the release of the *Great Britain* from Dundrum Bay Brunel devoted his time to other engineering problems but he never completely lost touch with, or interest in, maritime matters and in 1851 he once more associated himself with the steamship. The Australian Mail Company solicited his opinion on the best size and class of ship to operate a mail service from Britain to Australia. After some consideration he advised the building of iron ships of 5000 or 6000 tons capacity, the size allowing them to make the passage with only one stop, at the Cape of Good Hope, for coal.[1] This idea upset a number of directors and the plans were scaled-down, but Brunel did become Consulting Engineer to the company. Two smaller iron steamships, *Victoria* and *Adelaide*, were ordered and built by John Scott Russell, the design work being done by Brunel. These screw-propelled ships of about 3000 tons burthen were framed on the transverse system, probably in order to obtain classification with Lloyd's Register of Shipping,[2] although Brunel was very much in favour of longitudinal framing for iron ships.

Whilst working on these ships Brunel must have given consideration to the problems associated with steamship operations over long distances, particularly to places where local bunker supplies were difficult to procure. The major problem with oceanic steamship operation was one of coal; invariably supplies had to be sent overseas on sailing colliers and such an operation was expensive. For a ship to carry sufficient coal for a return journey to Australia without the need to bunker anywhere, it would have to be very large indeed. Scale did not worry Brunel: it was just another engineering challenge which could be resolved by the application of sound reasoning, and plenty of money. As with all of his other projects he prepared well and collected much data relating to trade between Britain and eastern countries, particularly India and Australia. Using this information he formulated his proposal for the construction of large steamers to operate a service between Britain and these regions.

> In February and March 1852 I matured my ideas of the large ship with nearly all my present details, and in March I made my first sketch of one with paddles and screw. The size I then proposed was 600 ft by 70 ft, and in June and July I determined on the mode of construction now adopted of cellular bottom; intending to make the outer skin of wood for the sake of coppering.[3]

The ideas were there before any company had been formed and before there was any apparent need for the ships. Making the outer skin of wood, with copper sheathing to prevent attack by *Teredo Navalis* and other wood-boring worms, was a novel concept for an iron ship but was probably considered essential due to the ease with which an iron hull became fouled by marine growths. Such fouling had an adverse effect on the performance of iron steamers and on a long voyage in warm tropical waters heavy fouling could be expected with a consequent large reduction in speed. At that time anti-fouling coatings were not effective and copper suffered less than iron but copper could not be fitted directly to an iron hull due to the electrolytic effect.

Brunel discussed his ideas with Scott Russell, Christopher Claxton and a number of the directors of the Eastern Steam Navigation Company. That concern had been established in 1851 with the hope of securing mail contracts to India, Australia and China but in 1852 P&O had been awarded these contracts and the company no longer had a function. Brunel gave it one. In July 1852 a scheme was proposed for the construction of a large steamer which would carry all of its own coal for a complete round-trip to Australia or similar distant places and

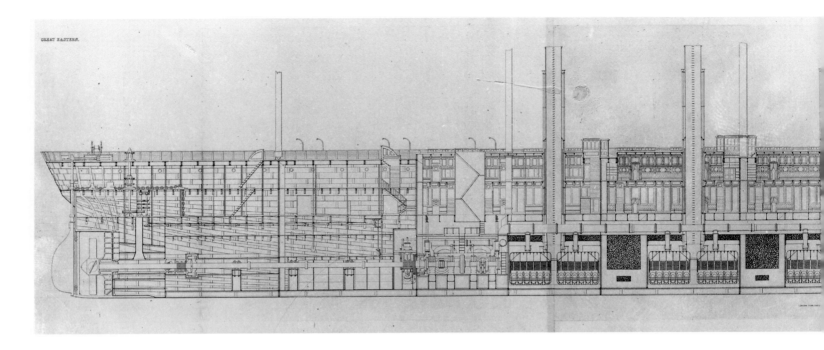

at the end of that year the directors agreed with the proposal. Brunel was given permission to undertake more detailed design work and to seek tenders for the construction of a ship and its machinery.

STRUCTURE

Sketches in Brunel's notebooks, held by Bristol University Library, show a number of different ideas for the arrangement of the ship and it is clear that the size and propulsion system was the result of careful consideration. The proposed ship would require more powerful machinery than had been installed in a ship to that time and there were engineering limitations. A single-screw propulsion system would require a massive propeller shaft, much larger than anything ever built, and the thrust block would cer-

tainly present difficulties. Twin-screw arrangements were a possibility but there was little experience of such systems and the provision of twin propellers would require a novel stern arrangement. Paddle wheels were less efficient than screw propellers but they did have advantages, particularly at times of shallow draft, such as might be experienced when operating in certain harbours. An arrangement of paddle and screw propulsion was sketched in March 1852[4] and this was the scheme finally adopted. Such a choice influenced the internal layout of the ship. It has been argued that Brunel selected a combined screw and paddle system because of the engineering difficulties involved in manufacturing the very large engine, propellers and propeller shaft which would be needed for a single-screw installation. Experience shows that Brunel thrived on engineering problems

Appropriately for the largest ship of the day, the plans were published in one of the largest books ever published, John Scott Russell's monumental Modern System of Naval Architecture. *(National Maritime Museum neg SRU95)*

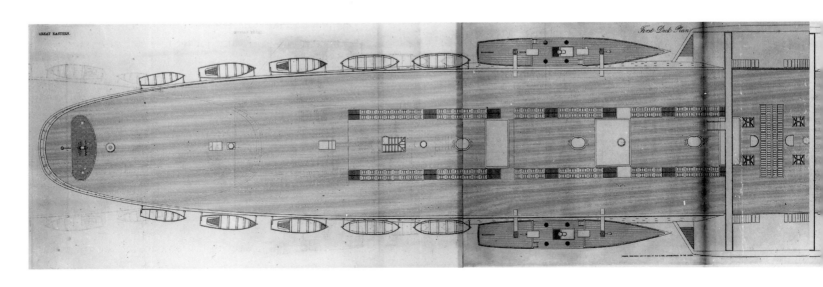

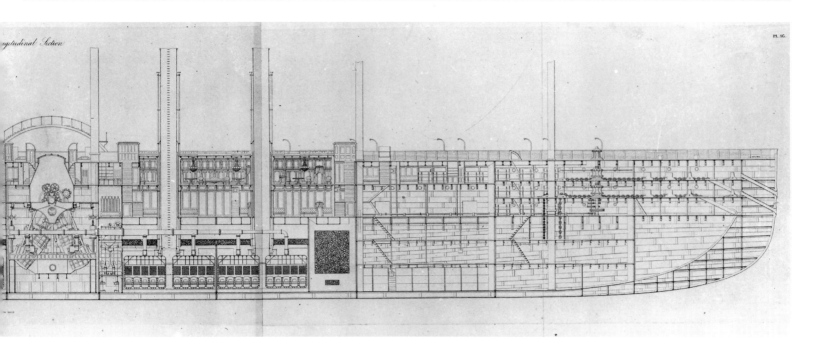

Longitudinal Section   PL. 95.

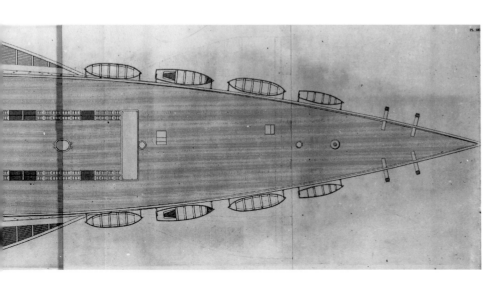

PL. 96.

and he did not disregard an idea because it had not been done before. The choice of a combined system was more for operational reasons than for any engineering concerns.

Brunel was responsible for the design of the ship, for preparing the contracts and for detailing the specifications; his powers were considerable indeed. The contract for constructing the hull was let to John Scott Russell and he agreed to very strict terms, financially and in many other respects. The contract, signed in December 1853,

The upper deck draught from Modern System of Naval Architecture. (National Maritime Museum neg SRU96)

Provided for the construction, launch, trial and delivery of an iron ship of the general dimensions 680ft between perpendiculars, 83ft beam and 58ft deep according to the drawings annexed signed by the Engineer, I. K. Brunel.

... No cast iron to be used anywhere except for slide valves and cocks without special permission of the Engineer. The ship to be built in a dock ... All calculations, drawings, models and templates which the contractor may prepare shall from time to time be submitted to the Engineer for his revision, alteration or approval. The Engineer to have entire control over the proceedings and the workmanship.

Russell's price for the hull was £275,200, exceptionally low as Brunel would have realised considering the cost of constructing the *Great Britain*; Russell even offered to reduce the price to £258,000 if he was awarded the contract for the second ship (it was originally intended to construct two vessels).[5]

Russell had a shipyard at Millwall on the Thames but it had no building dock and there was no dock large enough in which such a ship could be built. Quickly it became obvious that construction of a dock would be prohibitively expensive and a decision was taken to build the ship above high-water level and launch her into the water. That form of construction also presented problems due to the height of the hull and the fact that plates and frames would have to be handled with the primitive lifting gear which then existed. The angle of the slipway for a conventional lengthwise launch would have resulted in the highest part of the hull (the forecastle) being some 100 feet above ground level causing major difficulties in the absence of suitable cranes; the hull would also have been subjected to high

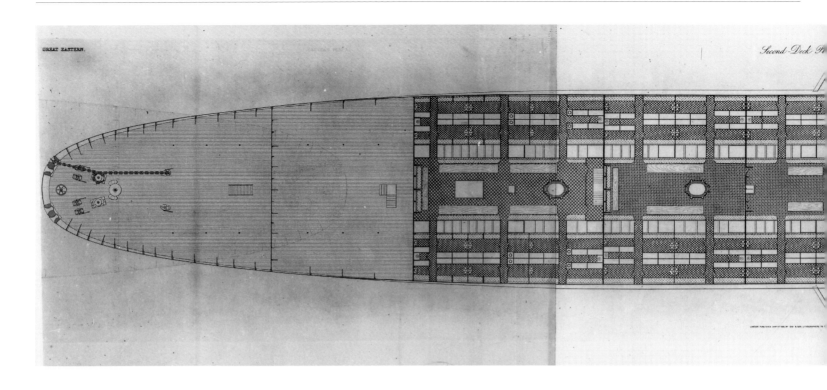

strains during launch when the stern was afloat but the bow was still supported by its cradle on the slipway. A sideways launch was the only possibility. The area in which the ship was to be built and launched had to be strengthened by timber piles driven into the ground. Some 1500 piles, 24 feet long, were driven into the solid ground below the surface and these were bound together by longitudinal and transverse timbers before a thick bed of concrete was poured between them. Iron rails were laid on the launching ways which were constructed in the same manner.[6]

Brunel had his own ideas on iron ship construc-

tion, particularly with respect to large ships, and these had been evolving even since the building of the *Great Britain*. From that earlier experience he developed his idea of longitudinal framing and then combined this and transverse strengthening in his cellular concept. But Brunel was not alone in this and Scott Russell had been building iron ships since 1834 when he constructed the 70-foot vessel *Storm* using longitudinal framing. Brunel had built the *Great Britain* using a clinker system for arranging the plates but this resulted in gaps between the overlapping plate and the frame and tapered strips of iron had be used to fill the gaps. Russell had the idea of

The second deck draught from Modern System of Naval Architecture. (National Maritime Museum neg SRU97)

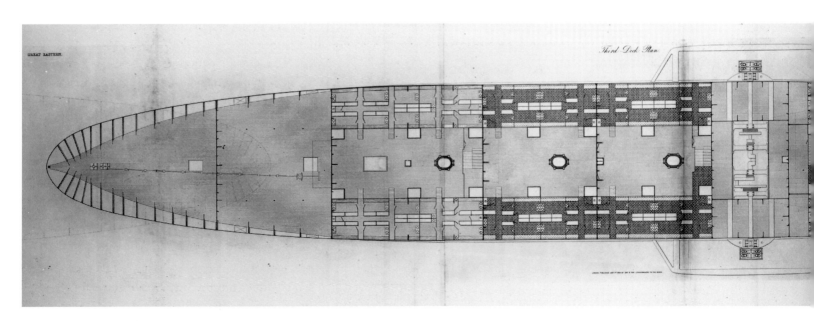

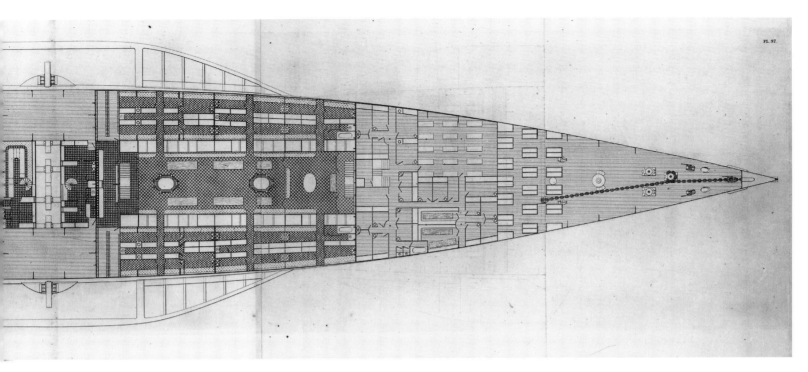

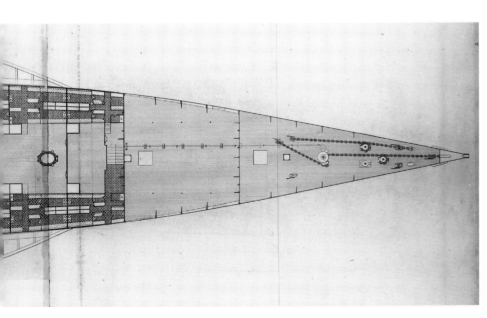

The third deck draught from Modern System of Naval Architecture. (National Maritime Museum neg SRU98)

arranging plates in an alternate manner, sometimes called 'in and out', where alternate plates were riveted directly to the frames and the plates connected to these were raised above the frame; the gap between these plates and the frames were filled with parallel strips of iron.[7] Brunel approved of the 'in and out' system of plating but was not happy with the use of the filler strips.

In a memorandum written in February 1854 after checking some of Russell's detailed drawings he wrote:

> It is evident that large weights may most easily be wasted or saved by a careless or close consideration of the best application of iron in every single detail. I found, for instance, an unnecessary introduction of a filling piece or strip, such as is frequently used in shipbuilding to avoid bending to angle irons; made a slight alteration in the disposition of the plates that rendered this unnecessary; found that we thus saved 40 tons weight of iron, or say £1200 of money in first cost, and 40 tons of cargo freight – at least £3000 a year.[8]

This was part of the genius of Brunel: he could mastermind a ship larger and more powerful than any that had been built but at the same time take care to look at the detail and consider the savings over the entire ship. He went on to state:

> The principle of construction of the ship is in fact entirely new, if merely from the rule which I have laid down, and shall rigidly preserve, that no materials shall be employed at any part except at the place, and in the direction, and in the proportion, in which it is required, and can be usefully employed for the strength of the ship, and none merely for the purpose of facilitating the framing and first construction.

As far as Brunel was concerned every piece of iron which went into the ship had to serve the purpose of adding to the strength and that included the

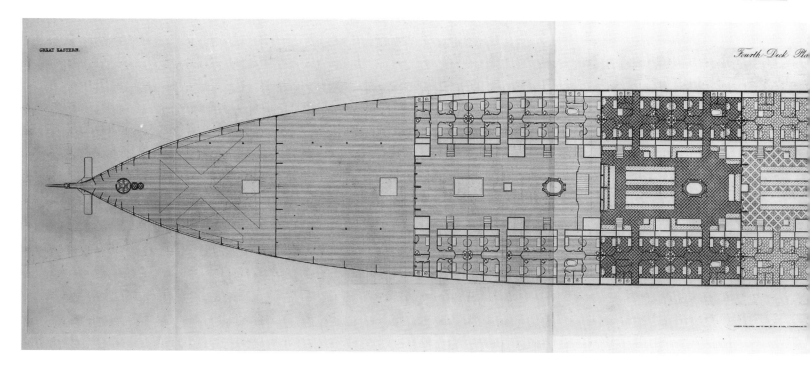

GREAT EASTERN.

Fourth-Deck Pla

The fourth deck draught from
Modern System of Naval
Architecture. (National
Maritime Museum neg
SRU99)

framing; frames were not used simply as places to which the side plating was attached, they were actual strength members of the hull structure.

> In the present construction of iron ships. . . . Nearly 20 per cent of the total weight is expended in angle irons or frames which may be useful or convenient in the mere putting together of the whole as a great box, but is almost useless, or very much misapplied, in affecting the strength of the structure of the ship. All this misconstruction I forbid, and the consequence is that every part has to be considered and designed as if an iron ship had never before been built; indeed I believe we should get on much quicker if we had no previous habits and prejudices on the subject.[9]

Only the best design practices were to be allowed and those practices were dictated by Brunel. Within the statement is a rebuke to Russell for employing the earlier ideas he had used for smaller ships; this new venture broke all existing bounds of scale and new rules had to be devised. There is also an indication of the rivalry between the two men with regards to who should be considered the father of the ship, and this rivalry simmered and occasionally erupted throughout the years of construction. Brunel considered himself as both the originator of the project and designer of the ship and took offence when he felt that he was not being given due cred-

it. In November 1854 a long article about the ship appeared in one of the London newspapers and it only mentioned Brunel once: 'Mr Brunel, the Engineer of the Eastern Steam Navigation Company, approved of the project, and Mr Scott Russell undertook to carry out the design.' Brunel wrote to the secretary of the company reiterating his personal stake in the project and expressing his displeasure:

> It surely cannot be necessary to remind the Directors that the very unusual stake which as a professional man I have been willing, perhaps imprudently, to risk on the success of this project – I mean stake of professional character, not merely pecuniary risk.
>
> I … am much annoyed by it. I have always made it a rule … To have nothing to do with newspaper articles. This article … bears rather evidently a stamp of authority and it may acquire the character of being an authorised statement; and, as such, I am individually much annoyed by a great deal that is in it, and by the omission of much that might with propriety have been introduced.
>
> And lastly, I cannot allow it to be stated, apparently on authority, while I have the whole heavy responsibility of its success resting on my shoulders, that I am a mere passive approver of the project of another, which in fact originated solely with me, and has been

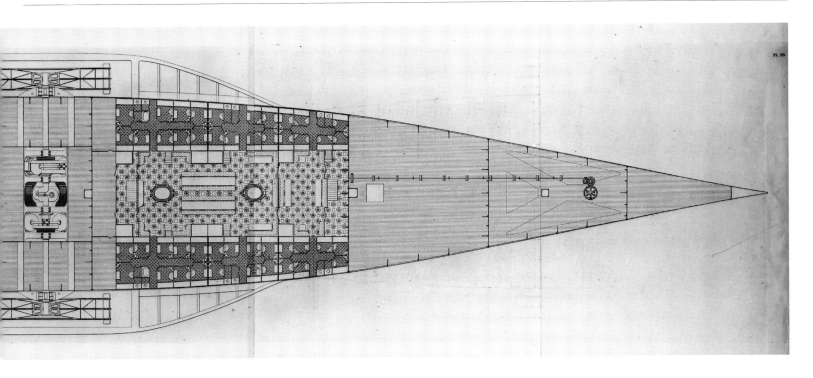

worked out by me at great cost of labour and thought devoted to it now for not less than three years.[10]

A little later, following a visit by Prince Albert to Millwall, Brunel received a letter from Russell in which he stated that he told the Prince that Brunel was the 'Father' of the ship. The letter was obsequious to a fault and Russell appears to have been trying to curry favour with Brunel. Rolt, who quoted the letter, left it to the reader to draw any conclusion[11] but it would seem that Russell had a hand in the newspaper article. In a letter to *The Times* in April 1857, Russell appeared to be glowing in his praise and confirmed his earlier expressed opinion that Brunel originated the concept of the ship and was responsible for the design. At the time the Eastern Steam Navigation Company was in serious financial trouble and Russell may well have been trying to distance himself from responsibility for any failure. 'My share of the merit and responsibility is that of builder of the ship for the Eastern Steam Navigation Company. I designed her lines and constructed the iron hull of the ship and am responsible for her merits or defects as a piece of naval architecture.'[12] He was clearly accepting no blame for the financial situation, although he had grossly underestimated the construction cost, nor did he want people to believe that he had anything to do with the launching due later that year.

In explaining Brunel's part in the project Russell did give an insight into the principle upon which construction was based. 'It is to the company's engineer, Mr I K Brunel, that the original conception is due … It was his idea also to introduce a cellular construction like that at the top and bottom of the Britannia Bridge into the construction of the great ship.' Unwilling to give too much praise, he then claimed to be the originator of the construction methods used: 'Her lines and her structure in other respects are identical with those of my other ships, which are constructed like this on a principle of my own, which I have systematically carried out during the last twenty years, and which is commonly called the "wave" principle. In other respects, also her materials are put together in the manner usual in my other ships.' Russell's wave-line principle was used to determine the ideal shape of the hull in order to reduce the energy loss in making waves. It was one of the first attempts to analyse hull form and its influence upon ship resistance, but it was erroneous and not until the work of William Froude was published some years later was ship resistance and wave-making put on a true scientific basis.

Russell certainly had been building iron ships for some time but there was a clear disagreement between the two men as to who was responsible for the practical shipbuilding design work. Brunel insisted that all previous ideas be ignored whilst Russell considered that the ship was built using his long-established methods. As the Company's Engineer Brunel had overall responsibility for the ship and he was authorised to look at, and amend where he though necessary, all drawings before any work was carried out. This means that any work undertaken on the ship had to be authorised by him. Any plans or ideas had to meet with his approval and if they did not he would have them changed, as he did with respect to the use of filler pieces between the plates and frames.

In a seaway the hull of a ship bends when it is supported by waves. If two waves support the ends of the hull the centre section tends to fall and this is known as 'sagging', whilst if the supporting wave is at the middle of the ship the bow and stern sections then fall and this is called 'hogging'. Such bending has to be resisted and a strong hull is required. Should the vessel ground there are different conditions but the hull is still subject to strain.

The fact is that Brunel did a considerable amount of preliminary work with respect to the design and construction of the ship and he was particularly concerned about the strength of the ship; his notebooks are littered with drawings and calculations reflecting the most severe conditions the ship would be likely to encounter. Treating the ship as a beam he investigated the loading if the vessel grounded on two points 400 feet apart, a highly unlikely condition. From the calculations he formed the conclusion that the bottom of the ship would need to be made from iron plate 90 feet wide and 4 or 5 inches thick if the stress was to be kept within limits. This may have been an extreme case and the use of iron plate 4 inches thick was, obviously, not practical but consideration had to be given to such conditions. From such analysis Brunel may have evolved the alternative idea of employing a cellular structure at the bottom and top of the hull in order to form a rigid box arrangement similar to that used for the Britannia Bridge, completed in 1850, with which he was familiar. The hull of the ship, any ship as far as Brunel was concerned, could be treated as a beam which was supported by waves when in the water or by a series of point supports when grounded or on a gridiron. The box structure of the Britannia Bridge tubes were no different except that they were beams carrying internal load and supported at their ends. Brunel did not originate the concept of a cellular structure or of a box-type girder but he did apply them to iron ships. As William Fairbairn said in 1860, 'The *Great Eastern*, which is probably the strongest vessel in proportion to her size ever built, is con-

structed on this principle [box section with cellular upper and lower chords], and the designer, the late Mr Brunel, was too sagacious an engineer to lose sight of the cellular system, developed first in the Britannia Bridge, to neglect its application to the deck as well as the hull of the monster.'[13]

The work in Brunel's note- and calculation books[14] indicates how rigorous he was in ensuring that the ship was designed correctly to meet all reasonable conditions. It was obvious to Brunel that such a large ship could not be dry-docked because there were no facilities in existence or even planned and so she would have to be grounded on a gridiron in order to enable routine hull maintenance to undertaken. He informed the directors of the action he had taken to allow for this, 'We have flattened the floor and strengthened it considerably so as to allow of the vessel being safely grounded on a gridiron or even if partially waterborne on a beach.'[15]

This grounding requirement, and possibly the implications of operating the ship far away from good repair facilities, may have led him to consider the idea of the watertight double bottom. He was certainly aware of the consequences of flooding should the hull plating be punctured from his experiences with the *Great Britain* at Dundrum Bay. The cellular structure did not have to be watertight and making it so did present additional constructional problems, but Brunel certainly saw the advantages and the watertight double bottom extended from the keel of the ship to the normal loaded waterline. Inner and outer skin plating was 1 inch thick and the plates were spaced 2 feet 10 inches apart; the longitudinal frames in the double bottom were placed 6 feet apart. The upper cellular structure was constructed in a similar way and additional longitudinal strength was given to the ship by two longitudinal bulkheads, 350 feet long and 36 feet deep, located in the middle part of the ship and placed each side of the engine and boiler rooms.

In addition to the need for the hull to withstand the strains resulting from hogging and sagging, it was also necessary for the hull to resist strains due to the action of waves which cause the ship to roll. As a ship rolls there is a tendency for the hull to distort transversely and move from a rectangular shape to that of a parallelogram; a similar situation can be imagined if the outer casing of a matchbox is collapsed. Brunel was well aware of this condition and arranged for the necessary transverse strength and rigidity to be applied to the hull. Russell produced the basic hull design and Brunel inspected it, making amendments as required. Transverse bulkhead provided rigidity and also divided the hull into several watertight compartments.

In February 1855 Brunel reported to the directors on the general hull design.

The whole of the vessel is divided transversely into ten separate perfectly watertight compartments by bulkheads carried up to the upper deck, and consequently far above the deepest water lines, even if the ship were waterlogged, so far as such a ship could be; and these are not nominal divisions, but complete substantial bulkheads, watertight and of strength sufficient to bear the pressure of the water, should a compartment be even filled with water; so that if the ship were supposed to be cut in two, the separate portions would float. Besides these principal bulkheads there is in each compartment a second intermediate bulkhead, forming a coal bunker, and carried up to the main-deck, which can, in an emergency, also be closed. There are no openings under the deep-water line through the principal bulkheads, except one continuous gallery or tunnel near the water line through which the steam pipes pass, and which will be so constructed as to remain closed, the opening being the exception, and the closing again being easy, and the height being such that, under the most improbable circumstances of damage to the ship, ample time would be afforded to close it leisurely, and to make it perfectly watertight.

Such was the interest in the construction of this mammoth vessel that a whole series of photographs were taken to chronicle progress. This relatively early view shows the transverse bulkheads.
(By courtesy of Denis Griffiths)

Besides the main transverse bulkheads, at about 60ft intervals, there are two longitudinal bulkheads of iron running fore and aft, at about 40ft in width, adding greatly to the strength of the whole.

The transverse bulkheads being perfect, there being only one door – and that of iron – in each, at one of the upper decks, all currents of air or means of communicating fire may be completely cut off; and with . . . the most ample means of supplying water, I believe that all possibility of danger from fire may be completely prevented.[16]

Not only had Brunel considered the strength requirements of the hull to resist hogging, sagging and racking, as well as the watertight subdivision to safeguard against the risk of sinking, but he was also well aware of the need to contain fire should it break out. This is one of the earliest applications of fire doors as well as watertight doors in bulkheads.

The eminent naval architect Sir Westcott Abel was impressed by the design: 'It must be agreed that Brunel's handling of the design of the *Great Eastern* before 1860 stands out as a milestone in the progress of building ships of iron and later steel.'[17]

MACHINERY

From the early days of the project Brunel devoted much time to the question of propelling the great ship and after giving consideration to a variety of possibilities came to the conclusion that a combined screw and paddle arrangement would best suit the ship. 'In February and March 1852 I matured my ideas of the large ship with nearly all my present details, and in March I made my first sketch of one with paddles and screw.'[18] In July 1852 Brunel

The huge hull towering over the slipway on the Isle of Dogs river front. (By courtesy of Denis Griffiths)

estimated that some 2500 nominal horsepower would be needed for the ship[19] (this would equate to about 6000 actual indicated horsepower).

That the screw propeller was superior to the paddle wheel Brunel had no doubt but it was not a simple matter of choosing one over the other; this ship was the largest yet envisaged and it was intended to operate in shallow river estuaries, particularly the Hoogly in India, as well as in deep oceans. Although the deep-water draught of the ship was to be about 30 feet, a maximum draught for entering the Hoogly would be about 23 feet. A single screw to transmit the intended power would have had to be about 28 feet in diameter and so it would not be completely immersed in the river resulting in poor manoeuvrability.

A twin-screw arrangement could have been chosen but there was little or no experience of constructing and operating twin-screw steamers at that time, and the installation of the machinery would have presented problems for hull construction. The eventual choice of a combined system seems reasonable in the light of the information available to Brunel at that time although control of two entirely separate propulsion systems was likely to present problems. It has to be realised that Brunel was designing a ship to operate to India and Australia and he had to consider the restrictions applicable to these areas and not the conditions which could be found crossing the Atlantic.

Initially Brunel considered that both screw and

The horizontal screw engine built for Great Eastern *by James Watt & Co.* (Drawing by Denis Griffiths)

paddles should transmit the same power and he was particularly keen that all measures be taken to ensure operational efficiency. There had to be an excess of boiler power – he was obviously learning from experiences with the *Great Western* and *Great Britain* – and boiler pressure should not be less than 20psi, although he had a preference for 25psi. Expansive working should apply to the engines permanently and all cylinders, valve chests and steam pipes should be steam-jacketed. Jacketing was a recent introduction to marine engine practice and was employed to minimise the condensation of steam on entry to the cylinder with the consequent reduction in power developed. The arrangement posed problems for manufacture and was not widely used as the improvement in performance was marginal at best; for the *Great Eastern* jacket steam was to come from an auxiliary boiler operating at 10psi more than the main boilers. Although jacketing formed part of the contracts for the screw and paddle engines, both engine builders objected to it and it was never fitted to the engines. Brunel regretted this but it is highly unlikely that it would have improved performance. However, another idea would have had a greater impact had it been adopted during building. He proposed making experiments to whether it would be worth heating the steam immediately before it entered the cylinders, a form of superheating or steam drying which would have been less expensive and have a greater effect on performance than steam jacketing.

Throughout the period he was considering the power plant Brunel was in constant communication with his friend Joshua Field and the pair did disagree on a number of points. Field considered that the steam pressure should not exceed 15psi on the grounds that mechanical problems increased with pressure but the gains did not increase at the same rate. Brunel agreed – 'There seems much truth in this' – but retained an open mind as to what the final steam pressure would be as there was, at that point, still a great deal to be done as the final power requirements had not then been decided. Field was very much against steam jacketing. By 17 July 1852 Brunel had decided that the screw engines should deliver 60 per cent of the required power and the paddle engines 40 per cent.[20]

In a memorandum dated 28 April 1853 Brunel wrote, 'We are now seeking tenders for the engines and ship of the following dimensions: Length 680 feet; beam 83 feet; mean draught about 25 feet; screw engine, indicated horsepower 4000; nominal horsepower 1600; paddle, indicated horsepower 2600; nominal horsepower 1000; to work with steam 15lbs to 25lbs; speed of screw 45 to 55 revolutions; paddle 10 to 12.'[21] Three proposals were submitted for the machinery: 'Mr Blake, of the firm Watt & Co, and Mr J S Russell and Mr Humphrys, have as I had before reported, devoted much attention to the subject: from these gentlemen I have received distinct well-considered designs of the screw and paddle-engines.'[22] It is evident that Brunel worked closely with these parties whilst they were devising their systems in order to ensure that nothing would be incorporated to which he might object. 'I have been in frequent communication with these gentlemen, and have seen their plans while in progress, and have made my suggestions upon them, and assisted more or less in maturing them, and at all events in preventing the adoption of any principle or arrangement that I should afterwards object to.' This was the duty of a Consulting Engineer and Brunel took his obligations seriously.

He considered the screw engine to be the important part of the propulsion system:

> The principal part of the propelling power of the ship will be thrown upon the screw; and upon these engines therefore will mainly depend the performance of the ship, and particularly upon their constant never-failing working, probably for thirty or forty days and nights, must depend the certainty of the ship's performance … The extreme simplicity of Mr Blake's engine [Watt & Co] leads me to prefer it.
>
> As regards the paddle engine, I unhesitatingly give preference to that proposed by Mr Russell.[23]

The screw engine was of the horizontal direct-acting type and consisted of four cylinders arranged in two opposing pairs driving a two-crank crankshaft, the cranks being at right angles to each other. The nominal power was as requested in the tender but the engine could develop 4890 indicated horsepower from cylinders of 84 inches bore and 48 inches stroke when working at 38.8rpm; at 50rpm and without expansive working the engine could develop 6000 indicated horsepower. Each piston had two

The oscillating paddle engine built by John Scott Russell for the Great Eastern. *(By courtesy of Denis Griffiths)*

rods attached to a crosshead which moved in guides. The starboard cylinders each had a single connecting rod which attached to the respective crosshead and crank-pin but the port cylinders had two connecting rods and these were located on the crank-pin each side of the associated starboard engine connecting rod. Steam for the screw engines, at a pressure of 25psi, came from six double-ended, tubular boilers of the box or rectangular type. Each boiler was 18.5 feet long, 17.5 feet wide and 14 feet deep with six furnaces at each end; there were two boilers in each boiler room and one funnel per boiler room. Engines were arranged for expansive working and the condensers were of the jet type.[24]

The four-cylinder oscillating paddle engine was of 1000 nominal horsepower. It weighed 836 tons, the cylinders being 74 inches in diameter and the piston stroke 14 feet. Each opposing fore and aft pair of cylinders connected to the same crank, cranks being positioned at right angles to each other. Air pumps were driven by means of cranks on the intermediate section of the crankshaft. Cylinders were arranged for expansive working of steam and with a pressure of 15psi, at one-third stroke steam cut-off, could develop 3000 horsepower when operating at 11rpm. With a pressure of 25psi and without expansive working of steam some 5000 indicated horsepower could be developed at 16rpm. Four double-ended boilers, of the same type as the screw engine boilers except with five furnaces at each end, supplied the steam, these being arranged in two boiler rooms forward of the paddle engines.[25]

Brunel monitored construction of both sets of engines but he appears to have played a significant part in the design of the screw machinery and consulted with Blake on many matters; this was, obviously, part of his duties as Consulting Engineer but he knew that the operational performance of the screw engine was critical to the success of the venture. The paddle machinery was, it would appear, ancillary and he left much of the design work to Russell; however, he checked drawings and inspected parts at various stages of manufacture. This is evident from a memorandum of 10 March 1854: 'Engaged all afternoon at Millwall . . . Settled and signed drawings of crank and piston rods.'[26]

This indicates more than just a passive role in the venture but one of active involvement as he had to approve of all engineering which went into the ship.

Brunel became almost obsessive with regards to the adequate sizing of bearings as they were critical to prolonged operation of the engines. A memorandum of 3 March 1854 mentions a meeting with Blake: 'Mr Blake called, and went fully into the general drawings which he brought. On the necessity of large surfaces he quite concurred with me.' A few days later he recorded, 'Blake here again. Found, as I had thought, a mistake of ten to one in his calculations of bearing surface.' The engine as originally devised by James Watt & Co had opposing horizontal cylinders connected by two piston rods and these rods attached to a single crosshead running in guides. From the crosshead was a single connecting rod which attached to the crankshaft. This scheme

Hoisting in the crank shaft of the paddle engine by derrick. From the Illustrated London News. *(By courtesy of Denis Griffiths)*

The frame of the gigantic paddle wheel can be seen far left as the ship nears readiness for launching. (By courtesy of Denis Griffiths)

was much simpler than giving each of the cylinders its own crosshead and crankshaft and Brunel originally approved of the plan, but he began to have doubts, particularly over the loading which would be imposed on the bearings. 'Have been thinking a great deal over Blake's arrangements and have come to the conclusion that double piston rods carried through to the opposite engine cannot, unless with a very low steam pressure, leave room for a properly proportioned crank. Wrote long letter to B. on the necessity of resorting to two distinct connecting rods.'[27] Brunel did have an influence on the engine design even though he was not the actual designer.

Even though he was engaged in a major shipbuilding work, and was involved with other projects, Brunel still had time to consider the detail and apply new and imaginative ideas. He was aware of the need for adequate governing of engine speed even before he learned of the incident aboard HMS *Agamemnon* on 9 November 1853 when serious damage resulted due to over-speeding of the engine after she lost her screw. 'August 7 – Memorandum for engines – Very sensitive governors to be applied to both engines to prevent running away.' After the *Agamemnon* incident he wrote, 'There is no reason why a sensitive governor should not act in less than one revolution of the crank, and act upon a tumbler which should shut off instantly the expansion valve.'[28]

An idea adopted from the *Great Britain* was for the use of feed water heaters located around the base of the funnels. Neither Russell not Field were happy with the idea, but Brunel insisted that they were fitted to the two forward funnels, from the paddle engine boilers. Each heater jacket, constructed from 0.5-inch iron plate, extended from the top of the boiler uptake to the main deck and formed a 6-inch annulus around the funnel uptake. Feed water was pumped into the heater and flowed upwards to an outlet near the top of the heater from whence it passed to the boiler; unlike that fitted in the *Great Britain*, these heaters employed force-feed of water to the boilers and not gravity-feed. A vent pipe was fitted at the top of the heater annulus and this extended upwards about 30 feet before venting into the stokehold. The vent pipe was fitted with a stopcock which could be closed in order to allow the heater annulus to be pressure tested but should have been open in normal service. Unfortunately, during the first passage from London the cock on the forward funnel heater was closed allowing pressure to build up as water turned to steam. Eventually an explosion occurred resulting in furnace blowback and the fatal injury of five stokers. The dying Brunel did not hear of the incident, which was the result of human error not his engineering failure.

THE LAUNCH

A view of the ship from the river by the artist J W Carmichael. (National Maritime Museum neg PW6224)

Without doubt Brunel's biggest technical failure with respect to the *Great Eastern* was the launch. The event has been covered in Brunel's biographies as well as all books concerned with the ship and can be looked upon as an event in itself instead of just an episode in the history of this ingenious engineer and his most remarkable ship. Initially he had advocated the use of a patent slip which could have been dismantled and moved to a terminus port to enable the ship to be slipped for overhaul. This was abandoned on the grounds of cost and a more conventional form of slip devised, this having an inclination of 1 in 12. Brunel would not consider a free launch due to the inherent dangers this posed to the hull and to the river; it had to be a controlled launch, one which he could control. The tops of the launching ways were covered with rows of iron rail and the lower faces of the cradles were faced with iron strips which

ran parallel to the axis of the ship. This he considered would reduce friction. The large cradles had a support area of some 19,200 square feet which produced a bearing pressure of about 0.6 tons per square foot, much less than that accepted for free launches at that time. There should have been no problem in keeping the ship moving and Brunel considered that the difficulty would be in regulating the speed of descent down the slipway.

In order to regulate the descent, two brakes were fitted, one to each cradle. Heavy chains were attached to the cradles and these were wound around 9-foot diameter drums, 120 feet long, the chain being paid out as required by the descent. Band brakes were fitted to each of the drums, thus

allowing the rate at which the chain was paid out to be controlled. A system of chains, pulleys and windlasses was arranged so that an initial pull could be exerted on the hull in order to get it moving. Technically the system was all that should have been required but nature, in the form of friction and gravity, decided otherwise.

The ship did move, but grudgingly, and it became obvious that things were not going according to plan. However, Brunel persisted: he had no alternative as the ship had to be moved from the building area due to possible litigation. After many attempts, during which movement could be measured in inches rather than feet he resorted to brute force and decided that the ship needed to be pushed down the

Efforts to side-launch the ship by conventional means failed, and it took three months of extreme exertion to get the ship into the water. The carnival atmosphere of this painting conveys relief as much as joy. (National Maritime Museum neg PU6762)

The extraordinary size of the ship is somewhat exaggerated by the small craft in the foreground, but at sea Great Eastern *must have been an imposing sight.* (National Maritime Museum neg X991)

incline. Hydraulic rams were the solution and Tangyes of Birmingham came to assist. Even then progress was slow and it was not until the end of January 1858, some three months after the launching process started, that the *Great Eastern* was afloat.

Brunel had certainly made mistakes in his assessment of the situation and to make matters worse the launch was conducted in the full glare of the public as the directors of the company had sold tickets in order to recoup some of the expenditure. The launch took much longer than it should have but it was a triumph of sorts as Brunel never gave up on the job. His engineering solution, with the aid of hydraulic force got his ship in the water.

Bibliography

Primary Sources and Contemporary Sources

Brunel Letter Books. Wills Memorial Library, University of Bristol.

Claxton, C, *The Logs of the First Voyage of the Steamship Great Western* (GWSS Co, Bristol 1838).
Log books of the ship together with copies of journals written on the first voyage.

—, *Description of the Steamship Great Britain* (GWSS Co, Bristol 1845).

—, *The Great Britain Released from Dundrum Bay* (GWSS Co, Bristol 1847).
Correspondence between Claxton, Brunel and the GWSS Co.

Fairbairn, Sir William, 'The Strength of Iron Ships', *Transactions of the Institute of Naval Architects (Trans INA)*, Vol 1 (1860).

GWSS Co. Directors' Reports. Brunel Collection, PRO, Kew. Reference; Rail 1149. (Copies at Bristol Reference Library).
Note. This collection also includes other documents related to the GWSS Co. and to the building of the *Great Eastern*.

Glances at Atlantic Steam Navigation, The Field Papers. The Science Museum Library.

Gray, Macfarlane, 'Steam Steering Apparatus fitted in the Great Eastern', *Trans INA*, Vol 10 (1869).

Guppy, T R, 'The *Great Britain* Iron Steamship', *Proceedings of the Institute of Civil Engineers* iv (1945).

Jordan, C, 'Some Historical Records & Reminiscences Relating to the British Navy & Mercantile Shipping', *Transactions of Lloyd's Register Staff Association*, Paper No 10 (1924-5).
The author commenced his apprenticeship with Messrs. J. Scott Russell & Co. in 1855 and was present during most of the building period of the *Great Eastern*

Lardner, Dionysius, 'Atlantic Steam Navigation', *Edinburgh Review*, Vol 65 (April 1837).

Report from the Select Committee on the Halifax and Boston Mails, Parliamentary Papers, August 1846

Russell, J Scott, 'The Wave Line Principle of Ship Construction (Parts 1-3)', *Trans INA*, Vols 1 & 2 (1860 & 1861)

Seppings, Sir Robert, 'On a New Principle of Constructing Ships in the Mercantile Navy', *Philosophical Transactions, The Royal Society* (March 1820).

Weale, J *The Great Britain Atlantic Steamer* (Weale 1847)
Very good drawings and description of the *Great Britain*.

Papers

Barr, G E, 'History & Development of Machinery for Paddle Steamers', *Transactions of the Institute of Engineers & Shipbuilders in Scotland (Trans IESS)* Vol 95 (1951-2).

Corlett, E C B, 'The Steamship *Great Britain*', *Trans RINA*, Vol 113 (1971).

Dyer, Henry, 'The First Century of the Marine Engine', *Trans INA*, Vol 30 (1889).

Elgar, F, 'Fast Ocean Steamships', *Trans INA*, Vol 35 (1894).

Farr, G, 'The *Great Western*', *The Mariner's Mirror*, Vol 24, No 2 (April 1938).

Forbes, D A, 'The Launch of the Great Eastern & the Aftermath', *Trans IESS*, Vol 136 (1992-3).

Fuller, R G, 'The *Great Eastern*', *Transactions of the Institute of Marine Engineers (Canadian Division)* (1961).

John, W, 'Atlantic Steamers', *Trans INA*, Vol 28 (1887).

Kidd, A, 'The *Great Britain*', *Trans IESS*, Vol 34 (1890-1).

Smith, E C, 'The Centenary of Atlantic Steam Navigation', *Transactions of the Newcomen Society*, Vol 17 (1937-8).

Books

Ball, A, and Wright, D, *S.S. Great Britain* (Newton Abbott 1981).

Beaver, Patrick, *The Big Ship* (London 1969).

Brunel, I, *The Life of Isambard Kingdom Brunel* (London 1870).
The biography of Brunel by his son.

Corlett, Ewan, *The Iron Ship* (Bradford on Avon 1975).
The standard work on this ship.

Emmerson, George S, *John Scott Russell* (London 1977).

—, *The Great Eastern* (Newton Abbot 1984)

Gardiner, Robert (ed), *Conway's History of the Ship: The Advent of Steam: The Merchant Steamship before 1900* (London 1993).
Good coverage of the steam powered ship with two chapters on the introduction of the screw propeller

Goold-Adams, Richard, *The Return of the Great Britain* (London 1976).

Griffiths, Denis, *Brunel's Great Western* (Wellingborough 1985).
Complete biography of the ship.

—, *Steam at Sea* (London 1997).

Pugsley, Sir Alfred (ed), *The Works of Isambard Kingdom Brunel* (London 1976).

Rolt, L T C, *Isambard Kingdom Brunel* (London 1957).

Rowland, K T, *The Great Britain* (Newton Abbott 1971).

Smith, E C, *A Short History of Naval & Marine Engineering* (Cambridge 1927).

Notes

Introduction

1 Gardiner, R (ed), *The Steam Warship, 1815-1905* (London 1992), pp16-17.
2 Hylton, A, *Charles Babbage; Pioneer of the Computer* (Princeton 1982).
3 Ibid, p147.
4 Ibid, p162.
5 Rolt, L T C, *Isambard Kingdom Brunel* (London 1957), p386.

Chapter 1

1 I Brunel, *Life of Isambard Kingdom Brunel* (Longman 1870), p233.
2 Ibid, Preface.
3 R A Buchanan, 'I K Brunel & Port of Bristol', *Transactions of the Newcomen Society*, 42 (1969), pp44-7
4 Brunel Letter Book No 2a. 20 February 1844. Bristol University Library. Brunel sent a cheque for £100 to the GWSS Co in payment for the last instalment of £5 due on each share indicating a holding of 20 shares of £100 each.
5 *Bristol Mirror*, 5 March 1836; G.W.S.S. Co. proposal document, PRO, Kew, piece No Rail/1149/60.
6 Eng-Capt E C Smith, 'The Centenary of Transatlantic Steam Navigation', *Transactions of the Newcomen Society*, 17 (1937-8), pp130-1.
7 Rolt, *Brunel*, pp31-2.
8 *Liverpool Albion*, 14 December 1835.
9 *The Times*, 27 August 1836.
10 Report of proceedings of the British Association on the Mechanical Arts. Meeting held in Bristol in 1836. Article VI (April 1837), pp118-46.
11 C Claxton, *Logs of the first voyage of the steamship Great Western*, GWSS Co, (Bristol 1838), p55.

Chapter 2

1 Directors Report GWSS Co 1836. PRO, Kew. Rail 60/1149.
2 *Bristol Mirror*, 5 March 1836.
3 I Brunel, *Life of I K Brunel*, p234.
4 Brunel Manuscript about ships: In Henry Brunel's hand and probably prepared by him to help with his brother's biography of their father. Brunel Collection, Bristol University Library.
5 *Bristol Mirror*, 22 July 1837.
6 Brunel Letter Book No 1, p121. Brunel Collection, Bristol University Library.
7 Brunel Letter Book No 2, p83. Brunel Collection, Bristol University Library.
8 E Corlett, *The Iron Ship* (Moonraker Press 1975), p15.
9 Claxton, *Logs of the First Voyage of the Great Western*, p61.
10 *The Sun*, 28 March 1838.
11 Claxton, *Logs of the First Voyage of the Great Western*, piii.
12 Ibid, pp1-2.

13 I Brunel, *Life of I K Brunel*, p243.
14 C Claxton, *Logs of the First Voyage of the Great Western*, pp1-34.
15 Official Engineer's Log Book for the First Voyage, Bristol Reference Library.

Chapter 3

1 I Brunel, *Life of Isambard Kingdom Brunel*, Vol I, pp285-6.
2 Rolt, *Brunel*, pp282-5.
3 W O'Byrne, *A Naval Biographical Dictionary* (London 1849), p198 suggests that Claxton was close to Admiral Sir Thomas Hardy, Nelson's friend and the Liberal First Sea Lord 1830-34. His stories were critical of Tory boards.
4 Henry Brunel Private Journal 12.2.1863: Brunel Collection, Bristol University Library. Courtesy of D K Brown, who notes that L T C Rolt did not have had access to this material when writing his biography.
5 W C Church, *Life of Ericsson* (New York 1907), Vol I, p87.
6 Sir W L Clowes, *The Royal Navy: A History* (1901), Vol VI, pp196-8.
7 E C Smith, *A Short History of Marine Engineering* (Cambridge 1937), p68.
8 John Wright to Admiralty 2.4.1850 ADM 12/528; Brunel to Burgoyne 29.8.1856 in Wrottesley, G, *Life and Correspondence of Field Marshal Sir John Burgoyne* (London 1873), Vol II, pp357-9
9 D K Brown, *Before the Ironclad: the development of ship design, propulsion and armament in the Royal Navy, 1815 - 1860* (London 1990), p99.
10 A D Lambert, *The Last Sailing Battlefleet: Maintaining Naval Mastery 1815 -1850* (London 1991), pp27-38
11 Ibid, pp27-38, 67-87.
12 Ibid, p116.
13 A Parry, *Parry of the Arctic, 1790-1855* (London 1963), pp197-209 esp. p203.
14 Thomas Lloyd. Evidence to the 1848 Select Committee PP. 1848 p.430
15 Lambert, *The Last Sailing Battlefleet*, p159 re HMS *Warspite*.
16 Ibid, p90.
17 J Hewish, *The Indefatigable Mr. Woodcroft; the legacy of invention* (London 1979).
18 Edye Evidence PP.1848 p.186: see A D Lambert, *Battleships in Transition* (London 1984), p55 *et seq*.
19 J Barrow, *An Autobiographical Memoir of Sir John Barrow Bt.* (London 1847).
20 The deadwood is the solid mass of timber, faired in two planes where the stern and the keel are connected. This area was critical to the strength of a sea-going wooden ship.
21 W M Petty, 'The Introduction of the Screw Propeller' Unpub. University of London MA Thesis 1969. The work of Stevens, Owen and Ressel failed from the

inadequacy of contemporary engine and boiler technology. Ressel's effort, in the Austria of Metternich, was brought to a premature end by the secret police. Wilson's valuable work with hand-cranked screws, which anticipated the correct position for the propeller, was never linked to an engine, while Marc Brunel did not realise the idea was sufficiently novel to be worth patenting
22 Journals of the House of Commons Vol 94 1839.
23 H I Dutton, *The Patent System and Inventive Activity in the Industrial Revolution 1750-1852* (Manchester 1984), esp. pp69, 72, 78-80, 86, 93-4.
24 Sir J Rennie, *An Autobiography* (London 1882).
25 Evans to Rear-Admiral Sir W Parker (Second Sea Lord) 28.10.1839 in G H Guest, *A Record of the Services of Admiral George Evans* (London 1876), pp11-14.
26 SPC to Admiralty 6.7.1842 ADM 12/402 ProS 480.
27 Reports of Lloyd and Chappell 2.5.1840; ADM 12/385 Digest.
28 Request SPC to detail terms for hire 23.5.1840. Ibid.
29 Brunel: 'Report to the Directors of the Great Western Steamship Company on Screw Propellers' 17.10.1840' in I Brunel, *Life of I K Brunel* vol II Appendix II pp539-558.
30 E Corlett, *The Iron Ship: the story of Brunel's Great Britain* (London 1990), pp48-55.
31 Brunel to Caldwell 8.7.1840: Brunel Letter Book (LB) 2B p77.
32 Brunel to Captain Chappell 8.10.1840: LB 2B p94.
33 John Barnes (1798-1852) godson of James Watt and sometime partner in Miller & Ravenhill, the Thames marine engineers. An early convert to the screw, he built the engines for the first French screw steamer, the mail packet *Napoleon*.
34 Possibly G H Phipps, who published paper on ship resistance with the Institute of Naval Architects in 1864.
35 Robert Bright, a Director of the Great Western Steamship Company.
36 Brunel to Claxton 12.10.1840: Brunel Coll. Bristol Library Great Britain Box DM 1758.
37 Brunel to Directors October 1840. Printed in Brunel 1870 Vol. 2 pp539-558
38 Parry to Claxton 6.11.1840 ADM 92/4 S420-1.
39 Brunel to Guppy 23.11.1840: Ibid, p117.
40 Brunel to Chappell 18.12.1840: Ibid, p130.
41 Controller of Steam 19.12.1840 ADM 12/375.
42 D Griffiths, *Brunel's Great Western* (Wellingborough 1985), pp53-4.
43 F E Hyde, *Cunard and the North Atlantic*

(Manchester 1975), pp3-6.
44 Admiralty to Surveyor 4.11.1840 ADM83/25 S5055.
45 Surveyor to Admiralty 16.11.1840 & 16.1.1841 ADM92/9 S340 & 413. Minto endorsed the latter. Admiral Sir Charles Adam, First Naval Lord, to Minto 18.11.1840L: NMM ELL/228.
46 Parry to Admiralty 14.12.1840 ADM 92/4 S423-4.
47 Surveyor to Admiralty 16.1. & 12.2.1841 ADM 92/9 S413, 432.
48 Brunel to Claxton 19.3.1841: Brunel DM800. Brunel's letter to Chappell of the following day in LB 2B p.166 is very non-committal, but his relationship with Claxton suggests that the letter to his friend was more explicit than that to a recent acquaintance.
49 Brunel to Symonds 30.4. & 6.5.1841 LB 2B 175 & 177.
50 Brunel to Caldwell 3.7.1841 & Brunel to Parry 3.7.1841 LB 2B pp190 & 192.
51 Edye Minute 26.7.1841 *Report on the Naval and Ordnance Estimates* 1848 Parliamentary Papers p1031.
52 Parry to Brunel 31.7.1841. ADM 92/4 S446-7.
53 Parry Minute sent to Symonds 28.9.1841. ADM 92/4 S453-4.
54 Surveyor to Admiralty 26.10.1841 ADM 92/10 S165.
55 Smith to Admiralty 1.7.1841 ADM 12/388.
56 Board Minute 3.3.1843 ADM 12/417.
57 I Brunel *Life of I K Brunel* Vol I pp285. Rolt 1957 pp. 284-5.
58 Brunel to Guppy 21.9.1841 LB 2B p214.
59 Brunel to Captain W A B Hamilton, PS to Lord Haddington 25.8.1841. LB 2B p215
60 Brunel to Guppy 20.12.1841: LB 2B p241.
61 Admiralty to Surveyor 1.1.1842 ADM 83/25 S1928.
62 Admiralty to Surveyor 10.1.1842, with notes by Symonds and Parry of 13.1.1842: ADM 1/5522 S2018.
63 Brunel to Cockburn 17.1.1842 LB 2B p253.
64 Brunel to Parry 28.1.42, to Symonds 7.2.1842 (twice) to Smith 7.2.1842; LB 2B pp259-67
65 Brunel to Admiralty 16.2.1842 LB 2B p271.
66 Endorsement on above 18.2.1842 signed Sidney Herbert (Political Secretary).
67 Brunel to Parry 7.3.1842: LB 2B p280.
68 She would be the third *Rattler*. One of her predecessors, a sloop, secured a battle honour for the 'Glorious First of June' 1794.
69 Admiralty to Surveyor 19.2.1842 endorsed in Symonds' hand 22.2.1842: ADM 1/5522 S2407 Admiralty to Surveyor 24.2.1842, endorsed 6.4.1842:

ADM 83/25 S2458.

70 Surveyor to Captain Fisher (Captain Superintendent of Sheerness Dockyard) various April to July 1842 ADM 83/25

71 Lambert, *The Last Sailing Battlefleet*, pp108-123.

72 Surveyor to Admiralty 17.1.1842: ADM 92/10 S2156. Rolt p.286 quoting a letter from Claxton to Henry Brunel.

73 Smith to Surveyor 4.6.1842: ADM 87/12 S3361.

74 Brunel to Claxton 22.7.1842 LB 2C p16.

75 Admiralty to Brunel 9.8.1842 ADM 83/26 S3942.

76 Brunel to Admiralty Clerk Waller Clifton (to whom he was directed to refer all requests for material relating to this project.), 1.8.1842: LB 2C p33.

77 Brunel to Smith 10.8.1842 LB 2C p38.

78 Surveyor to Admiralty 3.9.1842 ADM 83/27 S4354.

79 Brunel to Admiralty 17.9.1842 endorsed by Cockburn 28.9.1842: ADM 83/27 S4335.

80 Brunel to Guppy 23.11.1843, 27.11.1843 and to Harmer (chief Engineer at Bristol) 6.2.1844, 12.2.1844 on propeller design and pitch. LB 2C pp264, 283, 294 & 303.

81 D K Brown, *Paddle Wheel Warships* (London 1993), esp. p19.

82 Shipwright Officers to Captain Superintendent Sheerness: 8.3.1843. confirmed 9.3.43: ADM87/13 f5676

83 Admiralty to Surveyor. 11.7.1843 ADM 83/29 f6866.

84 Smith to Brunel 19.7.1843: LB VIII 47.

85 Brunel to Field 14.8. & 15.9.1843: LB 2C pp193, 208-9.

86 Report on the Trials of the *Rattler* Bound Vol.: Brunel MS Bristol University Library

87 Admiralty Order 27.10.1843: ADM 83/30 f7780. 28.10.43 *Rattler* to leave from East India Dock gate at 1.00 pm Ibid. f7791.

88 J Bourne, *A Treatise on the Screw Propeller* (London 1855), p134.

89 Brunel to Field & to Parry 30.10.43: LB2C pp234-6.

90 Brunel to Field & to Smith 31.10.1843: LB ibid pp236, 238

91 Smith to Admiralty 1.11.1843, endorsed to be done: ADM 12/417.

92 Brunel to Barrow & to Parry 7.11.1843: LB pp240-1.

93 Brunel to Parry 8.11.1843: LB p244.

94 Brunel to Smith & to Field 13.11.1843: LB pp247-8.

95 Brunel's Secretary to Parry 14.11.1843: LB p246. Brunel to Parry 17.11.1843: LB p250. Brunel to Barrow & to Lloyd 18.11.1843: LB pp252, 255.

96 Admiralty to Surveyor 23.11.1843: ADM 83/29 f8039 & ADM 12/417.

97 Brunel to Smith & to Guppy 23.11.1843: LB pp257, 260.

98 Brunel to Guppy 27.11.1843: LB p264.

99 Admiralty to Surveyor. 4.12.1843: ADM 83/30 f8136.

100 Brunel to Parry 18 & 20.12.1843: LB p283.

101 Brunel to Parry 29.12.1843: LB p285.

102 Brunel to Smith 24.1.1844: LB p288.

103 Brunel to Parry & Barrow 5.2.1844: LB pp292-3. Admiralty to Brunel 6.2.1844: Brunel DM 1406 VIII 2.

104 Brunel to Harmer (GWSS Co.) 6 & 12.2.1844: LB pp294, 303.

105 Brunel to Field 5.2. & to Maudslay (official) 8.2.1844: LB pp292, 297.

106 Brunel to Barrow. 10.2.1844: LB p300.

107 Brunel to Smith 11 & 13.2.1844: LB

pp302, 304.

108 Smith to Brunel 15.2.1844: Brunel DM 1406 VIII 47.

109 Brunel to Parry 18.2.1844: LB p311.

110 Brunel to Lloyd 22.2.1844: LB p314.

111 Admiralty to Surveyor 1.3.1844: ADM 83/31 f512.

112 Brunel to Caldwell 3.3.1844: LB p320.

113 R Morriss, *Cockburn and the British Navy in Transition* (Exeter 1998), p251. Morriss makes clear the extent to which Cockburn guided the process, and that he set the criteria.

114 Corlett, *The Iron Ship*, p88 and quote at p96.

115 Brunel to Smith 6.3.1844: LB p323.

116 Brunel to Smith 12.3.1844: LB p324.

117 Brunel to Lloyd 12.3.1844: LB p325.

118 Brunel to Smith 12.3.1844: LB p327.

119 Brunel to Smith 19.3.1844: LB p328.

120 Brunel to Maudslay 20.3.1844: LB p331.

121 Brunel to Admiralty (Barrow) 23.3.1844: (LB3 3).

122 Brunel to Admiralty (Barrow) 29.3.1844: LB 3 p8. Brunel to Smith 1 & 2.4.1844: LB 3 pp8, 12. Brunel to Barrow 4.4.1844: LB 3 p.15 & ADM 12/417.

123 Admiralty to Surveyor. 28.3.1844: ADM 83/31 f792.

124 Brunel to Maudslay 19.4.1844. LB p22. Brunel to Smith 19.4.1844: ibid p23.

125 Admiralty to Controller of Steam 27.4.1844: ADM.

126 Brunel to Lloyd 2.5.1844: LB 3 p28.

127 Admiralty to Controller of Steam 30.4.1844: ADM.

128 Brunel to Lloyd & Field 20.5.1844: LB 3 p42.

129 Brunel to Lloyd 27.5.1844: LB 3 p47.

130 Brunel to Smith 27.5.1844: LB 3 p46.

131 Admiralty to Surveyor 31.5.1844: ADM 83/32 f1298.

132 Brunel to Admiralty (Barrow) 3.6.1844: LB 3 p59.

133 Admiralty to Brunel 25.6.1844: DM 1306 VIII 2.

134 Brunel to Lloyd 17.7.1844: LB 3 p91.

135 Brunel to Smith 23.8.1844: LB 3 p117.

136 Admiralty to Surveyor 23.8.1844 re Mr Sunderland: ADM 83/32 f1919.

137 Corlett (1990) pp91-8.

138 Brunel to Admiralty 10.2.1842: ADM 83/25.

139 Thomas Lloyd, Testimony before the Select Committee 9.5.1848 PP. pp430-5.

140 Auckland to Admiral Sir Charles Napier 7.9.1848 Add. MSS. 40, 023 f278.

141 Lambert 1991 pp86, 155-6.

142 Admiralty to Surveyor 12.6.1848: ADM 12/497.

143 Wright to Admiralty 2.4.1850: ADM 12/528 ProW 705.

144 H I Dutton, *The Patent System and Inventive activity during the Industrial Revolution 1750 -1852* (Manchester 1984), pp155-6.

145 Solicitor 13, 20 & 22.9.1851 ADM 12/544. Currie to Admiralty ADM 1/5641.

146 Brunel to Scott Russell 21.7.1852 in G S Emmerson, *John Scott Russell* (London 1977), p66.

147 Palmerston to Smith 21.1.1855 *On the introduction.....* (London 1856), p61.

148 Brunel to General Sir John Burgoyne 29.8.1856 *Burgoyne* Vol. II pp357-9

149 Burgoyne to Brunel 8.1.1856; 29.8.1856. DM 1306 VIII Bristol Univ.

150 D L Canney, *The Old Steam Navy: Vol. One.* (Annapolis 1990), pp21-5 esp. p22.

Chapter 4

1 Puddling makes use of the phenomenon whereby the melting point of iron increases with its purity. Preheated charges of scrap iron and pig iron are placed in a puddling hearth and the temperature raised to about 1500°C. At this stage the impure iron melts and the slag and other impurities are drawn off leaving a molten charge which is slowly oxidising, reducing its carbon content, purifying itself and raising its melting point. A pure and less mobile ball of iron appears in the charge and this is manipulated by iron puddlers with long steel rods. Once this has reached a size of say one quarter of a ton, it is cut into billets of around 50kg, removed and hammered to remove slag and to produce handy billets of malleable iron.

2 The Directors of the Forth & Clyde Canal appointed a committee to advise on the construction of the *Vulcan*. The chairman was Sir John Robison and the members included Admiral John Schank, a noted experimenter on ship hull form, and James Watt, the world-famous engineer and canal builder.

3 The Institution of Engineers and Shipbuilders in Scotland was not founded until 1857 and the (now Royal) Institution of Naval Architects in 1860.

4 Some frigates built of Baltic fir for the Royal Navy in the 1790s were calculated to have had lives of 8 years, whilst others built in 1812 of North American fir lasted a mere 4 years!

Chapter 5

1 *The Bristol Mirror*, 29 September 1838.

2 GWSS Co Directors' report 7 March 1839. PRO Kew, Rail 60/1149.

3 British Library, Add. 37191, f.39.

4 C Claxton, *Description of the Great Britain Steamship* (Bristol 1845), pp11-23.

5 GWSS Co Directors' report 7 March 1839. PRO Kew, Rail 60/1149.

6 Nasmyth Sketch Book (vol. 4), Institute of Mechanical Engineers; Nasmyth letter Book No 3, Salford Archives.

7 Directors' report for 1842. PRO Kew, Rail 60/1149.

8 GWSS Co Directors' report 7 March 1839. PRO Kew, Rail 60/1149.

9 Brunel Manuscript about ships.

10 Brunel Letter Book No 1, p350, 21 November 1828. Bristol University Library.

11 Brunel Letter Book No 1, p336, 22 October 1838. Bristol University Library.

12 Brunel Letter Book No 1, p347, 29 October 1838. Bristol University Library.

13 Brunel Manuscript about ships.

14 I Brunel, *Life of I K Brunel*, pp249-50.

15 Brunel Manuscript about ships.

16 Ibid.

17 I Brunel, *Life of I K Brunel*, pp251-2.

18 GWSS Co Directors' report 11 March 1841. PRO Kew, Rail 60/1149.

19 Brunel Letter Book No 1, p273. Bristol University Library.

20 Brunel Letter Book No 1, p270. Bristol University Library.

21 *The Bristol Mirror*, 28 March 1840.

22 Brunel Letters to Guppy, 15 January 1839; DM1306, held at Bristol University Library.

23 Brunel Letters to Guppy, 17 January 1839.

24 I Brunel, *Life of I K Brunel*, p252.

25 GWSS Co Directors' report 26 March 1840. PRO Kew, Rail 60/1149.

26 Nasmyth letter Book No 5, Salford Archives.

27 I Brunel, *Life of I K Brunel*, p252fn.

28 Brunel Letters to Guppy, 20 December 1839.

29 Brunel Letters to Guppy, 8 January 1840.

30 Brunel Letters to Guppy, 15 January 1840.

31 *Civil Engineer and Architects Journal*, Vol 5 (1842).

32 RMSPCo Special Reports Book, p72. University College London Library.

33 Private Diary volume 2; DM 1306, Bristol University.

34 Brunel Manuscript about ships.

35 Brunel Letters to Guppy, Spring 1840.

36 Brunel Manuscript about ships.

37 I Brunel, *Life of I K Brunel*, p253.

38 Brunel Letter Book No 2, p96. Bristol University Library.

39 Pamphlets for meetings, PRO Kew, Rail 60/1149.

40 GWSS Co Directors' report 3 March 1842. PRO Kew, Rail 60/1149.

41 Admiralty Archives at PRO, Kew. ADM 12/388.

42 Admiralty Archives at PRO, Kew. ADM 12/402.

43 I K Brunel, *Report to the Directors of the Great Western Steamship Company on Screw Propellers* (1840); I K Brunel, *Life of I K Brunel*, pp539-58.

44 E Corlett, *The Iron Ship* (Moonraker Press, 1975), pp56-65.

45 I Brunel, *Life of I K Brunel*, p254.

46 GWSS Co Directors' report 11 March 1841. PRO Kew, Rail 60/1149

Chapter 6

1 GWSS Co. Directors' report 28 February 1843. PRO Kew, Rail 60/1149.

2 E Corlett, *The Iron Ship*, pp64-5.

3 Brunel Letter Book No 2b, p110, 29 October 1840. Bristol University Library.

4 Brunel Letter Book No 2b, p130, 18 December 1840. Bristol University Library.

5 Brunel Letter Book No 2b, p190, 3 July 1841. Bristol University Library.

6 T Guppy, 'The Steamship *Great Britain*', *Proceedings of the Institute of Civil Engineers*, 4 (1845), pp160-1.

7 Ibid, p161.

8 GWSS Co. Directors' report 28 February 1843. PRO Kew, Rail 60/1149.

9 GWSS Co. Directors' report 14 March 1844. PRO Kew, Rail 60/1149.

10 Ibid.

11 Brunel Letter Book No 3. p34, 10 May 1844. Bristol University Library.

12 Reported in *Mechanics Magazine*, No. 1107 (26 October 1844), p288.

13 Quoted I Brunel, *Life of I K Brunel*, p261.

14 E Corlett, *The Iron Ship*, p124.

15 Brunel Letter Book No 4, p170, 19 December 1845. Bristol University Library.

16 Brunel Letter Book No 4, p247, 20 April 1846. Bristol University Library.

17 I Brunel, *Life of I K Brunel*, p264.

18 Ibid, pp264-7.

19 Ibid, pp267-72.

20 E Corlett, *The Iron Ship*, p140.

21 Letter from Brunel to GWSS Co. directors dated 4 May 1847. Printed in *The Great Britain Released from Dundrum Bay*, pub GWSS Co., 1847.

22 *The Great Britain Released from Dundrum Bay*, pub GWSS Co., 1847.

Chapter 7

1 C Claxton, *Logs of the First Voyage of the Great Western*, GWSS Co. (Bristol 1838).
2 Sir Robert Seppings, 'A New Principle of Constructing Ships in the Mercantile Service', *Philosophical Transactions of the Royal Society* (9 March 1820).
3 Claxton, *Logs of the First Voyage of the Great Western*, p61.
4 Ibid.
5 *The Bristol Mirror*, 31 March 1838.
6 Log books of voyages 1 & 43 (Bristol Reference Library) and voyage 23 (Bristol Museum).
7 GWSS Co. Directors' report 11 March 1841. PRO Kew, Rail 60/1149.
8 GWSS Co. Directors' report 3 March 1842. PRO Kew, Rail 60/1149.
9 GWSS Co. Directors' report 28 February 1843. PRO Kew, Rail 60/1149.
10 *Mechanics Magazine* Vol 27 (23 September 1837), p414.
11 Claxton, *Logs of the First Voyage of the Great Western*, p59.
12 Ibid, various pages.
13 *United Services Magazine*, 170 (June 1843), p5.
14 Claxton, *Logs of the First Voyage of the Great Western*, pp36-47.
15 Log book for voyage 23, Bristol Museum.
16 T Tredgold, *The Steam Engine* (1856), p140.
17 GWSS Co. Directors' report 14 March 1844. PRO Kew, Rail 60/1149.
18 *The Artizan*, October 1844.
19 J Bourne, *A Treatise on the Steam Engine* (London 1876), p212.
20 Details of the engines and original boilers are drawn from a number of sources including contemporary journals such as *Civil Engineer and Architects Journal*, Vol. 1 (1838) and *The Athenaeum* (1838). In addition information was included in *A Treatise of Marine Engineering* by Bourne (1846 & 1876) and the *Treatise on Marine Engines and Steam Vessels* by Murray (1868). The Science Museum in London holds a number of drawings in the Maudslay Collection and these show the engines and boilers located in the ship.
21 GWSS Co. Directors' report 14 March 1844. PRO Kew, Rail 60/1149.
22 J Bourne, *A Treatise on the Steam Engine* (Artisan Club 1846), pp63-4.
23 Ibid, p64.
24 Brunel Letter Book No. 4, p171. Bristol University Library.
25 RMSP Co Special Reports Book, April 1847. University College London Library.
26 Parliamentary papers 1846, Vol. 563 p24, Question 186, p31, questions 301-303
27 *Herapath's Journal & Railway Magazine* (6 April 1844), p383; (8 June 1844), p677; (22 June 1844), p736. *The Times*, 15 June 1844.
28 I Brunel, *Life of Isambard Kingdom Brunel*, p244.

Chapter 8

Sources
This study is based on the twenty-three Log Books of hms *Rattler*, her entry in the Admiralty Progress Book and the Navy Lists of the Period. These sources have not been cited in the footnotes,

Progress Book ADM 180/14

Log Books ADM 53:
53 /3001-2 December 1844-September 1847
53/1848 to 53/1856 February 1849-March 1851

53/4953 to 53/4963 August 1851 to October 1855
53/5011 October 1855 to May 1856. W R O'Byrne, *Naval Biographical Dictionary* (London 1849), pp1085-6.
2 Report by Captain H Codrington, J Robb, and Commander J Crawford Caffin 24.4.1845: *Select Committee on Naval Estimates, 1848*. Appendix (F) pp914-6.
3 D K Brown, *Before the Ironclad: Development of ship design, armament and propulsion in the Royal Navy 1815 - 1860* (London 1990), p112.
4 J Bourne, *A Treatise on the Screw Propeller* (London 1855), pp117-22; ADM 53/3001 *Rattler's* Log.
5 Brown, *Before the Ironclad*, pp111-4, 206, provides a technical discussion.
6 Morriss quoting from Cockburn to Lord Haddington 9.6.1845 at p.252.
7 Admiralty to Surveyor. 14.4.1845: ADM 83/34 f3857.
8 O'Byrne, *Naval Biographical Dictionary*, p1085.
9 Cockburn to Haddington 9.6.1845: ADM 1/5533 & Peel MS.
10 Admiralty to Surveyor 24.9.1845: ADM 83/36 f5200.
11 Admiralty to Surveyor 31.10.1845 & 5.11.1845: ADM 83/36 f5616, f5659.
12 A D Lambert, *The Last Sailing Battlefleet* (London 1991), pp161-2.
13 Admiralty to Surveyor 11.5.1846: ADM83/38 f7526.
14 Commodore Sir Francis Collier to Admiralty 29.5.1846: ADM 1/5559 V6.
15 Ellenborough memorandum 7.7.1846: ADM 13/185 f32.
16 Parker to Rear-Admiral Bowles 9.8.1846: A Phillimore, *Life of Sir W Parker* (London 1878), Vol 3, p72.
17 Lord Auckland, to Parker Admiralty 24.8.1846: Phillimore, *Life of Sir W Parker*, Vol III, pp76-7.
18 Parker to Earl Haddington 26.11.1846 (at Lisbon): Phillimore *Life of Sir W Parker*, Vol III, pp96-7.
19 Admiralty to Surveyor 6.10.1846: ADM 83/40 f8890.
20 O'Byrne, *Naval Biographical Dictionary*, p780.
21 Parker to Auckland 24.12.1846 (At Lisbon); Phillimore *Life of Sir W Parker*, Vol III, p110.
22 For Howden's mission to Buenos Aires, and the Rio Plata War, see D Maclean, *War Diplomacy and Informal Empire: Britain and the Republic of La Plata* (London 1995), pp126-48.
23 Auckland to Sir Charles Adam on Surveyor to Admiralty of 27.3.1847:ADM 1/5581.
24 Admiralty to the Controller of Steam 26.4.1847: New *Rattler* class vessels.
25 Admiralty to Surveyor 2.11.1847 improved *Rattler* ordered as *Miranda*. David Lyon has pointed out that *Rattler* had no direct sisters, and that *Miranda* was of a different design (Lyon to Author 6.11.1998). *Rattler* was the only screw ship to use Symonds' lines, being a copy of his *Polyphemus*.
26 Admiralty to Messrs Whitworth 14.5.1849: ADM 2/1393 f102.
27 Admiralty to Joshua Woods 20.6.1849: ADM 2/1391 f213.
28 Select Committee on Naval and Military Estimates, evidence of Captain Ellice, Controller of Steam 13.4.1848: Parliamentary Papers, 1847-8 pp214-5.
29 Steam Dept. to Portsmouth. Dockyard. 4.9.1848: ADM2/1389.

30 O'Byrne, *Naval Biographical Dictionary*, p251.
31 S Roberts, *Charles Hotham* (Melbourne 1985).
32 See generally W L Mathieson, *Great Britain and the Slave Trade 1839-1865* (London 1929), esp. pp22, 102 & 114-136.
33 O'Byrne, *Naval Biographical Dictionary*, pp753-4.
34 For this war see: G Bruce, *The Burma Wars, 1824-1886* (London 1973), pp129-50, and J E Hubback & E C *Jane Austen's Sailor Brothers* (London 1906), pp278-81.
35 J H Schroeder, *Shaping a Maritime Empire: The Commercial and Diplomatic role of the American Navy, 1829-1861* (Wesport Conn. 1985), pp167-79.
36 G S Graham, *The China Station: War and Diplomacy 1830 - 1860* (Oxford 1978), pp276-96.
37 J S Gregory, *Great Britain and the Taipings* (London 1969), pp28-46.
38 A lorcha was a vessel of European hull form with a Chinese rig, common in the Macao area.
39 Gregory, *Great Britain and the Taipings*, p33.
40 Ibid, pp39-41.
41 Ibid, pp42-4.
42 J Y Wong, *Deadly Dreams: Opium and the 'Arrow' War (1856-1860) in China* (Cambridge 1998), pp140-7. This book is essential to understanding Anglo-Chinese relations, and the diplomatic origins of the Second Opium War.
43 See generally J B Williams, *British Commercial Policy and Trade Expansion 1750-1850* (Oxford 1972), p333 and W G Beasley, *Great Britain and the Opening of Japan: 1834-1858* (London 1951).
44 O'Byrne, *Naval Biographical Dictionary*, p352
45 R E Johnston, *Far China Station: The US Navy in Asian Waters 1800 - 1898* (Annapolis 1979), p79.
46 *On the Introduction* (London 1856) pp58-9.
47 A D Lambert, *The Crimean War: British Grand Strategy against Russia 1853-1856* (Manchester 1990), pp335-8; A D Lambert & S Badsey (eds), *The War Correspondents: The Crimean War* (Gloucester 1994), pp305-320 for the *Times* report.
48 The next *Rattler* was another wooden screw sloop, built at Deptford in 1862, and wrecked on the coast of China in 1868. She was followed by a composite gunboat of 1886, which lived on as the Navigation School hulk hms *Dryad* until 1924. The most recent *Rattler*, an *Algerine* class minesweeper of 1942, was renamed in 1943, and then sunk by a U-boat in 1944.

Chapter 9

1 Details of the hull construction have been taken from E Corlett, *The Iron Ship* (Moonraker Press 1975), Ch 5, and T Guppy, 'A description of the Great Britain Iron Steamship', *Minutes of Proceedings the Institute of Civil Engineers*, Part 4 (1845).
2 I Brunel, *Life of I K Brunel*, p259.
3 C Claxton, *Description of the Great Britain Steamship*, p20.
4 Brunel Letter Book No 1. p336, 22 October 1838. Bristol University Library.

Chapter 10

1 I Brunel, *Life of I K Brunel*, p290.
2 Sir Westcott Abel, *The Shipwright's Trade* (Cambridge 1948), p117.
3 I Brunel, *Life of I K Brunel*, p291.
4 Brunel Calculations Book, March 1852;

Bristol University Library.
5 Quoted in L T C Rolt, *Isambard Kingdom Brunel* (London 1970), pp312-3.
6 W S Lindsay, *History of Merchant Shipping and Ancient Commerce* (London 1876), Vol IV, pp496-7.
7 Sir Westcott Abel, *The Shipwright's Trade*, p122.
8 I Brunel, *Life of I K Brunel*, p310.
9 Ibid, pp310-1.
10 Ibid, p313.
11 L T C Rolt, *I K Brunel*, p319.
12 W S Lindsay, *History of Merchant Shipping*, Vol IV, pp492-3.
13 William Fairbairn, 'The Strength of Iron Ships', *Proceedings of the Institution of Naval Architects* (2 March 1860), p79.
14 Calculations and Note books in the Brunel Collection at Bristol University Library
15 Quoted, Sir Alfred Pugsley (ed), *The Works of Isambard Kingdom Brunel* (Institute of Civil Engineers 1976), p153
16 Quoted in I Brunel, *Life of I K Brunel*, pp316-8.
17 Sir Westcott Abel, *The Shipwright's Trade*, p119.
18 I Brunel, *Life of I K Brunel*, p291.
19 Ibid, p304.
20 Ibid, pp304-5.
21 Ibid, pp308-9.
22 Brunel's report to the directors on the tenders received, quoted I Brunel, *Life of I K Brunel*, p302
23 Ibid.
24 H P Spratt, *Marine Engineering* (The Science Museum, London 1953), p38 and W S Lindsay, *History of Merchant Shipping*, Vol IV, pp502-3.
25 H P Spratt, *Marine Engineering*, pp27-8 and W S Lindsay, *History of Merchant Shipping*, Vol IV, pp503.
26 I Brunel, *Life of I K Brunel*, p311.
27 Ibid, p311 and L T C Rolt, *Isambard Kingdom Brunel*, p323.
28 I Brunel, *Life of I K Brunel*, p309.

Index